LISTEN TO THE LAMBS

LISTEN

TO THE

LAMBS

Johnny Otis

Foreword by George Lipsitz

University of Minnesota Press
Minneapolis • London

Originally published in 1968 by W. W. Norton and Company

First University of Minnesota Press edition, 2009

Published by the University of Minnesota Press
111 Third Avenue South, Suite 290
Minneapolis, MN 55401-2520
http://www.upress.umn.edu

Library of Congress Cataloging-in-Publication Data

Otis, Johnny, 1921–
    Listen to the lambs / Johnny Otis ; foreword by George Lipsitz. —
1st University of Minnesota Press ed.
        p.   cm.
    Originally published: New York : W. W. Norton, 1968.
    Includes bibliographical references.
    ISBN 978-0-8166-6531-0 (pb : alk. paper)
    1. Otis, Johnny, 1921–   2. Rhythm and blues musicians—United
States—Biography.   3. Watts Riots, Los Angeles, Calif., 1965.   I. Title.
    ML419.O85A3   2009
    781.643092—dc22
    [B]   2009006773

Printed in the United States of America on acid-free paper

The University of Minnesota is an equal-opportunity educator and employer.

16 15 14 13 12 11 10 09   10 9 8 7 6 5 4 3 2 1

Contents

FOREWORD

Listening to the Lambs

GEORGE LIPSITZ

THERE HAS NEVER BEEN A BOOK quite like Johnny Otis's *Listen to the Lambs*. What started as a personal letter to a friend giving an eyewitness account of the 1965 Watts Riots grew into a powerful and prophetic book, a manifesto that delineates in clear and direct prose the causes and consequences of white supremacy in the United States. Published in the year that an assassin's bullet took the life of Dr. Martin Luther King Jr., *Listen to the Lambs* boldly exposes the limits and fragility of the victories won by the civil rights movement. In the face of massive unemployment, oppressive poverty, pervasive police brutality, overcrowded slum housing, systematic residential segregation, and unequal access to education, the formal equality promised by the 1964 Civil Rights Act and the 1965 Voting Rights Act did little to address the most pressing needs of the people of Watts. In this book, Johnny Otis insists that the desperate acts of the rioters grew inexorably out of the everyday despair that he had seen growing in the ghetto for more than two decades. Saddened, frightened, but also strangely energized by the boldness of the insurrection, Otis announces: "A man who has been completely oppressed in the past, is being economically strangled in the present, and who has no hope for the future, has nothing to lose by going berserk" (Chapter 21, "Your Mama!").

Johnny Otis was forty-six years old when *Listen to the Lambs* was published. He was a high school dropout who had never written a book before. But he knew the riot area and the entire city of Los Angeles thoroughly from nearly twenty-five years of experience in the region as a working musician, recording artist, talent scout, record producer, radio disc jockey, television host, businessman, civil rights activist, and candidate for political office. He had been writing a weekly column for a local Black newspaper *(The Sentinel)* since 1961 and had frequently warned his readers about the explosive social conditions in the city. Restrictive covenants, mortgage redlining, and outright discrimination prevented Blacks from moving out of their neighborhoods and left them vulnerable to exploitation and abuse. His columns criticized stores that charged exorbitant prices for inferior goods, merchants who owned profitable stores in the ghetto but refused to hire neighborhood residents, absentee slumlords who neglected the dwellings they owned despite receiving high rental payments, and an educational system that relegated Black children to overcrowded, underfunded, and culturally insensitive schools.

Worst of all, these conditions were maintained largely by force. Officers from the Los Angeles Police Department and the Los Angeles County Sheriff's Department treated the ghetto like an occupied colony, subjecting citizens to arbitrary traffic stops and arrests on flimsy charges. Yet these officers were nowhere to be found when asked to respond to actual crimes committed against Black people. In a column in the *Sentinel* in 1962, Otis reported: "The detestable attitude of many Los Angeles policemen toward Negro citizens continues to boil as a major issue in the community. Almost every letter received by this column now deals with the problem."[1] It came as no surprise to him that the incident that provoked the riots involved brutality by police officers after a seemingly routine traffic stop near the corner of 116th Street and Avalon Boulevard on August 11. That small spark ignited a huge flame as rioters poured into the streets to break windows, loot stores, and burn buildings. Fourteen thousand soldiers from the National Guard and fifteen hundred police officers tried to restore order. They arrested nearly four thousand people. By the time the smoke cleared, more than forty million dollars worth of property and six hundred buildings had been either damaged or destroyed. Soldiers and police officers killed thirty-four people and wounded nearly nine hundred others.[2]

In this book, Otis asks his readers to view the destruction in Watts in August 1965 as a product of pressures built up over centuries. Rather than viewing the riots as the product of deranged or criminal elements in the community, Otis depicts the uprising as a political statement by people deprived of any other meaningful way of getting their grievances heard. Otis insists that the riots emerged out of a complex of constraints that shaped life and death in the ghetto. In one poignant passage he asks: "Do we bury the dead in American flags . . . or canceled welfare checks . . . or Baptist choir robes? . . . or Los Angeles Police Department handcuffs? . . . or eviction notices . . . or selective service questionnaires?" (Chapter 1, "First Letter to Griff").

Otis presents the riots as a defining moment for the nation. Although shocked by its force and fury, the conflagration did not surprise him. He knew that frustration had been building for years, that freedom had long been promised but never realized. Otis once had high hopes for racial justice, but those hopes had been dashed again and again. In the years immediately following World War II he recalls, "I saw the whole community lifting. I thought we were going to realize the American dream. We'd say 'It's a bitch, there's still a lot of racism, but it's going to be OK because our kids will realize a fresh new democratic America.' Oh, how wrong we were. Things were grim and I realized my original appraisal was accurate and that my enthusiasm and happiness were not well founded, that the majority did not give a shit about Black folks, and in fact, despised them."[3]

Just a few months before the Watts Riots, Otis had won a citywide art contest with a painting depicting and honoring Nat Turner, the leader of one of the most violent slave rebellions in U.S. history. Turner had been a preacher who warned white America that God would not tolerate its wrongdoing forever. When the riots erupted Otis felt that the chickens had come home to roost. He thought of the gospel song that told about the lambs crying for the Lord to come by. "They wouldn't listen to the lambs," he writes in this book. "The lambs cried, and finally one day the lambs turned into lions" (Chapter 1, "First Letter to Griff").

Although his experiences and expertise positioned him perfectly to analyze the riots, Otis felt uncomfortable serving as a spokesperson for anyone other than himself. He held no elective office or position of authority in any community group. No one had asked him to speak for them. Even more important, despite the fact that many of his listeners, viewers, readers, business associates, and coworkers thought of him as Black, Johnny Otis was actually white. He was born in 1921 as John Veliotes, the oldest son in a Greek immigrant family. He grew up in a mixed but increasingly Black neighborhood in Berkeley, California, not far from the Oakland city line. Although his family belonged to the Greek Orthodox Church, he discovered that some of the Black churches in his neighborhood served chocolate milk and graham crackers to children who came to their services. In those years during the Great Depression when his family suffered financial reverses, chocolate milk and graham crackers were luxuries, so he started to accompany his young Black friends to church. He also liked the fact that the cutest girls in his neighborhood attended these churches and he could see them there. Yet as much as he liked the chocolate milk, the graham crackers, and the pretty girls, he soon realized that he was also entranced and enraptured by the services. He loved the singing of the gospel choirs, the intellectual and spiritual passion of the preachers, and the fellowship and love that members of the congregation showed to each other. "This society says no white kid can stay in Black culture," he observes. "But see, that culture had captured me. I loved it and it was richer and more fulfilling and more natural. I thought it was mine."[4]

Even outside of church, Otis found himself surrounded by Black culture. He loved the blues and jazz records that his neighbors played at parties, as well as the sounds that he heard wafting out of windows of nightclubs on Seventh Street in downtown Oakland. He began to think of himself as "Black by persuasion." Yet his affinity for Black culture sometimes got him into trouble with family members, school authorities, and the police. Johnny's immigrant father, Alexander Veliotes, had spent much of his early life in Greece and never really understood or condoned anti-Black racism. But Johnny's mother, Irene Veliotes, came to the United States as a young child and was more assimilated. When she learned that Johnny intended to marry Phyllis Walker, a Black woman, Irene tried to stop the wedding. When they got married anyway, she did not speak to her daughter-in-law for eighteen years. School authorities sent Johnny a similar message. One high school counselor took him aside and advised him to spend less time with his Black friends in order to protect his future. The advice made Johnny angry, and he promptly dropped out of school.

Having close friends who were Black also introduced Johnny to some of the pernicious ways that racism works in this society. In *Listen to the Lambs* he relates how he nominated his friend Rudy Jordan for membership in his Boy Scout troop only to learn that the group did not accept Black members (Chapter 2, "For Colored Only"). Later, he and Rudy tried to supplement their families' meager incomes by finding abandoned cars and car parts so they could sell them to salvage yards and junk dealers. One day police officers stopped and arrested them because of reports that someone had stolen some tires and siphoned gas out of a tank. Johnny and Rudy were not guilty, but the police felt free to abuse them. The officers put Rudy in handcuffs and slapped him around, but only asked Johnny why he was associating with Black criminals. When officers arrested the true culprit they let Rudy and Johnny go, but not before advising Johnny to associate with "clean-cut white boys." As had happened with his high school counselor, this advice backfired. "As a kid I decided that if our society dictated that one had to be either black or white," Otis explains in the Preface to this book, "I would be black."

While still in his teens, Otis started to play the drums in a small combo headed by Mississippi-born blues singer and pianist Count Otis Matthews. The band played for tips and jugs of wine at neighborhood house parties. When he went on the road as the drummer in all Black (except for him) territory bands, John Veliotes became Johnny Otis. He married a Black woman and together they raised children considered to be Black in this society. He traveled all across the nation touring with Black musicians, staying in Black hotels and rooming houses, and coming home from the road to a life in the Black community. In the 1950s, Otis threw himself into civil rights activism wholeheartedly, marching on picket lines, raising funds for the cause, and attracting so much hostility that one night a group of white vigilantes burned a cross on his front lawn. Always aware that his skin color and phenotype offered him privileges that might not be extended to his Black family and friends, Otis nonetheless thought of himself as Black.

Yet racial identities are not so easily taken on and cast off. We know today that all reputable researchers tell us that race is a biological fiction, that nothing of significance can be discerned about anyone simply because we perceive their phenotype or skin color. Yet this biological fiction of race in this society becomes a social fact, one that has disastrous and deadly consequences. Race *persists* because racism *exists*. Because opportunities and life chances remain skewed along racial lines, racial identities cannot be simply ignored or wished away. Regardless of our own personal choices, values, or beliefs, our racial identities are constructed as much from the outside through external ascription as they are created from the inside through personal affirmation. The Watts Riots forced Johnny Otis to face this reality in stark and unmistakable ways, to confront the limitations and contradictions of the choices he had made. He had lived much of his life as an antiracist white who was completely comfortable inside the Black community. But was there a place for him in an increasingly polarized society where even the best of personal intentions meant little in the face of the hate, hurt, and fear provoked by systemic structural racism and enduring injustice and inequality? Is it possible for any white person to be genuinely antiracist as long as the privileges and advantages of whiteness persist?

The Watts Riots forced Otis to experience his whiteness in new ways. As he relates in the first chapter of *Listen to the Lambs*, when he saw smoke and flames rising from buildings in Watts on August 13, 1965, his first instinct was to flee. But something compelled him to drive straight toward the riot area to witness it for himself. It was not that he wanted to participate in the destruction, or that he wanted to try to stop it, but rather that he recognized the riots as an event of great significance, something that he had to see for himself with his own eyes. It was only after he found himself in the heart of the riot area that Otis realized the problems with that decision. Despite his personal history, beliefs, and commitments, his skin color and phenotype still marked him as the enemy, as someone who bore more resemblance to the merchants, landlords, insurance collectors, and police officers who exploited the ghetto than to its permanent residents. Some people recognized him and extended friendly greetings, but to others he was just another white man in the way.

Otis relates these incidents with his characteristic self-deprecating wit. He tells about a woman who approaches his car and starts a conversation about members of his band as if they were in a park on a Sunday afternoon rather than in the midst of a riot. Yet it seems likely that Johnny Otis faced an awful crisis at that moment. The riots not only threatened to obliterate physical spaces that held precious memories for him but also called into question whether a life like his was even possible: whether the racial divide created by white supremacy pervaded society so systematically that even the most well intentioned antiracist white person could not escape it. It was not just that the rioters might see him as white even though he had lived much of his life being perceived as Black. It was that Otis believed they had every right to their resentment and rage—even if he got caught in its wake.

Given these circumstances, it would have been understandable if Johnny had written a different kind of book than *Listen to the Lambs*. He could have written about how unfair it was for him to be seen as an enemy of Blacks. He could have celebrated his long and distinguished history of antiracist activism, proclaimed his love for his Black family, and enumerated his contributions to Black culture. He could have presented quotations from Black people testifying to his good intentions and great accomplishments. He could have listed the awards he had received over the years from Black organizations. These would have been thoroughly understandable and completely human responses to the crisis he confronted because of the Watts Riots. Yet in this book he does something else. Rather than making an effort to justify himself or enhance his own reputation, Otis uses these pages to explain and support resistance to white supremacy. This would have been a remarkable decision for any writer, but for an entertainer dependent for his livelihood on the public and on the gatekeepers in the culture industry, it was a brave and noble act. By identifying himself with the rage of the urban poor, with the alienated and disaffected opponents of white supremacy, Otis showed that his principles, commitments, and beliefs mattered more to him than money, fame, and prestige.

The unconventional form of *Listen to the Lambs* flows fully from the aims of its author. Rather than make himself and his racial choices the center of the story, Otis devotes thirty pages in his book to testimony by community residents who have important things to say. These observations and commentary by friends and neighbors who witnessed the violence firsthand are reports from the front lines. They present evidence that was ignored at the time by the corporate media and political leaders, and which is still rarely mentioned today in histories of the uprising. Rather than conforming to the dominant political, journalistic, and social science view of the ghetto as a tangle of self-created pathologies, these testimonies trace the tragic violence of ghetto looters and arsonists to their origins in the pervasive presence of police violence in Watts before, during, and after the riots.

"My own experiences were quite limited compared to those of many others," Otis says with delicate understatement in introducing testimony by Lily Fort, Taft W. Hazely, Maxy Filer, and Stan Saunders (Chapter 4, "The Watts Riots"). Lily Fort (aka Ethel Fort) performed with Ray Charles's Raelettes and recorded popular vocals on her own as Lily of the Valley. Johnny's son, Shuggie (John Veliotes Jr.), had made his first record at the age of twelve backing Fort on a song that Johnny produced titled *I Had a Sweet Dream*. In *Listen to the Lambs*, Fort appears not as an entertainer but as a witness to the brutal tactics employed against the ghetto in the wake of the insurrection. Fort presents a wrenching firsthand account of the execution of a teenage looter. The young man entered a store with two friends, who ran away when a police car approached. The youth did not see the officers, but from their vantage point outside the store Fort and her brother-in-law did. They yelled at him to leave, but he did not hear them.

An officer approached the store, looked inside, and aimed his gun at the youth. Fort tried to scream but was so frightened no sound came out. The officer yelled, "Halt!" at the same moment he pulled the trigger of his gun. Watching the youth fall to the floor, the officer turned around to his partner in the squad car and made a "bull's eye" sign with his fingers. Fort says it was "just as though he had shot a tin can off a fence, not a human being." The officers waited for an ambulance to arrive before checking to see if the young man had been killed or not. When they found him dead, Fort says they dragged him out of the store "like he was a sack of potatoes." Soon the scene was swarming with police officers, some of whom were giving their version of events to the press. When Fort and her husband and brother-in-law tried to intervene and tell reporters what actually happened, the reporters simply drove away. A police officer ordered them to go back into their house. Fort's husband hesitated, which made the officer draw his gun. Seeing what she perceived to be a murderous look in the officer's eyes, Fort pulled her husband into their house so he would not meet the fate that befell the young man in the store.

Businessman Taft W. Hazely owned a cleaning and pressing shop in the riot area. In *Listen to the Lambs*, he contributes harrowing testimony about being unjustly arrested and about police officers and National Guard soldiers brutalizing citizens inside his store. Law student Maxy Filer reports seeing rioters commit "suicide by cop" during the rebellion. "These were people," he noted, "who had cracked under the social pressure piled on through the years. Here was the chance to go out like a man. They knew they were going to die, but with some Negroes it has come to that; just die and get it over with; nothing to live for really, anyhow." Rhodes Scholar and law student Stan Saunders relates his shock in reading a story about the riots in *Look* magazine, learning there about the death during the riots of his childhood friend Charles Fizer, once the lead singer in the popular rhythm and blues group The Olympics.

It takes a special kind of author to cede nearly thirty pages of his or her first book to the words of others, but this type of sharing flows fully and logically from the life Otis has led and from his practice of crediting the entire Black community for his artistry and accomplishments. It has not been an unusual occurrence for a white person in the United States to make a living off Black culture. Indeed, much of the history of popular music has revolved around precisely that dynamic. Yet it has been unusual to find any white person able and willing to connect that culture to the full history and social life of the Black community. In his musical career, Otis continuously did what he does in *Listen to the Lambs*— deflect the spotlight away from himself and turn it back onto the Black community. When his band enjoyed their first hit recording with "Harlem Nocturne" in 1946, Otis received many offers to perform before live audiences, but he felt funny about presenting himself as the star when he knew so many talented artists who did not get that billing. Following the practices he learned from touring with territory bands and observing Black vaudeville and tent shows, he presented a series of acts, a caravan of entertainers to make it seem as if a carnival had come to town. The Johnny Otis Caravan included Johnny and his band, but it celebrated the artistry of others. By the 1950s, the Johnny Otis Show included Little Esther Phillips, Mel Williams, Devonia "Lady Dee" Williams, and many others.

Otis never wavered from his emphasis on the group. His vocals on "All Night Long" and "Willie and the Hand Jive" enabled him to secure big sales, but he was prouder of his work as a producer and arranger on recordings by Little Esther, Johnny Ace, and Big Mama Thornton. He extended his sense of community and solidarity to all his endeavors. When he employed saxophonist Jackie Kelso as a producer for his record label and Little Esther Phillips as the lead singer with his band, he made them full partners in the business, sharing the profits with them as well as paying their salaries.

The statements by neighborhood residents that appear in *Listen to the Lambs* also evince Otis's love of Los Angeles's Black neighborhoods and the people living within them. Living in Los Angeles helped him see the importance of housing segregation to the skewing of opportunities and life chances along racial lines. The Los Angeles ghetto generally did not feature the multiunit tenement apartments characteristic of slum neighborhoods in eastern and Midwestern cities. Watts consisted largely of small bungalows with front and back lawns on streets lined with palm trees. Yet the physical isolation of Black neighborhoods made their residents vulnerable to exploitation. As early as the 1920s, Los Angeles emerged as the capital of restrictive covenants; these were deed restrictions that required white homeowners to pledge that they would never sell their property to nonwhites. When the Supreme Court declared such covenants unenforceable by the state (although still permissible as voluntary agreements among whites) in its *Shelley v. Kramer* decision in 1948, some Blacks in Los Angeles started to move into previously all-white neighborhoods. They faced ferocious opposition in the form of mob violence, cross burnings, and constant harassment. The California legislature passed a bill outlawing housing discrimination in 1963, but a ballot initiative sponsored by the real estate industry the next year promptly overturned that law, making it clear that the white voters in California intended to hang on to the privileges they derived from discriminating against people of color. Systematic segregation elevated the group interests of whites over the long promised but rarely implemented constitutional rights of Blacks, guaranteeing that the races in Los Angeles would live in separate and unequal places. As Otis explains in Chapter 23 of *Listen to the Lambs*, "Integrated housing has never actually existed in recent times in Los Angeles. A neighborhood may become integrated briefly, but it stays that way only as long as it takes the white residents to get out; then it becomes a part of the main body of the ghetto. The periphery inches out at a snail's pace and the ghetto gradually expands, but integrated housing remains an idealistic theory."

Yet while adamantly opposed to the effects of exclusionary segregation, Otis did not necessarily approve of integration as an end in itself. As he makes clear in *Listen to the Lambs*, he views the race problem as more a matter of power than of prejudice. In his view, there was nothing wrong with a Black neighborhood, as long as its composition came from voluntary choices and as long as it did not suffer because of the complexion of its residents. Black neighborhoods throughout the country served as resources for Black people. Out of necessity they made productive use of the spaces to which they were confined. They countered the de-humanization of white exclusion by cultivating a rehumanization grounded in Black solidarity. In the felicitous phrase of historian Earl Lewis, they turned segregation into congregation. Faced with the radical divisiveness of poor people's lives and constantly pitted against each other in competition for jobs, housing, romantic partners, and prestige, residents of ghettos like Watts cultivated their commonalities, continuously calling a community into being through creative, spiritual, and political activities. Thus, Otis could write that for all of its problems, "in Watts, as in any other spot on earth where the human spirit refuses to yield, there is deep and startling beauty. In the heart of Watts, one can feel the surging glory of the African character. It continues to endure like some indomitable, indefatigable, will-o'-the-wisp that denies the separation of thousands of miles . . . defies the span of hundreds of years, and tenaciously holds fast" (Chapter 6, "Where the Spirit Refuses to Yield").

Johnny Otis knew Watts well. Part of the pain he felt from the riots came from the destruction of places that had been impor-tant in his life. He sensed then that things would never be the same again, that the community that had done so much to shape him was gone forever. Otis had moved to Watts after the war, settling on a two-acre plot on 118th Street near Wilmington.

Watts was still partly rural in those days, and like many of his neighbors Johnny raised animals on the property: chickens, geese, ducks, rabbits, and pigeons. Bass player Mario Delagarde moved in with Johnny and his family and helped him run a poultry and egg business, which they named the Progressive Poultry Company. Johnny built coops for the birds, and he watered, fed, slaughtered, and dressed the fowl for sale. They bought a used ice-cream truck, and Delagarde sold chicken and eggs from this truck throughout the neighborhood.

In those same years, Otis partnered with singer, guitarist, band leader, and master of ceremonies Bardu Ali and his wife, Tila, in ownership of a nightclub on Wilmington Avenue between 107th Street and Santa Ana Boulevard, not far from his house. The Barrelhouse club became the first in the nation to feature rhythm and blues exclusively. It attracted an interracial clientele that included future poet and activist Jayne Cortez and future world champion surfer Miki Dora. Otis also promoted concerts and talent shows at the Largo Theatre on 103rd Street. He discovered fourteen-year-old Esther Mae Jones in a talent show at the Largo. She did not win, but she sounded to Johnny like a young Dinah Washington. He signed her to his record label, recorded her, and together they had hit after hit in the early 1950s under her stage name, Little Esther.

From his base in Watts, Otis made connections to the rest of Black Los Angeles. He played music in the clubs close to downtown along Central Avenue and at the nearby Lincoln Theater. He admired the socially conscious preaching and community outreach activities of Reverend Clayton Russell's People's Independent Church. He enjoyed the intellectual flair and political acumen of newspaper publisher and fair housing activist Charlotta Bass. In the early 1960s, Otis joined a Black political awareness group organized by Mervyn Dymally that hosted a distinguished set of guest speakers, including James Baldwin and Malcolm X. Although he originally thought of his work as a painter and sculptor in primarily recreational terms, he eventually became friends with some of the city's leading Black artists, such as John Outterbridge and Charles Dickson.

These associations and affiliations help explain the expansive intellectual vision that pervades *Listen to the Lambs*. In some ways it is a work of improvisational art, a book written quickly in the heat of the moment, a virtuoso performance of verbal bravado designed to salve a community's wounds and lift its spirit. It is a vernacular text, a message from and for a particular place and time, speaking to contemporary issues in contemporary terms, filled with the new slang words and the new language patterns being forged in the wake of the upheavals of the 1960s. But it also resonates with the long fetch of history, with the cumulative lore and lessons learned by Black people in the United States from centuries of exploitation, oppression, and brutality. Through his unique life experiences, Otis had learned how to be successfully pro-Black in a society where the rewards for being anti-Black were enormous. His bold statements in *Listen to the Lambs* about the depths, dimensions, and duration of white supremacy draw deftly on well-established intellectual and political traditions in the Black community. He embraced the tradition that emphasized a commitment to global justice and world transcending citizenship over narrow allegiance to a temporal homeland. In this book, Otis connects racism at home to U.S. foreign policy overseas, treating white supremacy as both a national and a global issue. He cites W. E. B. Du Bois in arguing that the capture and exploitation of African labor provided the necessary precondition for the creation of wealth in North America. Following the lead of Malcolm X, Dr. King, and many others, he points to the hypocrisy of a government willing to police the world but unwilling to defend the lives, labor, and property of its own Black citizens. He describes the war in Vietnam as unjust and immoral, as a drain on resources needed to fight poverty and racism at home, and as symptomatic of the unrestrained arrogance and imperial ambitions of a white supremacist nation. Like Du Bois and many pan-Africanists, Otis seeks a global rather than a purely national solution to racial oppression, suggesting "it might be an idea now to examine the entire world in terms of white and non-white" (Chapter 10, "The Negro Wars").

At a time when the Moynihan Report and a massive apparatus of social science experts attributed many of the disadvantages that Black men faced not to white racism but to the purported existence of a matriarchy in the Black community, Otis devotes a memorable section of his book to a defense of Black women. Acknowledging that one aspect of white supremacy entailed efforts to infantilize Black men, Otis points to Rosa Parks as evidence of how the strengths of Black women work to the benefit, rather than the detriment, of the Black community. Addressing the charges of Black matriarchy directly, he insists on the importance of viewing gender as a political as well as a personal identity, asserting, "Because the American black man has been preempted, the Negro woman has been forced to assume the impossible role of both mother and father, breadwinner and homemaker. The entire world of womanhood stands taller and prouder as a result of the American Negro woman's historically supreme job of holding her race together with her bare hands. In the finest tradition of womanhood, Rosa Parks struck the spark that lighted fires in twenty million hearts, and started an emotional surge that transcended mere survival" (Chapter 10, "The Negro Wars").

For a book with such serious purposes, *Listen to the Lambs* proceeds in ostensibly peculiar ways. Otis intersperses autobiographical vignettes from his past throughout the book, interrupting his sustained attacks on white supremacy with personal reminiscences about joining the Boy Scouts, learning about sex as a teenager, his first days on the road as a working musician and his first experiences at Central Avenue's famed Club Alabam, his memories of the Barrelhouse, his encounters with Jim Crow segregation in the South, his fondness for fishing, hunting, and raising pigeons, and his nervousness about being a new parent. It is almost as if the political points he wants to make are so harsh that he has to lighten things up with personal reminiscences. Yet all of these stories also serve serious purposes. They are not so much matters of personal biography as illustrative anecdotes fashioned to teach lessons about racism, designed to connect the macrosocial structures and conditions he condemns to the actual lived experiences of ordinary people like himself.

Otis might have used the occasion of writing a book to augment his reputation as an artist, to ingratiate himself to readers by entertaining them with stories about his life as a celebrity. For that reason, it is amazing to ponder what is *not* in this book. You will not read in *Listen to the Lambs* that Johnny Otis has been a success at nearly every thing he has attempted. You will not learn here that he placed seventeen hit records on the rhythm and blues charts and three on the pop charts, that he played drums on Big Mama Thornton's "Hound Dog," performed on vibraphone on Johnny Ace's "Pledging My Love," and played piano on his own "Willie and the Hand Jive." He does not acknowledge in these pages that he wrote the Fiestas' "So Fine" and Gladys Knight and the Pips' "Every Beat of My Heart." He does not say that he played on records with Ben Webster, Lester Young, Paul Quinchette, and T-Bone Walker. You will not learn in this book that he mastered the complex musical demands of big band jazz, rhythm and blues, and rock 'n' roll. He does not tell readers that he has been one of the world's great talent scouts, that his discoveries include Little Esther, Hank Ballard and the Midnighters, Etta James, Little Willie John, Jackie Wilson, Linda Hopkins, Margie Evans, and many more great artists. You will not learn here that his hobby raising birds has put him in correspondence with leading avian biologists, that his paintings have won prizes, that he is a magnificent cook. Otis does not tell you in these pages that he hosted the highest rated music programs on radio and television in Los Angeles throughout the 1950s, that he introduced

Black music to an entire generation of white listeners and viewers, some of whom went on to make music themselves, including Frank Zappa, Brian Wilson, Dave Alvin, and John Stewart. You will not learn here that the shows he promoted at El Monte Legion Stadium and the Angelus Theater opened up rock 'n' roll to an entire generation of talented Chicano/a artists. He does not tell you that he met Thurgood Marshall and Langston Hughes in nightclubs on Central Avenue in the 1940s, that he is friends with Maya Angelou, or that he played a key role in the careers of Gene and Eunice, the Penguins, and L'il Julian Herrera.

Instead, his autobiographical stories all serve as illustrative examples of how systemic structural racism makes its presence felt in the ordinary activities of everyday life. Rather than tooting his own horn, Otis tries to share what he has learned from life, especially from his struggles to become and remain antiracist in a white supremacist society. He phrases his conclusions simply and directly. Racism kills, literally as well as figuratively. Blacks have higher levels of infant mortality and shorter life spans not just because they are disadvantaged but because they are taken advantage of, because unjust and unfair impediments in their path carve out unearned riches for their oppressors. "This is not some biological phenomenon linked to skin color, like sickle cell anemia," he points out; instead, "this is a national crime, linked to a white-supremacist way of life and compounded by indifference" (Chapter 10, "The Negro Wars"). At a time when would-be experts of all sorts stepped forward with diagnoses about what was wrong with Black people, Otis correctly understood that the real problem lay elsewhere. "The real danger for the future," he explains, "grows not out of the Negro community's struggle for justice, but out of the white community's historical and continuing rejection of these demands" (Chapter 10, "The Negro Wars"). If the United States is ever to solve its "black problem," it must first deal with the problem of whiteness.

Listen to the Lambs ends with a warning that proved to be prophetic. "White America stands at a critical crossroad," Otis states at the beginning of the book's final chapter. "She can meet ghetto disorders with increased police power in the belief that oppressive punitive actions will make the problem go away, or she can start getting at the economic and social causes of the riots. Unfortunately, but typically, the trend is toward punitive police power." Four decades later we know that what emerged from the cry for justice that erupted in Watts in 1965 was not an honest reckoning with the tragic legacy of racism but rather a counter-revolution that promoted incarceration instead of education, that funneled resources away from the masses and toward the upper classes. Our problems today are so severe because warnings like Otis's went unheeded when they first appeared in print.

Reading *Listen to the Lambs* today compels us to confront the tragic consequences of our national failure to heed its clarion call. Certainly much has changed. As former basketball player and current sports broadcaster Charles Barkley quips, no one expected to see a day when the most popular golfer would be Black and the most popular rapper would be white. Yet the success of Tiger Woods and Eminem cannot hide how much has remained unchanged in our society or how insignificant some of the changes that have occurred have been. As Malcolm X used to say, racism is like a Cadillac: they make a new model every year. Its features may change, but its essence remains the same. This republication of *Listen to the Lambs* offers us an opportunity to face the deep roots of today's racial inequalities and antagonisms. It requires us to reckon with the consequences of four decades of prevarication and procrastination, of denial and disavowal of the powerful psychopathology of white supremacy. Yet *Listen to the Lambs* also offers ample reason to harbor hope for the future. The evidence, ideas, and arguments that Johnny Otis presented in this book (and in his many subsequent newspaper columns, radio broadcasts, night school classes, impromptu remarks at performances, and books) nurtured and sustained a generation of antiracist activists. Otis's perceptive analyses and passionate appeals have provided millions of readers and listeners with tools for understanding, critiquing, and combating racism. In this society, he stands out as someone who has chosen to honor the Black community and its culture, to champion its moral, intellectual, aesthetic, and political achievements. Perhaps even more important, he has exhorted others to do the same.

I am one of those people. Johnny Otis has been a part of my life ever since this book appeared. One afternoon in 1968 I was wandering through the music section of the stacks in the Olin Library at Washington University in St. Louis. The yellow spine of one book caught my eye. Its title, printed in black letters under a straight red line, was *Listen to the Lambs*. I removed it from the shelf, opened it up, and started to read. My life has never been the same since.

Although the book does not mention "Willie and the Hand Jive," I surmised that its author was *that* Johnny Otis, the one whose hit song blared out of the old gray radio in my bedroom in 1958 when I was ten years old. His hit song "All Night Long" was one of three favorites (along with Oscar Brown Jr.'s "Work Song" and Bobby Timmons's "Moanin'") that my fellow members of the Eastside High School marching band in Paterson, New Jersey, jammed to on our bus going to and from football games. I did not know until I read the book that Johnny was white, that he had been a jazz drummer, that he had ideas about racism, war, poverty, and power. Two completely separate parts of my life had come together. It helped me see that the radical political activist that I had become in college was also the consumer in training who listened to rock 'n' roll recordings like "Willie and the Hand Jive." The book revealed that the artist who recorded "Willie and the Hand Jive" was also a political thinker from whom I saw I had much to learn. The narrative voice of *Listen to the Lambs* reminded

me of the prophetic prose of James Baldwin. It exuded the vernacular wit and wisdom of the African American activists I had come
to know. Perhaps most important to me personally, it resonated
with the suppressed admiration for Black culture that often de-
velops in ethnic immigrant families (like those of my parents and
grandparents) whose efforts at assimilation entailed humiliating
subordination to white Anglo-Protestant propertied power.

On the day when I first read *Listen to the Lambs* my life was a
mess. For several years, I had been immersed in organizing, activism, marches, and demonstrations. Radical activism exposed
me to a world that I very much wanted to join. What Dr. King
referred to as "the bitter but beautiful struggle" pulled me onto
the streets of Montgomery, Alabama, in 1965 in the Selma to
Montgomery march for voting rights. It drew me into the massive
antiwar demonstrations at the United Nations and the Pentagon
in 1967. It introduced me to the insights and acumen of St. Louis
Black working-class organizers like Ivory Perry and Percy Green,
whose views of the world I quickly adopted as my own. Yet there
was a bitter component in all this beauty. The civil rights movement shocked me out of my middle-class complacency. It compelled me to meet people who lived in houses with dirt floors and
no indoor plumbing, whose children were so hungry that some
of them ate flecks of peeling paint from the inside walls of their
tenement dwellings, unaware that what tasted sweet to them contained deadly lead-based paint. I encountered mothers who stayed
up nights with the lights on and a gun in their laps so they could
shoot the rats who might bite their children. I saw sharecroppers
in the south and low-wage workers in the north risking all they
had to build a better world for others. I saw the legally constituted
authorities respond to them with indifference and disdain.

Then on April 4, 1968, Dr. King was assassinated. No one I
knew was really surprised. Ever since the passage of the Voting
Rights Act of 1965, Dr. King suffered defeat after defeat. His fair
housing marches in the Chicago suburbs provoked white racist

violence, but the press, the politicians, and most of the public blamed King for the trouble rather than the violent vigilantes who attacked the marchers. King was widely condemned for his opposition to the Vietnam War. In a visit to Marks, Mississippi, in 1967 he saw a level of poverty that was so overwhelming he decided to lead a Poor People's March on Washington to complete the unfinished work of the civil rights movement. In the last campaign of his life, he connected the Poor People's campaign to the struggle of striking sanitation workers in Memphis. In his last book, *Where Do We Go from Here? Chaos or Community* (now sadly out of print), Dr. King spoke apocalyptically about the necessity to address the fatal coupling of racism and poverty before it was too late. Four decades after his death, his challenge remains unanswered.

Reading *Listen to the Lambs* in the wake of the troubles and disappointments of 1968 made a tremendous impression on me. Everything about the book seemed to speak directly to me: its topics, its style, its perspective, its insistence on connecting politics and culture. The book seemed to understand what my college teachers, journalists in the corporate media, and elected officials did not: that progress came only with struggle, that the problems we face had to do with white power and privilege and not just with white prejudice. Perhaps most important to me at that time were Otis's perspectives on strategies for struggle in that particular moment. He expected the fight to be a long one, a contestation on many levels in many venues. "The enemy we face is a complex and well-rooted national disease," he argued. "We just have to resist and attack from now on, and in the meantime, try to figure the best way out" (Chapter 18, "Second Letter to Griff"). He had a special word of warning for young white radicals like me: "I wonder how recognizable many of today's idealistic young civil rights champions will be a few years from now when the combined forces of big business, organized religion, and their neighbors and relatives have had a chance to flog them back into line" (Chapter 20, "The New Bag"). I took this as a warning and a challenge, and I know many others of my generation did, too. If some of us have been able to remain true to the cause, to avoid being flogged back into line, I am sure that Otis's warning had something to do with it.

Listen to the Lambs quickly went out of print, but its ideas lived on in other venues. In 1970 Johnny Otis started a radio program that ran for nearly thirty-five years on listener-supported stations that featured his wise commentary, interviews with other musicians, and choice selections of rhythm and blues and blues music. For about ten years starting in the midseventies, he attracted a following as a Holiness preacher in the mostly Black but integrated Landmark Community Church in the Sugar Hill section of Los Angeles. His parishioners included many of his old friends from the music world, who made up one of the most amazing choirs and singing congregations ever. Otis preached a simple message in his sermons, asking members of the congregation to love one another, to help the homeless, to feed the hungry, to welcome the stranger, and to visit those who were in prison. He secured gallery shows for his art and published a book featuring his paintings and sculptures. In the midnineties, Otis reached a new audience when he began teaching a course on Black Music for a combined class of students from Vista Community College and the University of California, Berkeley extension division.

It is not possible to calculate the number of people who have been influenced by Otis's writing, speaking, art, and music. It is possible, however, to register the deep affection and respect people have for him. I know something about this because of his unexpected reappearance back into my own life. In 1986, I was researching an article on Chicano rock 'n' roll music in Los Angeles when I came across Ruben Guevara's essay "The View from the Sixth Street Bridge: The History of Chicano Rock."[5] Guevara mentioned that one of the first teenaged heartthrobs in Chicano rock 'n' roll was L'il Julian Herrera, who recorded for one of Johnny Otis's labels. Everyone thought L'il Julian was a Chicano, but Guevara revealed that the singer's real name was Ron Gregory. He was a Jewish Hungarian-American who ran away from his home back east and came to Los Angeles, hoping to move in with relatives in Boyle Heights. He did not find his relatives, but he did move in with a Mexican woman, who adopted him and raised him. It seemed appropriate to me that Johnny Otis—a Greek American who thought of himself as Black—was the person who discovered, recorded, and promoted L'il Julian, a Hungarian Jew who thought of himself as Mexican singing Black music!

I looked up Otis's business address in the library and wrote him a letter asking to come to Los Angeles and talk with him about L'il Julian. I wrote dozens of letters like this as a researcher but almost never got any replies. This time was different. On a cold day in December 1986, I was sitting in my office at the University of Minnesota. Outside my window, a typical Minnesota blizzard dropped nearly three feet of snow on the ground. I was speaking with a very smart graduate student who was asking me challenging and complicated questions, many of which I could not answer. Halfway through our conversation, the phone rang.

I identified myself, and in the uniquely resonant, throaty, and quintessentially musical voice that I would soon come to know well, the person on the other end of the line said, "Hey Professor, this is Johnny Otis. I got your letter. What I want to know is, are you a real professor who really knows things, or just a BS professor who just claims to know things?" Laughing, I replied that in my line of work that was sometimes a very fine distinction to make, but I was a professor who was *trying* to get things right. He invited me to come interview him, giving me the kind of directions that only a band leader would supply: "Now you vamp along the 110 Freeway until you hit your cue, which is Orange Grove Boulevard, then you come in there."

A few weeks later, I drove up to his house on a small street in Altadena. It was a Sunday morning, and a big orange tour bus was parked out front. I could hear the sounds of what seemed like hundreds of pigeons, chickens, parakeets, cockatoos, and other birds in coops behind the house. I rang the bell and waited a long time. It occurred to me that musicians played late on Saturday nights, and maybe it wasn't a good idea to interview one on a Sunday morning. Finally, Johnny came to the door wearing his bathrobe. A doo rag covered his hair, which he had just washed. Otis seemed only marginally awake, but when we sat down to talk his words flowed freely and I was mesmerized by his eloquence, the wonderful pace and rhythm of his speech, the humor and insight contained in his anecdotes, and the intellectual and political sophistication of his answers.

Just as reading *Listen to the Lambs* had done nearly twenty years earlier, this conversation spoke powerfully to me, to my deepest commitments and hopes. When we finished, Johnny said he thought we were kindred souls, that we shared many things. I felt the same way. He told me he wanted to write another book, that he had been saving drawings, observations, tapes from old radio programs, and character sketches that might make for a useful volume. Soon I was helping to edit his book *Upside Your Head!*, which was published in 1993.

We talked on the telephone frequently and corresponded often by mail. I met many of his family members, friends, and fellow musicians. We made presentations together when his book came out, and I gave guest lectures in his classes on Black music in Berkeley. But mostly, I just listened to Johnny and learned from him. Whether it was on his radio show, in his class lectures, during his onstage patter, or in everyday conversation, Johnny was always worth listening to, alternately intelligent, inspiring, philosophical, and funny. I am always impressed by the ways his many different interests, experiences, abilities, and ideas cohere around a unified sensibility deeply rooted in African American intellectual, moral, and spiritual traditions.

Four decades after the publication of *Listen to the Lambs*, voters elected Barack Obama to be the President of the United States. It would be an insult to Johnny Otis and the millions of other people who have struggled against racism in the United States and around the world to claim that nothing has changed over the years in this nation. Yet Obama's election by itself does nothing to improve the lives of ordinary Black people. Social conditions, opportunities, and life chances remain separate and unequal. Forty years after the publication of *Listen to the Lambs*, the passage of the Fair Housing Act, the Supreme Court's ruling in *Jones v. Mayer*, forty-two years after Dr. King's Open Housing marches in Chicago, one hundred and forty years after the signing of the 1866 Civil Rights Law, people of different races in the United States today remain relegated to different spaces.

More than four million instances every year of housing and lending discrimination work insidiously to skew opportunities and life chances along racial lines. We would make enormous progress toward racial justice if fair housing laws were only strengthened and enforced, if they included cease and desist orders or penalties sufficient to deter lawbreakers, if governments at all levels honored their affirmative fair housing obligations, if the Office of the Comptroller of the Currency and the Federal Reserve Board pursued cases against mortgage lenders based on evidence of policies with disparate racial impacts, if the property insurance industry was required to provide the kind of data that the Home Mortgage Disclosure Act requires from housing lenders, and if government agencies and officials at all levels enforced the law more actively and aggressively.

Yet stronger laws and better law enforcement alone will not be enough to counter the ways that race skews opportunities and life chances in our society. The patterns of the past impede the attainment of equality in the present and will continue to do so until we come to grips with the ways in which present policies increase the value of past and present discrimination by exploiting the cumulative vulnerabilities of aggrieved racialized groups. Gross imbalances of power always offer opportunities for profiteering and exploitation. Sites of cumulative violation and vulnerability yield unusually high profits. As organizers in the civil rights movement used to say, "water flows to the low places." Local, state, and federal governments do not do enough to combat discrimination to be sure, but even worse, they add to existing injustices and inequalities by providing subsidies for segregation and rewards for racism through putatively race-neutral policies that have disparate racial impacts and that frequently expand rather than narrow racial gaps in assets, wealth, opportunities, and life chances.

This republication of *Listen to the Lambs* provides us with an opportunity to assess where we stand today. Johnny Otis's words proved to be prophetic. Racism continues to be a matter of power as well as prejudice, a conflict of interests as well as attitudes. In the disgraceful response to the devastation enacted on Black people in New Orleans in the wake of Hurricane Katrina in 2005, we see the consequences of four decades of calculated cruelty and organized abandonment. Our national failure to listen to the lambs at the time of the Watts Riots in 1965 squandered an opportunity for meaningful change and moral growth. It postponed the day of reckoning with our vexed racial legacy. Because we did not listen to the lambs in 1965 or to Johnny Otis in 1968, the work we need to do now is harder, more difficult, and more costly. Yet the reappearance of this book could not come at a better time. It is just what we need now. At one and the same time a moving social history, a wise rumination, and a magnificent polemic, it speaks as powerfully to us today as it did the day it first appeared in 1968. It helps us see where we are, where we have been, and—above all—where we must go.

Notes

1. Johnny Otis, "Johnny Otis Says Let's Talk," *The Sentinel*, June 28, 1962, 6A.

2. Martin Schiesl, "Behind the Shield," in *City of Promise: Race and Historical Change in Los Angeles*, ed. Martin Schiesl and Mark M. Dodge (Claremont, Calif.: Regina Books, 2006), 144.

3. Interview with Johnny Otis, Altadena, California, December 14, 1986.

4. Ibid.

5. Ruben Guevara, "The View from the Sixth Street Bridge: The History of Chicano Rock," in *Rock 'n' Roll Confidential Report*, ed. Dave Marsh (New York: Pantheon, 1985), 118.

An Introduction

BY PRESTON LOVE

READING THROUGH the manuscript of this book prior to its publication, I repeatedly found myself pausing to ponder how unlikely it was that America, with all its sociological and environmental factors working against the probability, could produce an individual such as Johnny Otis. Even after more than twenty-seven years of the closest personal ties I am intrigued by the fact that my friend is genetically white but in all other respects completely black.

I first saw Johnny playing the drums in a Denver night spot in June, 1941. My first impression was that he was just another white kid down in the ghetto trying to learn to play like the Negro jazz musicians. I reasoned that the pretty brown-skinned girl with him was some little chick he had picked up in an extension of his effort to "get that colored feeling." I was very mistaken on both counts. The girl was his wife, Phyllis, and he was as "black" as I.

There were a number of factors that led Johnny and me to become inseparable, lifelong buddies. We were drawn together musically through our mutual love for the Count Basie band. The fact that we both have always loved hunting and fishing has had a lot to do with it also, but the thing that struck me most about Johnny was his fierce dedication to the cause of black people. I realize now that I met my first "black nationalist" almost thirty years ago. I can remember that from the first moment of our friendship until now I have found it impossible to think of Johnny as anything but an actual Negro.

From the first letter to Griff Borgeson to the end of the manuscript, I knew that this book would make fascinating reading for the average person, but to myself and to many others who know Johnny personally the autobiographical sections are a nostalgic delight.

As I read through the chapters dealing with the early forties I was reminded of our first joint musical venture back in Omaha, Nebraska. The Otis-Love Band. Our partnership dissolved when I went with Count Basie and Johnny joined the Harlan Leonard band on the West Coast.

After leaving Leonard, Johnny joined Bardu Ali's band at the old Lincoln Theatre in Los Angeles. Fortunately, I spent a lot of time on location in Los Angeles in those days with the Basie and Lucky Millinder orchestras and Johnny and I were together constantly. I remember how affectionately Bardu used to refer to Johnny as his son and how comedian Pigmeat Markham used to joke about the difference in skin tones.

In 1945 Johnny formed a big jazz group and became the house band at the popular Club Alabam on Central Avenue in L.A. A year later Johnny's first hit record, "Harlem Nocturne," gave him "name" status and paved the way for his first national tour and the many successes to follow. He formed his rhythm and blues combo in 1948 and a string of hit records with vocalists Little Esther and Mel Walker sent him off on extensive road trips that established him as a household word in Negro communities everywhere.

The strong identity that Johnny enjoys in the Los Angeles area is a result of his radio and television shows, which began in 1955. For years the Johnny Otis Show both on radio and TV were the only programs featuring rhythm and blues music exclusively. The radio show was a disc jockey program, the TV production a live weekly musical featuring Johnny's band and guest appearances by singers. Then came his hit record, "Willie and the Hand Jive," and Johnny became a kind of pied piper of rock and roll on the West Coast. At present Johnny's musical activities are divided between fronting his band, which now features his son, Shuggie, on guitar, and working as a producer for the Eldo Record Company in Hollywood.

A little-known fact about Johnny is his talent as a painter and sculptor. His paintings have been shown on occasion in the Los Angeles area. A strikingly prophetic oil of Nat Turner won Johnny first prize in a city-wide contest on historical Negro figures. It was prophetic in the sense that it portrayed insurrectionist Nat Turner leading his band of escaped slaves against a background of burning plantations. It was painted a few months before the Watts riots.

Johnny's love for the very flavor of the ghetto and the Negro community has far exceeded even mine. I have known countless Negroes who considered themselves avid race champions, but I perceived that their sincerity and their dedication to the black cause fell far short of Johnny's. For instance, I had two older brothers who were also very close to Johnny and who often engaged in verbal battles with him about America's race problem, and I always felt that Johnny was the Negro fighting for his people more so than my brothers, who were reasonably loyal Negroes and who were genetically Afro-American for sure. It was Johnny who always appeared on the defensive, or rather on the *offensive,* for our race in these discussions.

Johnny's position was never that of a white person identifying with the Negro community to offer it assistance. His life has been that of a black man joined with other black men to combat the outside—the hostile and unjust white establishment. I am reminded of Johnny when I read accounts of whites who lived their lives as Indians within the tribes of the early West. History records that they fought, lived, and died with their tribal brothers. I believe, however, that these were cases of white babies that were captured and raised within the tribes from infanthood. In any event, there is no evidence of any other "white" person becoming "black" as Johnny has unquestionably done.

Most of our mutual friends over the years considered it impractical of Johnny to sacrifice the many advantages he could have enjoyed in America by being white instead of identifying completely as a Negro. I partially agreed with this thinking but I could never get the point over to him. The closest we have come over the years to a downright rift was a shouting match in 1965 when I tried to prevent him from going into the heart of the Watts riot area during the peak of violence. "Someone won't recognize you, and you might be killed!" I yelled. But he went anyhow—moving freely among the black people as he has done for the past forty years in cities north and south, throughout the country.

There will be people, both black and white, who will ask where Johnny gets off writing for the black world and from within it. Johnny is the first to point out that he speaks for no one but himself. No one man can truly speak for the entire black race any more than one man can speak for the white. Black people are no more all one identical personality than any other. Only the environment that closes around us because we are black is uniform and therefore our culture is consistent. That environment closes around Johnny and his wife and children as surely as it closes around mine. Should the rising tide of black nationalism harden white society to the point of race war, Johnny stands with his black brothers as automatically as a Lyndon Johnson or a John Kennedy would stand with the United States against Red China in case of war. Johnny's lifetime as a black man in the Negro community, his involvement in the civil rights movement, and his accomplishments and experiences in the Negro show world give him the right, in fact the responsibility, to speak. I think Johnny Otis speaks well. But then, you may have noticed, I'm prejudiced.

January, 1968   *Preston Love*

Preface

THIS IS A BOOK that grew out of a letter to a friend. The letter, inspired by the Watts riots of 1965, caught the interest of a publisher who commissioned me to write a book. The prospect of having my say published set me off on a binge of typewriteritis that brought forth a series of pieces which darted here and there chronologically, some of which seemed distantly, if at all, related to the original subject of the letter. The Watts riots became a part, rather than the central theme, of the manuscript. It was particularly difficult for me to determine where to go and how to go with this project because I wanted to avoid the impression that I was presuming to speak for black people or anyone else (anyone but myself, that is) or that, because of my unique vantage point and lifetime of inside experiences, I was setting myself up as *the* expert on the matter.

I was born in Vallejo, California, in 1921. My parents, Alexander and Irene Veliotes, were Greek immigrants. (My surname, Otis, is a kind of abbreviation of Veliotes.) In 1922, my sister Dorothy was born and a year later the family moved to Berkeley, California. In 1928 my brother Nick arrived.

Until the late thirties, when the Depression forced him out of business, my father had a grocery store in Berkeley. We lived above the store in an integrated neighborhood that soon was to become an almost entirely Negro community.

There were a few white and oriental children in the neighborhood but the bulk of my childhood playmates, especially those with whom I had most constant and intimate contact, were black.

There is nothing particularly unique, I suppose, about a white child being raised among black folk in America. The difference in my case was that during my pre-teens and adolescence I didn't veer off into the white world. As a kid I decided that if our society dictated that one had to be either black or white, I would be black.

I did not become black because I was attracted to Negro music. My attitude was formed long before I moved into the music field. Nor did I become a member of the Negro community because I married a Negro girl. These eventualities were outgrowths of my life among black people.

I became what I am because as a child I reacted to the way of life, the special vitality, the atmosphere of the black community. Some people call this difficult-to-describe quality, Negritude. Today it is more popularly known as "soul."

No number of objections such as, "You were born white . . . you can never be black," on the part of whites, or, "You sure are a fool to be Colored when you could be white," from Negroes, can alter the fact that I cannot think of myself as white. I do not expect everybody to understand it, but it is a fact. I am black environmentally, psychologically, culturally, emotionally, and intellectually. To attempt to view my case anthropologically would be nonsense because the world, and surely America, is full of "Negroes" who are much lighter than I, and "whites" who are much darker.

There is one area where I differ from most Negroes: I am black by choice. But then, many white-looking so-called Negroes are black by choice, so I am not unique in this respect.

I leave it to the future social scientists to fathom, if they can, the special mysteries of black "soul." I simply know it exists.

White society has its energy and vitality also, but it's not the same. The black community throbs and vibrates with a live, animal heartbeat. The white world seems to me to generate a massive energy . . . but with a turbo-engine, ball-bearing quality.

Louis Armstrong once answered a question about jazz by saying, "If you don't feel it, you'll never know." This special quality possessed by American Negro people does not begin or end with music, dancing, or art; it grows out of the total life and atmosphere of the Negro Community—the way black people talk, laugh, walk, sing, cry, play, love, and live.

As a youngster in Berkeley I lived under constant pressure to abandon my social direction and become "white." I got this at school from teachers and counselors, from white friends, and especially from my mother. My father was not much concerned about race or color one way or another. Having come to America as an adult, he retained much of his early European-Mideastern point of view and was basically uninfluenced by New World racism. My mother, on the other hand, had come here as a small child and was raised in this country; she was quite Americanized and held a more negative attitude. In spite of her Christian posture and her American moralist convictions, she could not bring herself to practice fully what she felt she believed. She was a wonderfully dedicated and loving mother in every way but one—the one that counted most to me.

There were eighteen long years between the time Phyllis and I were married and the day my mother was able to finally meet and accept her daughter-in-law. It is a tribute to my wife's sweet, forgiving nature—typical of so many black people—that she could welcome my mother with love and understanding after such an incredible period of time. I resented the situation then, and I find it difficult to erase from my heart now, because it was an affront to my wife, my children, and my adopted people. But I suppose I lack some of Phyllis' compassionate nature.

I don't want to appear unduly harsh toward my mother, who has in recent years made a sincere effort to heal the wounds of the past and bring us all together, but it is, in addition to being a part of my story, a sad commentary on American life.

In the mid-forties my parents were divorced. Following his retirement in 1951, my father came to Los Angeles, where he lived with us until his death in 1957.

As I attempted to put this book together, I realized, with the thoughtful prodding of editor Eric Swenson, Preston Love, Stanley Saunders, and Lillian Adleman Polan, that if this book was to be more than a kind of detached analysis of the American black-white dilemma (after all, trained social scientists and writers have been and are doing that far better than I could), I would have to go more deeply into my personal life and experiences. Proceeding, then, with the knowledge that no one out there was particularly interested in the life history of Johnny Otis, per se, I have attempted to the best of my ability to put together something of interest and hopefully of value, in spite of its subjective, rambling, and at times, autobiographical character.

LISTEN TO THE LAMBS

ONE

First Letter to Griff

"I know my father told me yesterday that when he was a youngster the Negroes were promised a better future. He says now that here I am being promised a better future . . . that's the third generation. He says now this has been boiling up inside the Negro people for so long that they just couldn't hold it inside of them any longer and they just burst out the wrong way." — *Young girl, interviewed during the Watts riots.*

DEAR GRIFF: *August 17, 1965*

There were always three approaches to this question. Those who knew it COULD HAPPEN . . . and someday WOULD. Those who were smugly sure it COULD NOT happen . . . and those who swept the whole thought under the carpet and refused to admit consciousness of the subject.

Well, it finally hit the fan! Now, in the wake of the implosion, with Los Angeles' bowels exposed to the world and her dirty guts strewn all over the lot, will anyone believe it when someone hollers "HELP!" . . . And by the way, where are the leaders? . . . Who are the leaders? . . . Is this chess or checkers? . . . How come Hoyle doesn't know? . . . Do you win when you lose? . . . vice versa? . . . SOCIO-MILITARY QUESTION: How do you explain the phenomenon of poisonous fallout emanating from Glendale, Inglewood, Civic Center, etc., etc., suddenly blowing back to the inception point? Did Einstein work it

out? . . . Did   Teller? . . . Pauling? . . . Von   Braun? . . .
George Washington Carver? . . . Martin Luther King? . . .
Bert Williams? . . . Are you my mother?

Do we bury the dead in American flags . . . or canceled
welfare checks . . . or Baptist choir robes? . . . or Los Angeles
Police Department handcuffs? . . . or eviction notices? . . . or
selective service questionnaires?

Do we mark the graves with crosses? . . . asbestos or
kerosene-drenched? . . . How about marking them with frag-
ments of the Watts Towers? . . . or with the pens used to sign
the Civil Rights Act? . . . or swastikas?

Do the dead lie in Potter's Field or Forest Lawn? . . . Or
in the parking lot behind the old Watts Savings and Loan Association Building? . . . Or in the empty lot off 108th and Wilmington? . . . Or just plain on their ass where they've always
been anyhow?

Who's gonna cry? . . . Who's gonna cry besides Mama and
Papa and Sis and Bro? . . . And who is Bro? How many kinds
of brothers do I have . . . And what kind of keeper is this?
. . . now, who's gonna cry *real* tears besides Mama and Papa?
My pastor? . . . the Negro doctor? . . . Lawyer? Crying is "in"
in Watts. Crying is uncool in Baldwin Hills. Crying is a pain in
the butt in Beverly Hills. Hiding is the lick west of La Brea.

"Why can't they behave like civilized people? . . . It makes
it uncomfortable as hell for 'decent' Colored folk . . . and 'decent' white folk. . . ." Mexican-Americans, of course, ain't in it
at all, you understand. But how about Jewish people? They've
always been so sympathetic and all. Why make the merchants
suffer? Gee!

You know how come Billy Graham has such a huge following? 'Cause he knows where it's at, that's why! "Sinister forces in
the world are at work among the Negro people." . . . See what
I mean? INSIGHT!

How come the Communists exert such a strong ideological

influence among impoverished Negroes? Criminy Sakes . . . it's
un-American as hell! Just think, those Russians (or is it the
Cubans or the Chinese?) . . . anyhow, just think, foreigners
coming over here and inciting our Negroes to riot. Maybe now
we'll listen to Reverend Billy Hargis and Gerald L. K. Smith and
Robert Welch and all those guys who have tried to warn us.
WHAT? . . . it's a matter of people not having decent employment and housing? . . . Are you crazy? . . . *This is organized
insurrection.* . . . Now who told you that one-third of the men
in Watts were unemployed, . . . where'd you read that? . . .
the *People's World* or something?

WELL, what the hell . . . I'll tell you something, though, Griff,
it was a bitch! And I repeat, will anyone listen the next time the
ghetto cries "HELP"? Are you familiar with the gospel song, "Listen to the Lambs"? It goes:

Listen . . . listen . . . listen to the lambs,

They're crying for the Lord to come by . . .

I thought about it during the riot. They wouldn't listen to the
lambs. . . . The lambs cried, and finally one day the lambs
turned into lions.

Friday after work I decided to go by State Assemblyman
Merv Dymally's office (85th and Broadway) and try to talk him
into driving with me into the eye of the tornado. My daughter
Janice, who has a summer gig (secretary) at Congressman
Hawkins' office (same address as Merv), had gone home for the
day—she had called me when she left and I knew she was not
there. Up to this date the "riot" had been limited to the Watts
area only. As I pulled off the southbound Harbor Freeway onto
Manchester and Broadway, I realized that a different kind of
"business as usual" was about to be transacted in this area thick
with stores and storefronts . . . and that Watts wasn't going
to be the beginning and the end, nor was Manchester and Broadway. The place was alive with milling folk. It hadn't exploded

with destruction here yet, but it was about to. I had the feeling that I was looking at hundreds of neurotic ants reacting mechanically to invisible electric charges. I split.

The evening before (Thursday), light-skinned Negroes had been banged around by mistake. In fact, a number of Negroes' cars had been destroyed (burned and smashed) because the drivers and/or passengers had been mistaken for "Whitey." As a result, word was flashed around Friday morning that the secret password for light-skinned "bloods" was "BURN, BABY, BURN!" and that the signal while driving a car was three fingers held up with arm in the position of right turn. I knew what to do in case of a tie.

As I sped away from Manchester and Broadway I could see the fires raging to the southeast. My plan was to get to the freeway post-haste and make it to the pad. But, as I looked at the smoke in the distance, something weird gripped me. I know it was stupid . . . I know it was foolish, but I had to go! Nothing naïve like wanting to help or get into the mess, but I wanted to see. SEE WITH MY OWN EYES . . . even if I got the hell kicked out of me or worse. Griff, listen, we've got emotions sealed inside that we don't know about. I kept saying to myself, Listen, you are not going to live through this gloriously terrible hour and not be able to say ten years from now—or even ten minutes from now—that you didn't see it . . . didn't feel it . . . didn't smell it! I, Johnny Otis, was scared shitless but another "I" didn't give a damn . . . and this scared me even more. Who the hell was this other guy who didn't care if I was shaking all over?

I pulled left and headed for Watts. At Central I turned right and twice before getting to 103rd I used the three-finger signal. It worked. Now I felt better. Nothing to it. Now I wanted to see the charred remains of the 103rd business strip and over to 119th Street to see how our old homestead of the forties had fared, and then go home. But it wasn't that simple. I saw the tortured remains of 103rd from the Central Avenue end, but about a block away I ran into the real McCoy. I was third in a line of cars that ran into a howling wall of human anarchy. They converged upon the first car, bypassed the second, and three cats rushed up to me where I was sitting in my little MGA. At this point, scared-shitless Johnny Otis regained control of the debate. The other me was silent if not gone. I thought, Well, here it is. But my luck was with me. The second guy to reach me looked, hesitated, blinked and said, "Johnny Otis, are you out of your goddam mind? . . . Get the hell out of here before you get killed!" I said, "Man, I want to get out but I'm stuck in this mess!" Whereupon he got the other two dudes to help him clear a path behind my car, and I was able to back up to the point where I could swing right and make it straight to the pad. As they cleared a way for me they told the crowd things like, "It's Johnny Otis, let him back up here." . . . "Blood brother, blood brother, let him through." At one point a plump woman stuck her head in the car and said, "Hi, Johnny Otis," and so help me, we had a quick little small-talk session which included where was my old guitar player, Pete Lewis, and where was I playing tonight. I found myself chit-chatting like an idiot as though we were on a peaceful corner in some quiet community of some distant and misty land. Then I heard the "brave" me say, "What the hell are you doing having a delightful little talk at a time like this. *Let's get out of here!*" and I knew that he hadn't disappeared—he had finally gotten the message, and now the two ME's had blended into one unanimous, chicken-shit coward from head to toe!

As I write this, the curfew imposed upon the entire Negro community is still in effect. I mean all the way from Rosecrans to Olympic and from La Brea to the "boondocks" east of Watts and beyond. After 8 P.M. you keep off the street. All day and all night, trucks loaded with uniforms and machine guns and bayonets roll by our house and all other Negro houses. Like frozen iron porcupines they crawl down our streets and through our minds.

Saturday we had to go shopping. The stores in our area were either boarded up or burning, so we had to drive way out to a suburban shopping center in an all-white area—Laura and her baby, Shuggie, Nicky, Phyllis, and I. As we drive into the white neighborhoods the conversation turned to the riots and the possible hostility of the whites we would encounter. Phyllis finally said, "Well, the rest of you look white, so if they notice us at all they will probably think you captured me."

Now that the storm seems to have abated somewhat I read things in the daily papers that go like this: "The criminal elements that raged, rampaged, looted, and burned have disgraced the responsible majority in the Los Angeles Negro community. It is all the more senseless because here in California the Negro had it so good." So good! The misery and oppression visited upon the mass of black peoples in Los Angeles caused a spontaneous eruption and still there are those who think the Negroes have it "so good."

I'll tell you this: If the plight of the Negro in the big urban areas is not cured, and quick, we can expect plenty of the same. This thing is not going to go away. No piddling too late with too little war-on-poverty program is going to make a dent in this misery. Mounting unemployment, brutal police practices, discriminatory labor unions, teeming ghettos created by housing discrimination, inferior education for black children who are caught up in de facto segregated schools with poor facilities, overcrowded classrooms, uninterested and often lousy teachers . . . all these poisons contribute to the present condition. To even begin to remedy the brutal ills that afflict American Negroes, a massive, all-out effort must be the approach. The kind of billions that are spent on foreign aid and war must be spent in the Watts' of America.

The United States is willing to attempt to police the world, but is unwilling to defend black people against their domestic enemies. Plenty of legislation is passed and many inspiring speeches are heard, but this doesn't relieve the man at the bottom of the economic ladder of his immediate and crushing burden. Yes, many so-called Negro leaders are heard thanking the Great White Fathers for the civil rights crumbs that have been trickling down. And those modern-day Uncle Toms were the first to call down from their comfortable Baldwin Hills to "Stop the disgraceful rioting and looting." I heard one old apologist from way back exhort the rioters on radio and TV to "stop rioting and everything will be all right." But the people who were "working out" in the streets were too busy to be watching television, and if they weren't, they would spit at these self-appointed "leaders" who had performed so shabbily in the past.

I read somewhere once that when the French Revolution first broke out, the intellectual "leaders" of France responded with yelps of utter delight. "At last freedom is imminent! The people have risen and democracy is here!" But a few days later, when the heads began to roll, these same mental militants ran for the hills, horrified, with their tails between their legs. What I'm saying is that this thing in Los Angeles, just like any revolt, was terrible and regrettable, *but* it could have been avoided with a little justice and a lot of money and effort spent meaningfully. I can't read the American White Establishment's mind, therefore I don't know if they really see the handwriting on the wall. But I do know that if the black man is not cut completely free of his misery he will continue to rock the boat and rock the boat and rock the boat . . . and I don't mean nonviolent, organized demonstrations and marches led by pompous, sanctimonious preachers and self-declared "leaders."

And one more item, Griff. My son Shuggie, whom you and Jasmine love so well, is going to be spared the humiliation and degradation that his people have had to endure through the centuries or else—. He is going to be free . . . because attempting to keep him half-free is going to be very messy. If you think the present generation of young Negroes are insistent upon their rights, wait till you see Shuggie and his brothers and sisters.

I'll keep you posted on what's happening on this side of the drink. Please let me hear about your life in France, etc., and above all LOTS OF LOVE FROM ALL OF US TO YOU AND JASMINE . . . and that goes for your cat, too!!

Your buddy, Johnny

TWO

For Colored Only

Mid-west promoter to band leader Preston Love upon meeting him in person for the first time:

"By George, from your pictures I never would've thought you were Colored."

At a loss for anything else to say, Preston quipped, "You ever seen a Negro who wasn't colored?"

Promoter, undaunted . . . "But you're about the best-looking Colored boy I've ever seen."

I'M DRIVING DOWN the Harbor Freeway in Los Angeles. The car radio is tuned to an unfamiliar station. Chris, my son-in-law, and I are chatting about something . . . I don't remember what. The voice on the radio is going in the background. . . .

". . . he is deceitful and treacherous, my friends."

Something about the broadcaster's voice caught our attention. I guess it was the passionate tone, the urgency. Our conversation trailed off and we listened.

". . . he'll tell you a monstrous lie . . . time and again he'll repeat it . . . he knows it's a lie . . . he knows you know it's a lie . . . and he knows you know *he* knows it's a lie . . . but he tells it over and over again, because he gets away with it. And when he gets the chance he uses this lie to enslave you . . . to exploit you . . . to strip you of your rights and oppress you . . ."

I glanced at the radio dial, trying to get a line on what kind of program it was, or who we were listening to.

". . . he is full of talk about brotherhood and democracy and a world of blissful equality . . . he'll talk about freedom but he doesn't mean it . . . the freedom he means is the freedom he would deprive you of . . . to crush you . . . to suppress all that is sacred and precious . . . he is the enemy . . . the Communist!"

"Well, I could've swore he was describing the American white man," I said.

"Ha-ha," Chris laughed, "me too . . . and here the cat's talking about a Communist."

I wonder how I would've reacted to that broadcast had my father, some forty years ago, decided to settle in Glendale or Santa Ana rather than in the Negro community of Berkeley, California?

I can't remember as a child in Berkeley ever "wanting" to be white. But I can remember . . . as the baby days passed and the eighth, ninth, and tenth years of my life arrived . . . as I began to feel the knife of racial hypocrisy . . . how I wanted *not* to be white. And I remember, in my pre-teens and early teens, as my childhood pal Rudy and I grew even closer, how our white playmates grew farther apart. For young boys and girls the color line was traumatic enough, but as we moved into adolescence it took on deep, poisonous expressions with sexual overtones. Now it was more than a matter of not wanting to be white. I yearned with all my heart to be black.

As I look back I realize how strong the pressures to keep white and black apart really were . . . and, incidentally, still are. I remember the school counselor who gave us a very inspiring talk about equality and brotherhood one evening at a Christian Endeavor meeting. This was the same man who called me into his office at school some days later to suggest that I should cultivate some white friends.

"For your own good, John . . . don't misunderstand now . . . the Colored boys are just fine . . . but you must think about your future . . . you will soon be a young man . . . and there will be girl friends . . . and I know that you are an intelligent fellow and you understand. . . ."

I wanted to point out that it was a matter of *his* intelligence . . . and that I *did* understand but *he* didn't . . . and that I knew what lurked behind that pious, white Christian attitude . . . and that I was way ahead of him . . . and that there not only would be girls, but that there *were* girls.

To make my mama happy I became a member of Boy Scout Troop 25 in Berkeley. It was great fun and I was having a ball. I got interested enough to work up from Tenderfoot to 2nd Class Scout. One day I earned a Merit Badge in Cycling.

At first Rudy ignored the idea of joining the troop but I finally gained his interest, and at the next meeting I submitted the name Rudolph Jordan for membership. I realize today how fortunate we were that Rudy had to deliver papers that night and couldn't appear in person. As it turned out, he was spared a degrading experience. That night the happy world of Boy Scouts crumbled for me.

The meeting was held in a school bungalow. At the end of the meeting I went to the cloak room to get my jacket. I could hear the Scoutmaster and a number of other adult men talking behind a screened-off section.

"As long as I'm connected with this troop there'll be no damn Portagees in here with our white boys!"

Portagees? White boys? I wondered if they meant Rudy.

Oh, now I remembered. Earlier in the meeting an olive-complexioned Portuguese man had brought his little boy in to join the troop. The name Rudolph Jordan hadn't created any resistance because it sounded Anglo-Saxon, but I knew that if a Portuguese boy was being barred, my black buddy didn't stand a chance. I was crushed.

Rudy and I had big plans for the future. We were going to grow up and own a big auto-wrecking yard. We were about fifteen at the time. This was before I got the music bug and he decided he was going to own a big nightclub where my band would play. We figured the best way to prepare ourselves for the auto-wrecking business was to hang around the salvage yards. And we did.

One day my father gave me an old decrepit Model T Ford he kept stored in the garage. Here was our chance to work on a car. We were able, through trial and error, to put the old junk into shape. Rudy was studying auto shop at school and we salvaged parts from the junkyards.

We would ride around Berkeley and Oakland in the old Model T, looking for abandoned cars in empty lots and broken-down wrecks in garages, backyards, and driveways. The old cars had salvage value at the junkyards. It was Depression time and three or four bucks was like a fortune for us.

Eventually we worked up to an old Dodge truck and business was moving along fine. Pulling into one of the junkyards one day we were rushed by a group of policemen with drawn pistols. Someone had stolen some tires and siphoned some gas, and we were nominated.

They handcuffed Rudy and slapped him around. On the way to the West Oakland Police Station they asked me what I was doing associating with black criminals. I was too choked with tears and too scared to answer. In the station two other cops were booking a Mexican man. He had confessed to the crime that we had been apprehended for. After a few more racial insults to Rudy and a warning to me to start running around with "clean-cut white boys," we were released.

This experience had a turn-about effect on us. To that day we had never thought of stealing anything. After that we began stealing tires and siphoning gas. If we're going to be treated like dogs when we're innocent . . . we might as well be guilty, we reckoned. We had the idea that we were "gettin' even with the 'man'" every time we filched something. We not only used this reasoning to justify stealing, but we felt it actually gave our illicit activities a kind of Robin Hood righteousness.

The experience with the cops gave Rudy new ammunition in his own personal campaign to "whiten" me up.

"See what I been tellin' you," Rudy would lecture. "You've got to identify more with whites. It will help us in business. Fool, why do you think the cops slapped me in the mouth and put the handcuffs on me and only talked to you?"

"I know all about that."

"Yeah," but you ain't taking advantage of it. Some day when we get ready to open our business we're just gonna be two niggers . . . one dark and one light . . . and we won't get no kind of break."

"So what?"

"So goddamit, if you mingle with some white people and get contacts we can be successful, that's what. And another thing, we're both talking about what good we can do for black people when we get big. Well, a rich white man can do something if he wants to, but a poor black man can't do shit."

"Well, that's what I'm gonna do, I guess . . . I ain't gonna do shit."

"Listen," Rudy would reason, "white-looking people are no big novelty among Negroes. There's no problem there, but whites will always beat you back to the other side. They will always say, 'You're white . . . get over here . . . you're black . . . get over on that side, and stay there.'"

For a while he had both of us believing that the white world had some infallible, magic power that worked like a supernatural ray to keep people "in their place."

"If you look white, the 'man' says you *are* white and that's it," with Rudy's theory. He held to it until 1939 when we went to the Count Basie dance on Treasure Island during the World's

Fair. At the door a big cop told me I couldn't enter because the affair was "for Colored only."

"I'm Colored," I answered. "This is my cousin." I pointed to Rudy. The cop blinked from one face to the other.

"Hey, Bill," he called another cop, "come here. This punk says he's a spade . . . you're from Mississippi . . . take a look."

A big bruiser in a policeman's uniform . . . the type I would grow to know and despise later in my travels through the Deep South . . . sauntered over.

"Let me see your fingernails, boy."

He examined my nails with a professional, almost scientific, authority.

"Yeah, he's a nigra . . . let him in."

Once we got inside I turned to Rudy. "I thought you said if you look white you are white and the 'man' keeps you white."

"Okay, my black brother . . . I mean cousin," Rudy chided. "It's your funeral."

IN 1941, Phyllis and I eloped to Reno, Nevada. Rudy was the best man. Everything went fine until we applied for the marriage license.

The fact that Phyllis and I were mere kids didn't bother the clerk. He was bugged by our contrasting colors.

"I don't care who your cousin is, boy . . . you look white to me and we don't issue marriage licenses to black and white in this state."

I started to ask him to examine my fingernails, but Rudy pulled me aside.

"Don't worry about it. Phyllis and I will come back when this cat's not here and I'll get the paper in your name."

The following day, armed with a marriage license, we drove to an Episcopalian minister's home to tie the knot. A friend had taken the precaution of informing the minister (who was white) that I was a Creole from New Orleans, in order to avoid the kind of problem we had had with the city clerk the day before.

"Come in folks," the preacher called.

He placed his half-empty glass of beer on the mantelpiece, opened a book, and the ceremony began.

With the words "I now pronounce you man and wife," the preacher began a long dissertation about how he used to play with "cullud" kids when he was a youngster Down South. I glanced at Phyllis and Rudy. They were too busy wiping tears away and being sentimental about the wedding to notice what the preacher was talking about. With every reference to "black gals" and "clinker-top boys" I got hotter and hotter under the collar.

Finally I blurted, "Let's get the hell outa here!"

Rudy's glasses almost jumped off his nose. As we beat an awkward but hasty retreat, I got a lecture for being "too sensitive."

From Reno, Phyllis and I went to Denver, Colorado. Rudy went back to Berkeley. We never really saw much of one another after that. We moved on to Omaha and then to Los Angeles. When occasionally my band would play in Oakland and San Francisco, I'd see Rudy for a short time. Until his accidental death in the early fifties, we would write one another from time to time. Rudy's optimism about becoming a big-time club owner had waned.

THREE

Pogies and Miss Werensky

"In the way of showing them how they feel sometime, like they not the underdog all the time. White treat them like a dog and keep them down for the rest of they life. They tired." — *Man, interviewed during the Watts riots.*

IT WAS DURING THE SUMMER OF 1939 and I was seventeen. Our old truck was back in working order and Rudy Jordan and I were on our way to a West Oakland junkyard to pick up a spare tire. From there we were going to the old pier in Richmond to fish for a kind of sea perch called a pogie. We needed plenty of perch because we had promised to supply the fish fry and social our club was throwing that night at San Pablo Park. The early-morning sun shone through the old, battered windshield. Tiny beads of sweat had formed on Rudy's nose and forehead. They sparkled like rainbow diamonds against his rich chocolate face as he anticipated the good times we were going to have at the picnic party.

"We gotta have at least a hundred pogies to be safe for to-night. There's a gang of cats coming over from Alameda and they're bringin' some of them pretty Portuguese chicks with 'em," Rudy informed me.

There was a Portuguese colony in Alameda. Someone had told us they were originally from the Azores. Their skin was generally light brown, and the girls were much sought after by the young cats in Berkeley and Oakland. Rumor had it that they were very clannish and that the men did not take kindly to outsiders who cast eyes toward their girls. We had heard tales of woe from young Negro fellows who had had run-ins with the nationalistic color-conscious Portuguese men.

One night about three months before, Rudy and I had gotten wind of a party in the Portuguese sector. Our plan was to slip into the party. Rudy had a long-distance crush on a gorgeous Portuguese girl named Lorraine, who was to be at the party, but we had to be cool because she had two brothers who looked like Charles Atlas and who guarded her like hawks.

"We're liable to get messed up in that party," I chickened-out to Rudy. "You don't even know the girl . . . and how do you 'act' Portuguese anyhow?" I asked.

"Just keep quiet and walk through the door. . . . I'll get tight with her when we get in and then she'll get one of her girl friends and we'll slip out and have a ball," Rudy countered.

A stern-looking, middle-aged man challenged us in Portuguese at the front door. Rudy kept nudging me as though I was supposed to come up with an answer. I started to say, "What are you nudging me for, fool?" The look in the guy's eye changed from stern to murderous. We split.

Now Rudy swung the old Dodge around a corner. It groaned and chug-chugged in protest. Because the car lacked a second gear, Rudy kicked it from first to third and the truck struggled to gain speed. "What makes you know that some Portuguese chicks are coming to Berkeley tonight?" I asked.

"Don't worry about it, baby. It's all set. I sent Lorraine a note by a chick that goes to school with her, and two of my boys from West Oakland are going to pick them up near the Alameda Tube at seven o'clock. The old master knows what he's doing," Rudy explained.

"Did you actually talk to *her* about it?" I asked.

"Didn't I say it's all set? Don't worry about it, man, don't worry about it!"

Up ahead a new Packard sedan was sitting on a flat. A well-dressed, middle-aged woman was standing with her hands on her hips surveying the damage.

"Here's where the old master does his good deed for the day," Rudy declared, as he pulled the truck to the curb.

We jacked the Packard up and replaced the flat with the spare. All through the operation the lady praised us for being so kind and thoughtful. She kept referring to us as "kids." This disturbed Rudy and he tried with every word and action to create the impression of a professional auto mechanic.

"You see, ma'am, the new Packard line has quite a weight distribution toward the rear end. You should always maintain heavy-duty tires to avoid extra wear and tear on the treads," he improvised loudly; then *sotto voce* to me, "This old broad's got lots of money . . . look at that necklace . . . look at this brand-new buggy. . . . I'm gonna con her into making me her personal mechanic."

"This is so sweet of you boys. You know, kids nowadays are so irresponsible . . . but you are certainly good boys . . . your mothers should be proud."

"Well, a car like this requires special attention, you know. I know from my experience at the garage that I can't assign just any of the boys to service the new Packard. This model is a favorite of mine and I have done plenty of research on it. I usually handle these jobs personally because they're very tricky."

I handed Rudy the lug wrench. "Get it over with, man. We gotta go fishin'," I murmured.

"Don't rush me, we've got plenty of time."

When we were through, the lady insisted that we drive into downtown Oakland with her so that she could show her appreciation.

"I told you. Now watch what happens," Rudy whispered as

we climbed into the Packard.

She drove to a jewelry store and bought us each a nice monogrammed ring. Mine had a big letter J on the black onyx and Rudy had the jeweler put on three small letters, RLJ. They stood for Rudolph Lamerro Jordan. While the jeweler was getting Rudy's ring fixed up, the old conversation started up again.

"Yes, ma'am, you should think seriously about putting that fine Packard into the hands of a man who can really handle it right," Rudy said.

"You kids always remember how it pays to help others when you look at your rings," the woman kept repeating.

Back at the truck Rudy held his ring up to the light. "Kinda sharp, man!" he said.

"Nobody'll ever believe us when we tell them about this," I said.

I looked around as we pulled away. I hadn't noticed it earlier, but we were parked across from the building where I had attended Greek school a few years back. And there, walking slowly down the street was the same old bearded priest who had been the teacher. He looked little . . . bent-over and moth-eaten. Back in the days when my folks had visions of my becoming a Greek scholar, he had looked huge, hairy, and formidable. It was the same old man in the same wrinkled black habit, but he had lost his awesomeness. How I used to hate that basement school. All the other kids in the neighborhood would be out at the playground or the park having fun, and I was trapped in the dingy recesses of Greek school. Once a week I was sent . . . or rather *sentenced* . . . to suffer through a couple of hours of reading and writing lessons in a language I couldn't make head nor tail of; because it certainly was not the familiar folk-Greek that we spoke at home.

The old priest had a habit of walking to your desk before asking a question. Then, shoving his beard full in your face, he'd shoot the question at you in a cloud of garlic breath. Once, he rushed down the aisle, rheumy eyes blazing, and demanded that I hold out my hand. Startled out of a reverie and immediately obedient to the garlic shout, I put both hands out, palms down. I had responded to his angry order Pavlov-puppylike, and as I hurried to bring my wandering mind back to the classroom, I could hear him shrieking, "I told you if you didn't pay attention I'd punish you!" His words were punctuated here and there with a sharp, cracking sound. Suddenly, my sensory organs caught up with one another. The cracking sounds my ears had reported were caused by a switch that was beating my hands. The fire message reached my brain and I snatched back my hands and screamed. I was running for the door. The garlic beard in the vampire suit was after me, punishment stick held high . . . the kids were laughing . . . my heart died in a convulsion of hot humiliation and fear . . . my hands hurt like hell!

I told my father what had happened. He cursed and swore that if it wasn't for the fact that it would be considered sacrilegious he'd kick the priest's ass. I never had to go back. I vowed that when I was grown I'd seek out that brutal old codger and do exactly what my father had been reluctant to do. Seeing the pathetic old figure now, bent over and inching along, I decided to close the case.

WE GOT TO the pier about noon. It was almost deserted so we had all the "good spots" to ourselves. An old man sold us a can of pile worms for a nickel and we started fishing. They were biting, but not fast enough for us to fill our big bucket and be out of there in time to collect on my paper route later in the afternoon.

"Say, who says pogies won't bite on anything but pile worms?" Rudy asked.

"Everybody knows that pogies won't bite on anything but pile worms," I answered.

The old man who collected the worms at low tide and sold

them for five cents a can, chimed in. "Pile worms is they natural food. They won't touch anything else. You ever see anybody catch a pogie without he do it with pile worms? No, you ain't. And you ain't never going to either. It's against nature, see, so they don't eat nothin' but pile worms."

"I caught a pogie on some mussels once," Rudy announced, cocking a challenging eye in our direction.

"No stuff?" I asked.

"Damn right," Rudy said.

The old man was shaking his head and mumbling under his breath.

"You don't believe it?" Rudy asked him.

"You mighta caught somethin' look like a pogie on mussels but you ain't caught no sho' nuff pogie on nothin' but pile worms," the old man insisted.

"Look man, I caught a sho' nuff, SHO' NUFF pogie on mussels," Rudy said sarcastically. "I know a pogie when I see one, and it was a pogie . . . and I caught him on mussels."

"Well, maybe you had a little piece of pile worm on that mussel . . . maybe just a little taste, see," the old man suggested.

"Nope, didn't have no pile worms that day, just mussels," Rudy snapped with finality. The wind died down and what had been a choppy surface on the water became smooth and glassy. Under the shadow of the pier we could see fish skittering about by the thousands.

"Man, there's many a fish in the sea . . . look at that," Rudy said. He pulled his line up, rebaited and threw it back. He wedged his pole into a crack in the pier and stood up and stretched. "I'm going to get a bottle of pop to go with these sandwiches," he yawned. "You want one?"

"Yeah, bring me one, too," I answered. The sun was beating down full blast now, the wind had died down, and my mouth was like cotton. A few more people had arrived, but no one was catching many fish. There were thousands down there. We could see them, but only occasionally was one hooked and landed. An old lady let out a yell as she hauled in a small crab. In her excitement she wheeled him over her head and he landed at my feet. Watch it, baby, I thought, you're gonna hook somebody in the head! I reached down to retrieve the crab for her, but he had jarred loose from the hook and was crawling sideways toward the edge of the pier. I reached out gingerly to grab him behind his hind legs, but he hit a crack in the pier and fell through.

"I missed him," I said to the lady.

"Forget it. I didn't want that ugly bastard . . . oh, for crissake, my paper boy! Fancy meeting you here," she said.

It was the old lady who lived up on Sacramento Street who was always swearing at her husband and giving me hell for not throwing her paper up on the porch. "Hi, Mrs. Milford," I said.

"Yeah, say listen," she said, "since I ran into ya, do me a favor will ya? Put the paper on the porch will ya, for crissake! Half of the time I never see the goddam thing because some crumb picks it up. Put it up on the porch like you're supposed to . . . just like you do for that broad next door. Don't I pay ya just like she does, for crissake? . . . Yeah, the lousy chippy, she probably gives ya something extra special at that."

I threw the papers the same for both of them, but Mrs. Milford was probably jealous of the big, well-stacked blonde who lived in the next apartment. I wish Miss Werensky *would* lay a little something "extra-special" on me, I thought. Or maybe I should wish that I had enough nerve and experience to hit on her. But every time I'd go up to collect for the paper and she'd come to the door in that silk bathrobe and ask me to come in while she got the money, I'd freeze up. She was maybe twenty-five or twenty-six, and that was an *old* chick to my seventeen-year-old mind . . . but a sexy . . . *SEXY* old chick!

"Come in, honey," Miss Werensky would croon. The sweet

boudoir smells in the apartment would almost paralyze me as I awkwardly stepped across the threshhold. She would invariably pull the door shut and lock it, turn and refold the bathrobe which had cracked open, smile and say something like, "My, you look handsome today, honey." At that point I was always a nervous wreck. I'd try to put up a front and say something cool, but I was too shook up. I was at once burning with animal desire and dying of sex fright.

I stood there on the pier, daydreaming about Miss Werensky. "What do you see out there . . . a submarine or something?" Rudy cracked, as he handed me a bottle of orange pop.

"Oh, no, I was just thinking about that big, juicy stallion, Miss Werensky," I answered.

"Oohwee! She's a fine thing! If you wasn't such a no-pussygettin' cat you could score with her in a minute. She keeps lookin' at you like you was a lollipop, and you keep actin' simple," Rudy said.

"Now you know so damn much, how do you know I ain't already *got* some of that stuff?" I demanded.

" 'Cause you run out of there like you was scared or something, that's why. Shoot! If you was gettin' some of that good stuff you'd be in there longer'n a split second, wouldn't you . . . or are you a rabbit or something?"

"You wouldn't know it if I was gettin' some anyhow," I said.

"Man, if you got some of that good stuff, you couldn't wait to tell me about it!" Rudy said. He took a big bite out of one of the sandwiches we had brought along for lunch.

"That's what you think," I grumbled. A series of flashes in the water caught my eye. Crumbs from Rudy's sandwich had fallen to the water and the fish were diving over one another trying to get to the food. "Hey, look at that, man. The fish are going crazy over the bread crumbs you just dropped!"

"I thought pogies didn't eat nothing but pile worms," Rudy

said.

"Them ain't pogies . . . them smelts," the old man pointed out. "Pogies, they down deeper."

"That's how we catch smelt in Lake Merritt . . . that flour and water stuff . . . it's just like bread . . . yeah, those are smelt," I agreed.

"I'm gonna find out," Rudy said. He rolled a piece of bread up in a ball, put it on his hook, and dropped it into the water. A swarm of fish tore it to pieces.

"Hook's too big," I told him. "Smelts' mouths are too small."

"I ain't after smelt," Rudy said. He put a heavy sinker on, rebaited with a ball of bread, and dropped the hook down past the smelt zone.

Almost immediately his pole dipped and he pulled up a pogie. But what a pogie! This one was almost twice the size of the little three-or four-inchers we were used to.

I stood speechless. The old man's jaw dropped.

"Don't mess with the old master if you don't know what you're doing!" Rudy exclaimed. "Now, I'm gonna show you cats how to catch pogies!" With that, he put on a couple more hooks and started pulling up big pogies, two and three at a crack.

Word flashed around the pier and people started a mad search for bread. The old man hobbled up the pier and returned with two loaves of bread. Pogies weren't the only fish on a bread kick that day. Every now and then someone would shout, "That's a beavertail!" or "Wow! a marble-eye perch! I ain't seen one of them for years!"

The windfall lasted about an hour. Then suddenly nothing was biting on bread. But an hour had been more than enough. Our bucket was overflowing and we had a gunnysack full, too. We had enough pogies and other assorted perchlike fish to supply three fish fries.

The old man explained that once in every so many years the

moon affected the sea creatures this way. Rudy wouldn't go for
that. "Moon, my ass!" he snorted. "It's just some people got it
and some ain't. I happen to have the touch. I'm what's known as
an old master."

In the months to come we were to try bread bait again and
again, but never a nibble. Rudy had scored a bull's-eye that day
though, and he made the most of it.

After we cleaned the perch and delivered them to Pluty, the
chairman of our entertainment committee, it was time to deliver
my newspapers and finish my monthly collections.

"Well, let's go see Miss Werensky," Rudy cracked as he
started up the truck.

"What ya mean, let's go see Miss Werensky . . . I've gotta
see *all* my customers."

"Yeah, but *she's* the one you want to see . . . you just collect from them others . . . but you want to *see* that big, juicy
stallion. Only you're too scary to hit on her . . . ha-ha," Rudy
chided.

"You're fulla' crap!" I said. Now why did he have to start
that stuff, I thought. "I oughta deliver my papers on my bike,
anyhow," I grumbled.

"Oh, no . . . I'm gonna watch this action. If you go alone
you'll try to tell me how you made out and all that jive. Oh, no.
I'm gonna be a witness." Rudy had me cold-turkey. As much as I
tried to create the impression that I was cool about the situation,
he knew that I was nervous and flustered. We'd been bragging
teen-age style to each other for years about our sex conquests. I
knew he was lying, and he knew I was lying, but we would
rather die than admit our virginity.

"Watch where you're throwing, man. You almost knocked
that woman's flowers down then," Rudy said. The closer we got
to Miss Werensky's block, the worse my aim got.

"Hold it here . . . I've got to collect from this house," I told
Rudy.

"Okay, but hurry up. Those big legs are waiting for you up on Sacramento Street," Rudy teased.

"You go to hell!" I shot back. I rang Mr. Moore's doorbell. This was the cat who ran on the road and owned the big sporty Cord with the lights on the running board. During the Depression years he had been the most prosperous individual in the neighborhood. He lived like a king on his Pullman-porter earnings and with his stylish pinch-back, bell-bottomed tweeds and his flashy Cord roadster, he was the envy of all the young cats in the community. The door opened and a sexy-looking chick with a drink in her hand nodded to me and called out, "Sandy, it's the paper boy." The paper "boy." I'd be glad when I became a man! Then I could be like Sandy Moore. A different pretty chick every day he was in town and parties on the weekends and all that. Mr. Moore came to the door in his shirtsleeves; there was a smudge of lipstick on his face.

"How much I owe you, buddy-boy?" he asked. I told him and he turned to the girl and said, "Pay the kid for me, will you, sugar." The girl disappeared for a moment and returned with her hand in a large, flowered purse. She counted out the correct change and turned and put her arm around Mr. Moore. Boy! I thought. He sure got his chicks well-trained.

He said "Thanks, baby," to the chick and gave her a playful slap on the hip. He flashed me a smile and a wink and closed the door. I felt a thrill as I tried to guess what was going to happen behind the door. Miss Werensky flashed into my mind. I'm gonna be like Sandy Moore, I suddenly resolved . . . and starting today, too! This is it. No more chicken-hearted copping out. I'm gonna do a Sandy Moore with that big stallion, and won't Rudy be surprised. Even as I planned in my mind how I was going to move in on Miss Werensky, waves of nervous fear swept over me. If only Rudy would stop his damn agitating maybe I could get myself together.

"Did you see that sweet thing that Sandy Moore had in the

house?" I asked Rudy.

"I couldn't see her too good, but I know she was on the ball. He don't feature nothing but fine ones," Rudy answered.

"I'm gonna grow me a mustache like Sandy's," I said.

"I think I will, too," Rudy agreed. "Well, here we are. Why don't you get in there and take care of business? Look at her, she's peeking through the curtain."

My heart jumped into my throat as I saw the curtain drop back into place. I braced myself. Okay, I thought, get yourself together. If Sandy Moore can do it, you can do it. I took a deep breath. "Okay!" I said. My voice jumped out louder than I had intended. "Okay." I turned down the volume. "I might just knock this old chick out . . . I'm tired of fooling around anyhow."

Rudy sensed my determination. He giggled and punched me on the arm. "Now you're talkin', baby! Ain't nothin' to it." I felt stronger. Ole Rudy's gonna be surprised when I get through with this chick, I thought.

"Go ahead, man, what'cha waitin' on?" Rudy whispered fiercely. "She's in there right now, waitin' for her daddy. Ha-ha." There he goes again with that old jive, I thought.

"She's layin' in bed panting like an old hound dog . . . buck-naked!" Rudy said. All the butterflies in my stomach started churning again.

"Shut up, man . . . don't rush me!" I said.

The door cracked open. "Come in, honey." The words oozed through the crack like myrrh. Myrrh? What was myrrh? I had never seen myrrh. A Biblical word. Don't start thinking about the Bible at a time like this, I told myself.

"My, don't you look sexy in that leather jacket," she purred.

Wow! Not handsome this time . . . *SEXY!* She hadn't refolded her bathrobe. I tried not to ogle, but those two pink mountains almost peeking out of the robe had me hypnotized.

"I'll be right back, honey," she said, as she swirled away and through the bedroom door. A cloud of fragrant air blew over me. Myrrh. Back to the Bible again. As soon as she comes back in, I'm gonna grab her and kiss her, I decided. I might have done it, too, but she left the bedroom door open on her way back in and I felt electrocuted by the sight of her unmade bed with a pair of panties and a brassiere thrown across it.

"Come over here and sit by me, honey," she called. She had crossed her legs and her robe fell back. I tried to make out her receipt, but my eyes kept bobbing over toward the big thighs next to me. One of her powder-puff-looking slippers had fallen off and she was wiggling her toes.

She paid me for the paper and with a trembling hand I gave her the receipt. She then went into a line of small talk. The more time I spent inside the apartment, I thought, the more chance of convincing Rudy I had scored. After a few minutes of meaningless prattle she suddenly asked me if I had a girl friend.

"Naw, not no steady girl," I answered. The sudden personal turn in the conversation started the butterflies up again.

"How come, honey . . . a big sexy fellow like you?" she asked.

I couldn't come up with anything so I answered the question with a question. "Have you got a boyfriend?" I blurted a little too rapidly.

"Yeah, but we're not speaking right now. I'm getting rid of him anyhow . . . he's too jealous." She must have read the message in my eyes because she added, "Don't worry, honey, he usually only comes by on Sundays . . . and he can't get in anyhow."

Now I had two things to worry about: my built-in frustration because of my youthful inexperience and the thought of a jealous boyfriend busting in.

While I sat worrying, Miss Werensky took matters in hand. She reached over me and clicked out the lamp. With all the shades drawn, the room dimmed close to pitch black. Miss

Werensky snuggled up close to me and I could hear my heart booming in the dark. She pulled my head close and blew in my ear. Suddenly, the amorous scene was shattered by a frightful pounding at the front door.

"Oh Jesus! That lousy, jealous Vito!" she hissed. All the butterflies I knew I had, and a couple of hundred I didn't know I had, churned into action. My mother'll die, I thought. In a panic of rushing thoughts I could see my father secretly laughing. . . . My father'll die laughing, but my mother'll really die! Worse than that . . . *I'll* die if that jealous cat has a gun or something!

As I flew out the back door, I remembered I had left my receipt book on the couch. He'll track me down by my name on the receipt book! Can't go back now, though! The fence in the backyard was too high to risk getting hung up on. And a dog was barking on the other side. I slipped along the bushes down the side of the apartment building. I peeked around, and there at Miss Werensky's door stood not big bad Vito, but Mrs. Milford, the old lady I had seen earlier on the pier.

"And when you get through doing whatever the hell you're doing in there, bring me my damn paper . . . and put it on the porch . . . not in the street!" Mrs. Milford was shouting.

It was still daylight. People had begun to pop their heads out of doors and windows to see what was happening. Old lady Milford had broken up my little playhouse. As soon as Mrs. Milford went back into her apartment I stepped out of the bushes and up to the truck.

Rudy was bug-eyed. "What happened, man?"

"Drive off, man," I drawled. I leaned back and put my foot up on the dashboard. "What the hell you think happened. I *scored*, that's what."

Rudy was stunned. His glasses had fogged over and had slipped down on his nose. "You did score, huh!" he exclaimed. "Well . . . well . . . what was all the commotion?" The order to drive off had gotten half-through, and he was pressing the clutch and brake pedal and fumbling with the gearshift. His eyes, shining incredulously over the top of his spectacles, were trying hard to pull the story out of my face.

I rolled the window down and sailed a paper toward Mrs. Milford's porch. It bounced off a potted plant and into the geranium bed below. The pot teetered, spun around, and fell on top of the newspaper, covering it with dirt. Oh, oh! Now I'd done it! But I wasn't going to get out.

"Drive off, man!" I shouted.

Rudy, startled into action, snatched his foot off the clutch and we lurched away.

"Well, what happened?" he wailed. "What was that old lady hollering about . . . was that her mother?"

"No . . . I'll tell you . . . just drive on." My mind was racing. I had already proclaimed victory . . . now I had to put a good lie together.

In his excitement Rudy kicked the truck into second. The broken gears crunched and clattered and he quickly yanked the gearshift into high.

I remembered an old, half-empty pack of cigarettes in the toolbox under my feet. I reached down and pulled one out. Rudy's head kept darting from me to the road ahead. Out of the corner of my eye I could see him stealing glances at me as if he had never seen me before. I decided to play the moment for all it was worth. I lit the cigarette in the coolest Humphrey Bogart manner. I leaned back, slowly blew out a cloud of smoke, and drawled casually, "Man, that stuff was all right!"

As I described the experience, lying all the way, I realized that the time I'd spent in the apartment, combined with Mrs. Milford's noisy performance, had contributed heavily toward convincing Rudy that I had indeed "scored." I also realized that as the improvised tale unfolded, Rudy became ever more quiet and distant. By the time we finished delivering papers and making collections, an invisible wall seemed to have grown between us. I began to regret not telling him the truth. This was not like the teen-age bragging we'd done in the past, when we both knew the other guy was lying. This time Rudy believed me and felt left out.

"Well, I'll see you later on. What time are you gonna pick me up?" I asked as we pulled up to my house.

"Oh, I don't know . . . I'll honk the horn," he answered.

The party we had planned that evening never came off. Pluty and the fish had disappeared and without the fish we couldn't have a fish fry. We went instead to a party being thrown by two sisters named Curly and Leona not far from where I lived. It was a backyard affair and most of the kids we had expected to see at our fish fry were there. The girl who had delivered Rudy's note to Lorraine was there too. She was dancing with one of the guys in our club.

"What happened with Lorraine?" Rudy asked as they danced by.

The girl threw her hand up to her mouth and giggled. "I'll tell you in a minute," she laughed as they whirled away.

I hope everything works out for Rudy with Lorraine, I thought. That might help compensate for the damaged ego my lying had produced. I glanced around and my eyes fell on a pretty girl standing within a group of kids.

"Ooh, I could sure go for that chick over there," I told Rudy.

"Don't you remember her?" Rudy said. "That's Rogie's girl, Phyllis."

"I don't know her," I said.

"Yes you do. Don't you remember that little chick who lives down on 61st Street near the tracks . . . used to wear her hair in braids . . . looked kinda like she was an Indian?"

"Is *that* her? No, man, that can't be her."

"Yeah, she grew up, that's all. You better quit staring over there. Rogie might lower the boom on you," Rudy warned.

"I don't care about Rogie," I shot back as I took a quick look around for Rogie, just to play safe.

The girl messenger tactlessly told Rudy that Lorraine had laughed contemptuously and torn his note to bits. I wished I hadn't heard her tell him about it. Now Rudy had suffered *two* devastating blows in one day, and I was a frustrated witness to both.

"The hell with that hinkty bitch!" he said bitterly. "I'm glad she didn't come anyhow, 'cause I planned to spend the evening with my chick Helen, so all's well that ends well."

Helen was a little, homely girl who carried a torch for Rudy. He always avoided her, but now I saw him move across the yard and take Helen by the arm.

On the way home that night, I was acutely aware that my buddy, Rudolph Lamerro Jordan, had had a crushing day. He liked to imagine himself a dashing and worldly cat, but the events of the past few hours had diluted that image considerably. I wanted to get him off the hook, but I didn't know how to start.

"I was sure glad to see you give Helen your new ring. That girl sure is in your corner and that really knocked her out when you did that."

"Yeah, well, you know . . . she's a good kid . . . and I've been kind of rough with her. She ain't the greatest beauty in the world, but she's got class, man . . . and she's smart as a whip. A guy can use a good steady chick like that, you know what I mean." But his words lacked conviction.

"Yeah, I'm glad to see you give her a play. She's really all for you. She just waits patiently while you make it with all kinds of glamour girls and tonight you really made her happy. . . ." I shouldn't have said that about glamour girls. This was not one of our casual lying sessions, and as soon as he uttered his next words I knew I had put my foot in it.

"What other glamour girls?" he asked caustically.

"Well, you know, man, I mean, Helen's really in your corner and everything . . . and . . ."

"Yeah, I know . . . bull shit ain't nothin' but chewed up grass!" he ground out.

We pulled up in front of my house. The street light cast a sickly yellow glow into the cab of the truck. We sat silent for a while.

Finally, Rudy coughed and shifted on the seat as if to start the truck up. "Well, I'll see you tomorrow morning," he said dully.

This was the first time a truly strained and awkward feeling had developed between us. It had all started with my lying earlier in the day. The Lorraine rebuke had made matters worse, and now I had a painful case of the guilts.

"You know something," I started, groping for a lever to relieve the misery that gripped us, "I really like that chick Phyllis. I couldn't believe she was the same little girl that used to wear the braids. I'm gonna take her to the movie next week. Maybe you and Helen would want to go, too."

"Yeah, that sounds okay," he said quietly.

It was either close the evening out on a negative note or try to purge my conscience. I decided to come clean.

"Say, you know what?" I started.

"No, what?"

"I know you believed me when I told you I scored today, but I was lying . . . didn't nothing happen."

"How come you told me you did?" Rudy asked suspiciously.

"Same reason I tell you a lot of crap . . . same reason you tell me a bunch of jive sometimes . . . just trying to bullshit myself and you too that I was a big man," I explained.

"What'd you cool on the deal for?" The atmosphere softened. I thought I heard a hint of relief in his voice.

"Aw, man . . . I couldn't go for an old chick like that. She's too bogus anyhow . . . a nymphomaniac or something." I rushed the words, hurrying to get us back into our familiar groove.

"I'm glad you used your head for once, come to think of it," Rudy said philosophically. "Listen, a chippy like that . . . m-a-a-an! She's liable to give you a case of the Chinese Mong Gong or something. I had a deal like that once . . . big old blonde just like that one . . . always chasing me just like she was chasing you. . . ." We were back in tune and everything was back to normal. ". . . Suppose you met her sometime when you were taking Phyllis to the show or something? . . . Could be a d-r-a-g, man, a drag. . . ." I settled back in the seat at peace with the world.

FOUR

The Watts Riots

"It has to be violence. You fight fire with fire, that's an old phrase. This hadn't happened before. Maybe it should have, but it didn't have to . . . because no one could listen. . . ." — *Young man, interviewed during the Watts riots.*

BASED ON MY PERSONAL EXPERIENCE through the years, I have drawn certain conclusions about the Watts riots, which are set forth in the pages of this book. They include what I feel were the causes of the riots, their effect on the present and the future, and steps that I feel should be taken in order to ease the burdens and pressures that caused them. However, my own experiences were quite limited compared to those of many others. I have attempted to talk to as many people who were in the thick of things as possible. Their statements and accounts are presented as they were told to me, without abridgement or alteration, in the hope that the reader will find them of value in forming his own conclusions.

TAFT W. HAZELY, *1671 East 84th Street. Businessman, owner of a cleaning and pressing shop. Also a student at Jordan High School, attending adult classes at night*—I have two more weeks before I finish this course I'm taking now. And I'm also a beautician by trade.

Now, the first beginning of this riot, well, I was remodeling my home. I had two carpenters working with me. I had a Preston and Alfred Johnson working with me. So this riot started. Well, we didn't know anything about no riot. We heard the fire engines running, and the ambulance running, the police cars running, and then we noticed smoke. So Preston said, "Man, that looks like a fire over there by my house." See, he lived in Watts. I said, "Oh, man, that ain't nothing." So we went on back to work; we didn't pay too much attention to it. This was Thursday. So Preston said, "I think I better go home and check." I said, "Okay, Preston, I'll carry you home." So we jumped in the car and we went over to his home. He lives on Holmes Avenue near 103rd Street. Everything at his home was okay. His wife was kinda' nervous. We came on back. So that evening we knocked off approximately five o'clock. I had to go to school. That next morning, Friday morning, I went over and I picked Preston up and I went over and I picked up Johnson and brought 'em on over to the house and we started back to work. So man, it got so bad that evening that about three o'clock Preston's wife called and said, "Preston, come on home quick!" She was all nervous and upset. Then Mrs. Dorothey called for Johnson to come on home (I call him "Goat," that's his nickname), and I'm the only one that's got a car so I carried the two fellows home and, boy, 103rd Street was all in flames, and his wife was nervous and shaking and everybody's standing out there in the street: "Lord have mercy! I hope my house don't burn down!"

And so I said, "Well, Preston, I have to rush back home." So I rushed on back home and then by this time my wife she called me: "Taft, come over to the shop quick! Glass is falling all around me and I'm just so scared. I don't know what to do!"

I said, "Okay, Barbara!" I jumped in the car and I went over to the shop. My cleaning and pressing shop is at 39th and Normandie.

When I got over there I said, "Barbara, cool down," I say,

"Everything's all right!" I said. "Ain't nobody going to bother you."

And she was just so nervous. She was just sweeping glass off the sidewalk, you know, and some of my customers wanted to come in and get clothes at this particular time. The customers rushing in and I'm trying to wait on the customers and I'm hollering, "Come on, Bobbie, and help me," 'cause she's at the shop every day and she knows more about the business than I do, you see what I mean?

So, about eight o'clock that night the police, they came through and some people were standing on the sidewalk out in front of my shop.

So the police told 'em, "Get off the sidewalk!" Well, the first thing they did they came into my shop. Okay. One man stopped in the door of my shop there and was talking and I said, "Man," I said, "come on in the shop here." So he came in the shop and so the police they came up to the door and said, "I mean, you all stay off the sidewalk if you don't wanna . . . you know . . ." and they used a lot of vulgarity. And then one of the policemen reached in the door of my shop and hit a man in the head with his nightstick, you know. I said, "Man, come further in the shop!" And he had begun to bleed and I closed the door on the police. And then the police got together and left. But first, before they left, I forgot to tell you this: When they drove up, one the policemen jumped out the car and said, "I came down here to kick some ass!"

And I guess that's what he did when he hit this man with the nightstick—inside my shop now—private business. The man was inside the shop, a public business, you understand what I mean? One of my customers, too.

So okay, we stayed down the shop all night. My wife had a pillow, quilt, and blankets. So we stayed down there and we watched our shop and everything to keep people from coming there lootin'. We stayed down there all night Friday and Saturday. So that Sunday night, on the sixteenth, we stayed down there till approximately seven or seven thirty. So my wife said, "Taft, I don't feel like going home tonight. We'll just stay around one of the customer's homes."

I said, "Okay." So we have a man named Lishey; he stays at the shop and watches the shop. I had three weapons at the shop so I said, "Lish, I gonna leave my big weapon here by the cash register with you," and I say, "I'm gonna take the other two home with me." So I put 'em in the trunk of my car.

So we went around to the customer's house. We were all sittin' up and we had another customer there and she had six children at home and she was worried about them. She had to go home. Now, I'm the only one there got a vehicle. She lived on 39th Street. We were on 38th and Budlong.

I said, "Yeah, I'll carry you home, Daisy."

So the two other guys there, Patterson and James Lucky, so they live close to this lady and Lucky says, "Well, since you gonna carry her home, you can drop us off, too, bein' we all live close together."

And there was another fellow there named Oscar and he said, "Well, I'll go with you just for the ride and I'll come back with you."

I said, "Come on, Oscar." He didn't even have a shirt on.

So as we got in the car, the National Guard and the policemen they came up behind us and told us "Halt! Don't move!" and they instructed us to put our hands on the dashboard, and then instructed us to get out of the car with our hands above our heads, and we obeyed the officers and we did like the officers said.

They told the lady to come around the front of the car. And the lady went around to the front of the car. She was scared and nervous and worried about getting to her six children and next thing the police started hittin' her, with the nightstick, started beatin' her, you know. So, one of the fellows, James Lucky said,

"Man don't be beatin' the woman like that. We ain't did nothin'," you know just like that.

"SHUT UP! . . . if you don't wanna die!" you know. So the officer who said it took his shotgun and pushed it in the back of James Lucky's head. About this time we're up against the building. So he's still hittin' on the woman . . . and the woman's tellin' him, "Man, don't hit me! What you hittin' me for?"

He said, "Shut up. I said shut up!" and still beatin' on her.

And James Lucky said, "Man, don't be hittin' on that woman like that!"

I said, "Lucky," I said, "quiet man," I said. "Those are police officers," just like that, I said, "you ain't got no win. Just keep you mouth closed." Because I didn't want 'em to kill all of us. He done put the shotgun on the back of James Lucky's head, and got it cocked and everything. I didn't want him to accidentally shoot the man or kill somebody right there on the spot.

Then they put the handcuffs on us so tight they cut the circulation of our blood off. So 'bout this time, my wife was in the house, they had heard all this commotion outside so they came on outside and I was complaining about how tight the handcuffs were on my hands. So my wife tells me . . . I couldn't see 'cause I was facing the building. . . . Sergeant came around the corner and she asked the sergeant to loosen the handcuffs on me, please. You know, a little. So, he did. He told me to get down on my knees and bend my head over, and I did as the officer instructed me to do, and so he loosened up the handcuffs, just a fraction, just enough. So then they had the National Guard bring the trucks up and then they loaded us all up on the truck. They carried us to University Police Station. They instructed us how to enter the building.

In the meantime the arresting officers had gave my two weapons they found in the trunk of my car to a detective.

I was about ten feet away from a chair in the jailhouse and I was walking toward the chair. So an officer ran up behind me and said, "Sit down!"

I haven't made it to the chair yet, I'm still ten feet away. I said, "Man, give me time to sit down in the chair, I haven't made it to the chair yet." And he jumped up on my back and said, "I said sit down, godammit."

And I said, "Man, get off my back." So he got off my back and he left. Wherever he went I didn't see him any more. So I got to the desk later and there was a Negro officer sittin' at the desk. He got up and he pulled a chair up where I could sit down and I sat down. He straightened my shirt up for me which I appreciated after all the mean treatment I had got. There was a white officer standing at the end of the desk. Okay, so the Negro officer, he asked me for the information. So, I gave him the information that he wanted. Then he gave it to the white officer to sign.

And the white officer said, "What's wrong with you. You say you don't want to be involved?" You know, just like that.

So the Negro officer said, "Well, give me the paper back then." And he did and he signed it.

Then he told me to go over to the window and I did. There was another fellow standing in front of me and there was a Negro officer standing next to him and the other officer at the window was asking this fellow some questions. In the meantime, this Negro officer took a cigarette and burned the man on the arm. And the prisoner said, "Man," he said, "don't burn me with that cigarette!" Well, I was standing right behind him; I saw the man burn him with the cigarette, deliberately.

He said, "If I burned you with this cigarette, I didn't do it intentionally."

Now I know the man did it intentionally, you know, 'cause I'm lookin' at him. He stuck the cigarette to him. I said to myself, "Aw, man, this is something else!"

Then they told me to go to this other little cage. So I sat in this little room here and then I got fingerprinted and then they kept us locked up there for approximately two hours. Then they transferred us from the University station to the Central jail, and I think we stayed there approximately three hours and then they transferred us to the Lincoln Heights jail.

When we get to Lincoln Heights that morning on the bus there was a white fellow right in front of me when they were unloading us. The police officer asked the white fellow, "Where did you get arrested at?"

So the white fellow said, "On Exposition near 39th."

He said, "Yeah, what did they arrest you for?"

He said, "Well, I had a weapon in the car. They said the weapon was stolen, but I didn't know the weapon was stolen because my daddy gave me the weapon."

He said, "Are you a student?"

The prisoner said, "Yes, I'm a student. I study law."

The next morning, this white kid he was a free man. He walked out the jailhouse and everybody gave him phone numbers to try to get in touch with their relatives and people so someone could get them out of jail, because they wasn't givin' out no information.

They kept us locked up in that Lincoln Heights for six or seven days . . . no heat, no covers . . . we was sleeping on these steel beds and you know how cold steel can get, man, and the only way that we had to try to keep theirselves warm they'd go to the rest room and get this toilet paper, when they could find some, and try to wrap up in it. That's the only kind of cover that we had to put next to this cold steel.

Men were in the Lincoln Heights that was sick . . . real sick . . . with the pneumonia. They had fever, had chills. They wouldn't even give them no kind of medical attention. Men that they had beat up with those nightsticks, man, some of them cracked-up in there. They wouldn't even take 'em outa there until we guys got together and just kept up so much noise, beggin', man, to "take this man out the cell and give him some medical help."

One of the guys he cracked-up so he was just runnin' around from bunk to bunk—pulled off all his clothes—and jump off and jump against the door of the jail to try to kill hisself, man. Well, they had beat him crazy, over the head, you see what I mean? You get the idea? They had beat him crazy so the man was actually out of his mind! And they wouldn't do anything for him. Until finally we was keepin' up so much noise and beggin' them till they eventually came and got the guy. We don't know if we did the guy a favor getting him out of there or not, 'cause what eventually happened to the guy we don't know, 'cause we didn't see the guy any more. And the guys who were suffering with the pneumonia and the flu, they was still in the cells the same way when I left, with no kind of medical attention. I suffered in there for all them days. I don't know if they got air conditioning or fans in there, but they turned 'em on and just froze us to death.

We couldn't sleep. Get up and go in the rest room and try to stay warm, man, that's the only choice we had. Cuddle ourselves together, try to stay warm; we didn't have no cover, no fire, no kind of heat.

So they transferred me from Lincoln Heights, they sent me to the new County Jail. Well, the new County Jail, that's where we had a chance to get sprayed, get a shower, and they gave us some dungarees to put on. And the beds and the cells was fairly well comfortable and we got three meals a day and then every evening we could take a shower, a good hot shower, and I wished the poor guys at Lincoln Heights could have some too.

You understand, I hadn't done anything to be guilty. Now maybe some of the guys had done some wrong—I don't know —but even if so they deserved to be treated like a human being, not like a dog.

Then they transferred me to the old County Jail. All right now, this is something else. They didn't have enough beds to go around at the old County Jail (that's where we had to sleep on the floor; roaches runnin' up side the wall), but it was better than Lincoln Heights because they did give us a bedroll and cover, you see what I mean. Even though we did sleep on the floor and roaches and things, but we had a cover, you know, to kinda' stay warm.

From the old County Jail I had to go to court. The day I was scheduled to go to court they said they lost me or something, they couldn't find me. So they sent the other four . . . Daisy, Lucky, Patterson, and Oscar. No, they didn't send Daisy. They sent the other three that day; they said they couldn't find me.

Okay, so the next day they sent myself and Daisy. We went to court. So for the same reason I was carrying Daisy home, the judge let Daisy go home on her own recognition, without puttin' up any bail, because she had six children and they was sufferin' a hardship. You see what I mean? Man, that was the same reason I was carrying the girl home and got in this trouble, because she had children and they needed their mother 'cause they was scared in the riot. Well, the judge turned her loose and let her go home on her own recognition.

He set my bail at five hundred and fifty dollars. So okay, my wife got me out on bail but, man, let me tell you something. Before we entered the courtroom they had us in a little ole small room now—no air, no ventilation, and they had approximately about a hundred and fifty men or more in this little cell, and it's hot back in there, man. No place to sit down. You just have to stand up for something like eight hours until they call you to court. Just like a bunch of cattle, that's the way they did us.

About a week later I had to go back to court. I tried to get a public defender but I couldn't because they said I was able to pay. It just happened it was a Mr. Johnson there from the NAACP, and he said, "Yeah, I'll take the case."

So he took my case. The two police officers, they never ap-

peared against me; they said I was booked on burglary and re-
ceivin' . . . which I hadn't burglarized or received nothin'.
Bob's Loan Office . . . they said I burglarized that place . . .
which I didn't . . . because the two weapons belong to me and
I had receipts and papers and they're registered.

So the judge he dismissed the case against all five of us. And
so I asked Mr. Johnson how much he charged me and he said,
"Thirty-five dollars." And I gave him forty dollars, you know, because I appreciated what he did . . . he didn't have to say anything because the judge dismissed the case . . . he didn't have
to say one word, but I just appreciated havin' him sit there by
my side. And he advised me to wait approximately two weeks
before I called about my weapons.

So about two weeks later I went down to see about my
weapons. The police officer who was handling the case he
wasn't in. So they gave me his phone number and told me to call
him the next morning. So I did and I asked him about my weapons . . . when could I get my weapons back? So he said, "Well,
Hazely, I'm thinkin' about puttin' more charges against you."

I said, "You gonna put more charges against me . . . now
what you gonna charge me with this time?"

He hung the phone up in my face. So I went down there to
try to see him again, but I couldn't see him no more 'cause he
wasn't never in.

So in the meantime, my cousin died. I had to drive back
home to Texas for the funeral and when I came back I went to
school on a Monday night and when I came home my neighbor
said, 'Taft, the officers been over to your home . . . all around
your house."

So I said, "Now what they doin' around my house?" I said
"OOOH," to myself, I said, "Oh, yeah, the officer said that he
was going to file more charges against me."

So later the sheriffs they came and knocked on my door and
said, "We have a warrant for your arrest."

So they took me down to the Firestone Sheriff's Station, and we started talkin'. And we talked about two hours. Then they said, "Aw, Hazely, you're just a victim of circumstances . . . we got the wrong man," and they said, "we got to get off now . . . we got to change shifts so we got to book you and lock you up."

Now here they told me I was innocent and I thought I was on my way home, but I was on my way to jail again.

My wife and the bail bondsman had been there, sittin' out there waitin' to bail me out. So they locked me up, then they called me back and they fingerprinted me, and my wife bailed me out.

So then I had to go and get me an attorney again. Then I had a court date set. The officers weren't there to appear again. There were two other officers there. The prosecuting attorney came out and talked to me and I told him exactly what happened and how it happened. Well, the prosecuting attorney acted kinda' confused about how he was gonna prosecute the case . . . you understand? And then the prosecuting attorney went to the judge and they talked. They had violatin' the curfew, carrying concealed weapons, disturbin' the peace, and they had about ten charges against me. So I pleaded guilty to violatin' the curfew. I hated to do that 'cause I had a clean record through my life. So the judge said, "Six days in jail or twenty-nine dollars."

The attorney cost me three hundred and fifty dollars. We shook hands and parted from each other and that was it.

Question: "Mr. Hazely, what do you think caused the riots?"

Well, I think the cause . . . REALLY . . . the cause . . . first, unemployment . . . and second, police brutality. You see, what really happened in this riot situation, there were a whole lots of people that had been mistreated by the police and had been broke and out of work . . . you know what I mean? But during this riot, just like when the policeman stopped this kid down there . . . that was it. . . . There's a lot of people, man, that others don't even know how they really feel. Like when this thing first started . . . their real feelings just came out. There's a lot of good citizens around here, but you talk to them and eventually it comes out. . . . They tell you a little bit . . . a little bit more. People who never committed no crimes . . . but they have been stopped by policemen . . . harassed by policemen . . . some of 'em beat by policemen . . . for nothin'! See what I mean? It's just two main things that started that riot here now I don't care what they say . . . that's unemployment and police brutality.

STANLEY SAUNDERS, *age 23, Rhodes Scholar, Yale law student*—I think my first reactions to the riots were very much like what a white person's reaction would be. I was coming down Alameda Street, driving with a friend, when we first saw this large billow of smoke loom, and we knew right away that it was from 103rd Street, and we turned to one another. We almost guessed right from the beginning that it was one of the department stores. And we knew that if it was a riot it had taken a turn for something very new, something very different in American race relations. And quite frankly, when I got home I was disgusted. I called an old friend, and in talking to her on the phone, I think I used the term "nigger" for the first time in addressing a white person. I said something to the effect that, "Here we are out here . . . us niggers . . . burning and almost getting ready to kill ourselves, and the white man is going to go ahead and let us do it. The Fire Department is standing by watching the flames, and the Police Department hasn't begun to act, and 103rd Street has become a general melee!"

After this initial reaction, which I still consider to be somewhat of a "white" reaction because I was looking at it, if not like a white liberal, certainly like a middle-class Negro, I went down on 103rd Street and saw the conflagration and saw the fervor of the crowd—the heat of the activity that they were caught up in. Slowly and gradually I came around to a different orientation.

I had only been home for two weeks at the time. Two years I had spent in England, traveling on the Continent, playing on the beaches, reading, jotting down ideas. I was a young man having an existential experience, a real-life experience, as it were. And looking at the riots and fires against that background, I came to some very different conclusions. I came to conclusions, as I seemed to merge back into my old community, that I regard now as wholly Negro. For one thing, I realized that this wasn't something peculiar to Watts: riots had taken place in Harlem and in Rochester and riots were expected to occur in Newark, Washington, D.C., East Bay Oakland. I realized that this was some general phenomenon and that as far as Negroes in Los Angeles were concerned it was now their time; it was now happening to them. So my reorientation that Friday became only part of the general phenomenon of being a Negro in America.

That night I was hired by a national magazine because they had no Negro reporters and therefore none of their staff could enter the riot area. I traveled with two Negro out-of-town reporters who, like me, had had some experience outside the country to reflect on their own characters as individuals, as men, and who came to find out who they were, irrespective of color, irrespective of their former backgrounds. But we were suddenly facing ourselves as individuals who must come to grips with themselves at some time in their lives.

The three of us rode around, and probably one of the most interesting experiences in my life was this going from one part of the riot area to the next. As reporters we had to spread ourselves throughout the riot area—following fires, following police calls, trying to stay up on top of the events. And in vast Los Angeles this is no easy matter. Sometimes it would mean going all the way from 103rd and Wilmington, where there was a fire breaking out, to Vernon and Central, where there was a shooting, on up to Twelfth Street where there was looting going on.

But on the other side, we also had to solicit the cooperation of the law—the "man," who was imposing the control and trying to subdue the rioting. And this part of our night activities took us to the military compounds, to the several police headquarters in the area. In this world, which was the world of so-called "law and order," of the "public interest," of "law-abiding citizens," we encountered a very different kind of reaction. Here we had to button our top collars, pull our tie knots tight, remove our hats and comb our hair, and almost speak with a different intonation in our voices. In other words, we had to fall back into the old middle-class patois and speak the language of the suburbs rather than the language of the ghetto. And it was this dichotomy that we straddled for the entire night.

Traveling from a police station to a point of a looting where the police had just been. Trying to talk to the people there on the scene, the eyewitnesses, the Negroes who had seen the shooting or who had perhaps even set the fires. Trying, in spite of the telltale cameras around our necks and the pads and pencils, to dispel the impression that we were perhaps representing the man downtown; that we were, in fact, with them as brothers. Yet, at the same time, trying in reality to serve a broader purpose. Not of law and order necessarily, but the greater purpose of informing the public, both Negro and white, both within the ghetto and outside, and throughout the country.

So there was this difference. One shade was white and one was all black. And to us, three college-educated Negroes, all trained in white institutions, this was a startling contrast.

I was almost shot once during my reporting chores. The three of us were driving back into Watts at the crack of dawn. Saturday morning. Things on 103rd Street appeared quiet. What we didn't know while driving south on Graham Avenue was that a wild gun battle had taken place on that street only about a half hour earlier.

So, as we approached the National Guard barricade, completely unaware of what had preceded us, we were told to stop. I slowed almost to a stop, but I continued to let the car roll forward slowly so that we would have a shorter distance to walk when we finally came to a complete stop. As the National Guardsman hollered, "Halt!", I was leaning out of the car window shouting, "Press!" Our messages became garbled in the interchange. The Guardsman raised his rifle to shoot, and I stopped just in time.

A second feature that stands out in my memory of that night was an incident on Vermont Avenue. We arrived on the scene just as three ambulances were pulling away. And as we talked to the people about what had happened, we gathered that three young men had been caught in the act of looting a shoe store. The cops had been standing across the street and had told the young men that they were caught and they had better proceed to come out, drop whatever they had in their hands, and keep their hands high above their heads.

According to the eyewitnesses, who may also have been looting, the three boys came out of the store carrying boxes of shoes up above their heads. They dropped the shoes, raised their hands high, and began to walk across the street pursuant to the orders of the police officers who were standing there. As they got to the middle of the street, they were gunned down. And those were the three ambulances that we saw, taking the three boys away. They were shot in the stomach, in the leg, and one boy was shot twice.

The atmosphere among the crowd on the scene was one of smoldering hostility. Because they felt that this shooting was wholly inhuman and unnecessary; that the young men knew they had been caught, and they were following the instructions of the police.

The people on the scene felt that this was pretty much an indication of how the law and order was going to be restored

during the next couple of days. And the general impression we
gathered from this crowd that was getting larger and larger as
the story spread, was that this was a martyrdom and that whatever we did in the next couple of days we stood the threat of
being killed needlessly. So there was this strange kind of doom,
of fey, that hung over the whole area. Whether you were a re-
spectable citizen with a coat and tie on or whether you were just
one of the boys standing on the street corner twiddling your fingers, the fact that you were Negro was cause for apprehension.

A third incident, which was really part of the Friday night
burnings, took place on Avalon about 2 A.M. on Saturday. We
accompanied one of the sweep patrols of the National Guard
down Avalon from 51st to Slauson. One of the ironic things that
happened to me as I was walking along with the patrol was that
one of the caissons rolled by and a National Guardsman hung
his head out of the window and called, "Saunders!" And I wondered who in the world in the National Guard could know me
out here. And strangely enough it was one of my fraternity
brothers from Whittier College, a white fellow who was a very
good friend and who was now in the National Guard.

He jumped out of the truck and we talked. He tried to give
me his impressions. He seemed more startled and frustrated than
anybody because he had barely missed death earlier when a car
driven by a young rioter had rammed his patrol, just avoiding
him and almost killing the man next to him. And the way my
good friend related the story was that here was a community of
people, at least a segment of the community, who didn't care if
they died or not. The driver of the car was killed. There could
have been no question in his mind that he would lose his life
when he made the attempt to ram the patrol. And it was that
this kind of temperament prevailed among many of the rioters,
certainly among many of the riot dead, that was most shocking
to my National Guardsman friend.

The paradox of the two of us standing and talking about the

riot—both of us graduates of the same college, both of us members of the Lancer's Society, fraternity brothers, which is a very close bond on a college campus—and yet, we were miles apart on that particular night. The strange furtiveness about our conversation: he was telling me something and yet, it wasn't everything, and I was telling him my own reactions to it, but I was talking again in the language of Whittier College, not really in the language of Watts, because he could only understand in the language of the campus. He'd only known me as a Whittier College student and so to talk any other way not only would've been misleading, it would've been almost meaningless.

After the riots were over they became a matter of social interest, almost of intellectual interest to me. I was called upon to answer questions of the white world. Naïve questions, though I felt them stimulating, because some of the questions that had been lurking in my own mind while I was abroad, just about Negroes and about Watts and about the future of the civil rights movement, had really been challenged during these last couple of days; so I had to reevaluate, and I had to come to some new accommodation in my own thinking about the status of the Negro, about myself among Negroes, and about the future of my people in America.

It didn't really become a very personal experience, however, until after I got back to Yale. That was when I read in *Look* magazine that one of my very good friends had been killed during the riots. Somehow in Los Angeles I didn't get the information that my childhood friend, Charles Fizer, whom I'd gone to school with, who occupied a special place among my acquaintances, had lost his life during those days. Charles and I had a lot in common early in life. He was a singer, and for a brief while I tried to sing in a little group that he had organized. He was always organizing things. In fact, he went on to become the lead singer in the very popular Olympics group.

Through the years Fizer and I had grown apart. He had

gone his way into the entertainment world, and I had pursued my education. But still there was this intimate bond, that as little boys we had slept in the same bed, and as little boys had gone to grammar school together in the same class, and had walked that mile to junior high school every morning and to Jordan High. We had shared a lot of experiences together, and to learn that he had been riddled with bullets, that he had been practically blown out of his car, and that his family has suffered tremendous grief after the riots, touched me in a very personal way.

And I think *then* the riots took on every possible dimension that they could take on for me. They were of a sociopolitical interest, they were of an intellectual concern; now it was a personal involvement because a close friend had died.

After getting back to law school, and getting away from Los Angeles, and not always being identified with Los Angeles, or riots, or Watts, I began to think about the riots in a different light. There emerged in my mind this philosophical association of the riots with the Negro in America: I went back to this idea that being a Negro in 1965 was something very different from being a Negro in 1963 or even in 1964. Today it meant that you were an angry young man. And it meant that you were part of an avant-garde group that wanted something more than plain civil rights, than just voting rights; perhaps it wanted more than a political office, more than a good job, more than just a home in an integrated neighborhood or the chance to send your children to an integrated school. Here, in 1965, was a move abroad to win dignity for our whole community of people. I think this moral aspect, the idea of a people trying to dignify itself, appealed to me most. And I think it will be, if nothing else, the real question posed by the Watts riots. Because in a sense, Los Angeles is not of that sociological class of cities where crowded tenement houses and rat- and roach-infested, slummy areas prevail. Watts is, everybody agrees—the McCone Commission, the California

Advisory Committee on U.S. Civil Rights—in no sense a typical slum. Not all of the social factors contributing to the riots in the East were present in Watts. It had something to do with not *where* you were, but with *what* and *who* you were. The fact was that you didn't riot so much because you didn't have a job (although I feel that unemployment would increase the chances of active participation), but because you were Negro. Because during the riots it never occurred to me that I should be out there throwing stones. But after the riots, after I got back to New Haven and began to reflect upon all these things—the Negro in America, myself as a Negro in America—I became ridden with a kind of shame for not having gotten my stone in. I felt very much that I should have been down there rioting. The fact that I had been a student leader at an all-white campus impressed me even less.

I was from Watts. And my brothers, my good classmates from Jordan High School, were throwing stones and were breaking windows, and were BURNING! And for some strange reason I felt that *I* should have been throwing stones, that *I* should have been involved. And it was this kind of identity as a Negro that caused me to feel strangely Muslim in a way. In a way that I'd never felt Muslim before. These things were working on me not because of any intellectual merit, not because of any athletic or leadership merit, but because I was a Negro. And this feeling of becoming Negro in 1965 is, I think, the most profound thing that comes out of the Watts riots. These things are happening to Negroes, and what is happening to them is happening to *me*. And because we can't disassociate ourselves from the identity of our people anywhere, the feeling of being a Negro in America today will probably produce, if not more riots, spurts of spontaneous, uncontrolled activity and uncontrolled expression, much like what happened in Watts.

The colleagues whom I traveled with during the riots were from New York, and they came in with stories that they had heard there about events that were taking place in Los Angeles. I thought it rather strange that there would be that nexus between what was happening in Watts and what they knew was going to happen—that is, what the people in Harlem anticipated for Los Angeles.

My fellow reporters were told to watch out for a sort of Cuban-guerilla influence: the Panama hats, the red arm bands, things that would smack of guerilla effort. I took note of what they said, but I did not see any such evidence. And then there were these reports over radio and television, which I understand were later discounted, as part of the fiction that was mixed in with the facts about the events of those days. These included reports that people had been seen with Cuban hats and red arm bands, loading into trucks with rifles and guns and what not. Whether that's true or not I don't know, but what I *did* see while I was traveling along the freeway on Saturday, August fourteenth, was an airplane doing some skywriting. It spelled H-I-D-D-E-N, then there was a space, and this was followed by M-A-O-I and then a curlicue, which was obviously an unfinished S, and the rest of it, I suppose, would have come out T spelling out "HIDDEN MAOIST."

The skywriting stretched approximately from Santa Monica Beach to Redondo, over the ocean, so it could be read by someone in an easterly position.

And then I remembered that my fellow correspondent had alerted me to watch for evidences of what he had described as "urban guerilla warfare." The idea of the "hidden Maoist" struck me as rather foreboding, as did the whole idea of Negro urban guerillas residing in the Negro community by day, trying to disassociate the Negro community from the rest, and then fanning out at night into all parts of the city, looting and burning.

I traced the airplane to a particular company, but the owner refused to give me any information. I called on the phone. He wanted to know who I was, what, why, and so on, but no information.

I don't feel that any of this means that there was any organized guerilla activity or any deliberate pre-planning by any black nationalist organization, but it does present the possibility that there was this element within the riot group, that it was part of it. There is no certainty that there was direction from hidden Maoists, but there seemed to be at least some evidence that "Maoists," as it were, were a live possibility.

As far as the causes of the riots are concerned, I guess you could spell out any number of factors. First of all, on the political side, there was the fact that a lot of antipoverty money in Los Angeles had been bottled up as a result of political in-fighting and had failed to seep down to the poor for whom it was intended; and then the fact that Proposition 14, which nullified all previous California anti-discrimination statutes by giving most landlords and homeowners absolute discretion in the sale and rental of housing, was considered a personal affront by the Negro community. These sociopolitical factors are really outside of my own firsthand knowledge, however, because I was abroad at the time. But I think that there was one single cause that I would emphasize. That is the frustration of the young Negro male between the ages of, say, nineteen and twenty-five. The economist tells us that the person most likely to be unemployed in the United States is the young Negro male in this age group, who has a mere high school diploma, if he has a diploma at all, who is married, with one dependent. This is a basic cause because all of the causes seem to combine in this age group. They compound themselves, resolve themselves into a set, a class of individuals. And if there is any one cause I would say it is the characteristics and features of that young, unemployed Negro male who is trying to embark—or who is frustrated in his attempts to embark—upon a meaningful life for himself.

As far as what I feel the future portends, it is a very difficult thing to say. It's easy to be optimistic and say that what happened in Watts is merely an isolated incident, some historical freak occurrence, and that the causes that underlay this particular situation can be easily removed by massive Federal aid and local cooperation. But one can take a different tack, a pessimistic, almost cynical view, and say that really this is not an isolated incident, but an episode in an ongoing development of the Negro; that the Negro community, so long silent and mysterious, often reflected in the civil rights movement, but more often not reflected in the civil rights movement, is evolving—and who can say what direction that movement is going to take? America has never really dealt with the Negro community before. The white community has only dealt with the civil rights movement. And now it has to deal with a person and a class that has never really been of much importance. Now the Negro is aware of himself, he's conscious of the changes, and these changes are affecting him in a very deep way.

Black men in Africa are making states. Although unsettled, they are still forming a different philosophical basis. One that speaks of a racial ideology. One that is not to be disparaged. It's justifiable. It's a wholly valid premise to base an interpretation of the real world upon.

These are the factors of the future that will have to be dealt with as a result of Watts, not only because of Watts. But there is a Watts *because* of these factors. So it is both a cause and effect. What the future holds is probably more of the same because historical circumstances in America have created the energy, and it can work for ill or good, depending upon the response this energy generates among black men and white men.

And it is this energy that has led us to this cause and effect, this response and reaction, this Negro qua white man that will lead us either to more Watts' or possibly to a world where there is some accommodation between Negroes and whites.

MAXY D. FILER, *age 35, law student, President of the Compton, California branch NAACP. Married, father of seven children. Born, Helena, Arkansas*—I reached Watts, 103rd and Compton Avenue, about 3:30 P.M. on Friday. That was August the thirteenth. Well, I guess what they say about Friday the thirteenth really came true that day. The place was literally going up in flames. Store after store was being looted and then burned down. First they would break in, then loot, then burn. There was a definite pattern. In watching it I realized, as time wore on, that there was no preplanning. It was spontaneous. The pattern developed, and soon the routine was set in an almost business-like manner.

I started helping men from the United Credit Union to direct traffic. The police could not function at this corner. Bottles, bricks, pieces of steel—most anything was thrown at the police or any fire equipment that came into the area. You ask yourself, why? Because all the police and firemen were white. They symbolized "the man." Here was a chance to express long pent-up resentment.

The word was, "Negroes hold up three fingers and get 'Whitey.' Any 'Whitey.'" They all looked alike to the people in the streets that day. Loot, then burn every store that belonged to whites. Negroes put signs on their stores saying, "Negro-owned" . . . "Blood Brother" . . . "Peace Brother" . . . and like that.

I saw two liquor stores and two other stores looted and burned while I attempted to direct traffic. The store windows were systematically broken by one or two individuals, then hordes of people would rush in and clear out everything that was not nailed down, and some things, as I think back, that were nailed down. I saw a cash register broken from the counter, brought out on the street, and ransacked. Then a safe was brought out, loaded onto a truck, and carted away.

Cars would stop in the middle of the street. Husband and wife and children would go into the stores, help themselves to goods, get back in their car, and leisurely drive away.

Four children about four or five years old crossed the street, arms loaded with potato chips, Fritos, candy, and were roundly cheered by the teen-agers and adults. I was offered beer many times by girls. Listen, I mean girls, not young women—girls not more than twelve or thirteen years old, man. The boys would break, the girls would cheer and loot.

Many times I held one lady in my arms to keep her from falling. She had consumed too much liquor. She would come down the middle of the street and sit down (or try to sit down) on the hood of a slowly moving police car. I tried to help her. She kept getting into dangerous situations, but I tried to protect her even though she was drunk. You know why I did it, why any of us would do it? My mother is black. And although she is a devout Christian, I knew that there, but for the grace of God, goes my mother. Fortunately, the police were not interested in arresting her, so she was left in my care for about four hours, and I had to remove her from the street about every thirty minutes.

You know, we've seen many of the same people through the years in the civil rights movement here in town. Which reminds me, Johnny, when I heard that you were in the area that Friday I got worried that some brother would not know who you were and do you in. But at least when the chips were down, some of us were there trying to do whatever we could. There wasn't much anybody could do . . . but a few of us tried, right? Okay, that's the point I'm coming to. You see, and may I remind you some could have been elsewhere, but I saw exactly one elected official, two Negro attorneys (one Democrat and one Republican, incidentally), and no Negro ministers. Maybe they were elsewhere, but it seems to me that at least one could have been there with us at 103rd and Compton where the storm was raging.

Let me point out in all fairness that I have reliable information that a number of our ministers did perform valiantly in other areas, but I didn't know this at the time, and I kept wondering.

No matter how severe a situation gets, there's apt to be some levity. A lady and her husband went up to one of the furniture stores, walked through the broken-out window, and proceeded to pick out the stereo of their choice. After finding the one they liked, they picked it up and gingerly stepped through the window (for some reason nobody bothered to try to open a door), and carefully stopped for the red light at the corner. I was flabbergasted. I motioned for them to cross; they refused and waited for the light to change. They crossed the street, waited for another light to turn green, and gaily went about their business. I guess the moral is that they didn't want to break a traffic law.

Another individual brought his pregnant wife to the furniture store, helped her across the windowsill, and they picked out a baby bed. He carried the bed, she carried the mattress. When they drove off I didn't notice if they were parked in violation.

Later a policeman tried to shake hands with me for the effort I had made to keep traffic moving out of the area. I told him I'd rather not shake hands. I would have lost any little effectiveness I might have had with the people if I was seen shaking hands with "the man."

Finally, we were all herded off the street. A group of us wound up in an office. Included with us were two small children. You see, they were Negroes too, and when a policeman tells you to get off the streets, all Negroes look alike. This was brought home to me vividly by a riot gun pressed to my body. I wasn't hurt physically . . . just my pride. I tried to explain that I wanted to go home, to no avail. We sat and watched Watts burn down around us.

Earlier, while I was directing traffic, a fireman had to connect a hose in the middle of the crowd. He was immediately hit by a bottle. I begged them not to hit him. A voice spoke up from the rear, "Don't bother the fireman, we want the police."

The National Guard came and they blockaded the street. About 11 P.M. an old car sped through the line. About forty-five minutes later this same car came through going the other way. The order, "Halt!" was given, but this time the occupants opened fire as they tried to run through. They were cut down in a hail of gunfire. The bodies, riddled with bullets, were dragged out. This happened about five more times.

We stayed as low to the floor as possible. A man came through on a motorcycle, firing as he came. The motorcycle stayed. He wound up in the morgue, I guess.

These were people who had cracked under the social pressure piled on through the years. Here was the chance to go out like a man. They knew they were going to die, but with some Negroes it has come to that: just die and get it over with; nothing to live for really, anyhow.

Vietnam? We had it in Watts that Friday the thirteenth.

Was I glad to see the sun. There was a time clock in the office. I heard every second tick that night.

What in the world was I doing there? I asked myself as I drove home. After all, I don't have any money, but I do have a little house and a wife and children and a chance soon to become an attorney.

Well, the answer is, I guess, wherever a black man lives, he lives in Watts.

I think the reasons for the riot are clear. For years Watts was the butt of jokes and derisive insults. Nobody listened to the people who knew the terrible misery that existed under the surface: unemployment, poor school facilities, dirty shacks for housing, and a brutal Police Department. Maybe now they'll think less about the moon and Vietnam and more about the many Wattses in America. I hope so.

MRS. ROBERTA ANDERSON, *861 East 116th Street, Los Angeles. Domestic worker, housewife. Husband a mechanic. No children*

—This whole riot just made me sick. I was sick. I just asked myself, "Why did it have to happen?"

Now I'm one hundred per cent Negro, you know what I mean, and I stand behind my people, but truthfully, I have never experienced some of the things they say caused everything—like bad housing, insufficient food in the homes, no jobs.

I know they exist because I can see, but I'm lucky that I never encountered it personally.

I have sat and tried to reason this thing out. I just can't understand why these things have to be.

I do domestic work in different white homes and I hear the people talk. You know, I never express my opinion, just listen. Because if you just listen you'll hear a lot more than if you run your mouth. I just let them talk and I listen and try to see what it all means.

Most of the places I have worked, the people said they felt it was something that should have happened to open people's eyes to the real situation that so many of our people have to live in.

I absolutely believe that many of the white people know now that something must be done, and because of this I feel that something good will come out of a bad riot.

We live right around the corner from the place where the riot started.

We had guests visiting us from Cleveland, and after dinner we drove out to take them sightseeing.

When we got near the trouble I said to my husband, "Look at that crowd of people. There must have been a bad accident."

I asked a neighbor who was standing near the car what had happened, and she told me that the police had beat up a pregnant woman.

"Let's go!" I said to my husband. "Let's get away from here before some bullets start flying."

We got back into the community about a quarter to twelve.

My husband looked at all the people and said, "I bet it started a riot."

LILY FORT, *6610¼ South Broadway, Los Angeles. Lead singer with the famous Roulettes*—We watched from our front porch that Friday during the riot. People were everywhere. The liquor store across the street in a mess. But police cars were going up and down the street without stopping. People were taking stuff out by the carton. During this time it was like a game. Me hoping nothing bad would happen. A lot of our people were in the street, seeing if they could get free food and clothes and furniture and some of them taking liquor, too, but the white man was out for blood.

Then three boys came down the street, laughing and talking. They were teen-agers, about fifteen or sixteen years old. As they got right at the store they seemed to debate whether they would go inside. One boy started a couple of times to go. Finally he did. Now a cop car finally stops to investigate. Police got out of the car. Meanwhile, the other two boys had seen them coming and they ran. My brother-in-law and I were screaming and yelling for the boy to get out. He didn't hear us, or was too scared to move. He never had a chance. This young cop walked up to the broken window and looked in as the other one went around the back and fired some shots and I just knew he'd killed the other two boys, but I guess he missed. He came around front again. By now other police cars had come. The cop at the window aimed his gun. He stopped and looked back at a policeman sitting in a car. He aimed again. No shot. I tried to scream, but I was so horrified that nothing would come out of my throat. The third time he aimed he yelled, "Halt," and fired before the word was out of his mouth. Then he turned around and made a bull's-eye sign with his fingers to his partner. Just as though he had shot a tin can off a fence, not a human being. The cops stood around for ten or fifteen minutes without going inside to see if the kid was alive or dead. When the ambulance came, then they went in. They dragged him out like he was a sack of potatoes. Cops were everywhere now. So many cops for just one murder.

While they were dragging the boy out, a station wagon from one of the news agencies pulled up and we could see the police telling them a lie. We went out to the gate and called to the news reporters, but the driver just looked over, turned around, and drove off.

Then one cop yelled for us to get back. We moved back, but he hollered for us to get in the house. My husband hesitated and the cop raised his gun and aimed and he had that same murderous look in his eyes. I pulled my husband because I was scared for him, and I had seen what they had just done to the other kid.

FIVE

Getting a Gig

"We want jobs! I'm a man with seven children and I don't have one. I don't have a job. But I'm not illiterate; I'm not stupid. I have things to do. So these other fellows around here, they want jobs. You get them a job and they'll stay off the street." — *Man, interviewed during the Watts riots.*

I PLAYED MY FIRST cash-paying gig with Willard Marsh's Collegians, but the first time I attempted to perform publicly was on a talent show with a schoolmate named Jean Johnson who played the piano. Jean's mother must have thought she saw something in our drum-piano duet because every weekend she would take us to a neighborhood theatre somewhere in the Bay area, wherever a talent show was being held. Jean and I were about fifteen years old at the time and I can remember us getting on the streetcar, Jean with her music under one arm, my snare drum under the other, her mama with my tom-tom and cymbals, and me with the bass drum and trap case. That we never won a prize is a tribute to the audience's judgment, but even that fact fails to describe the "quality" of our performance.

My musical teeth were cut on "Count" Otis Matthew's West Oakland House Stompers. The group had no set personnel, just any cats he could get together for a gig. Count Matthews and I were the only permanent members. Some of the men who played with us from time to time were Al Levy, guitar, a cat

named Pops on clarinet, Bob Johnson on bass, and a trumpeter
with one hand, named Preston. House Stompers was a good
name for the band. Count Matthews set the tone with his rollick-
ing barrelhouse piano, and the rest of us "stomped" along in his
wake.

I don't recall ever making a dime in salary on any of the
Count Matthews gigs, but we did have one fairly regular "job"
at the old West Oakland boxing gym, where the promoter used
to pay us off with a big jug of wine. We even got canceled off
that gig one night because the promoter felt outraged and scan-
dalized when Count Matthews sang a blues that went:

> *Oowee, I ain't gonna do it no more,*
> *'Cause every time I do it . . .*
> *It makes my wee wee sore.*

The song that Count Matthews was famous for, though, was
a blues rocker done with a Bo Diddley rhythm the Count called
"Yes, Yes":

> *Mama bought a chicken, thought it was a duck,*
> *Put it on the table with its feet stuck up,*
> *Here come baby sister with a spoon and a glass,*
> *Tryin' to stir the gravy from his Yes, Yes, Yes!*

One day in 1941, Bob Johnson called Count Matthews and
me together to tell us he had an offer for a long-term job for a
drums-piano-bass trio in Reno, Nevada, that paid forty-five dollars a week per man. At last, a real gig that paid real money. We
read, over and over again, the letter the club owner had sent
Bob.

". . . am in a position to offer your trio $45 a week salary
for long-term engagement at Peavine Club here in Reno. . . ."

We packed up and made it to Reno. The hours were from
seven in the evening till 4 A.M., seven days a week! But that
wasn't the worst part. The salary was forty-five dollars a week,

for all of us. That amounted to fifteen dollars each.

"Damn man!" Count Matthews complained, "this ain't good as my wine gig in West Oakland. I usually drink fifteen bucks worth of wine a week!"

"But the man said we can keep all the kitty money," Bob argued, "and these gamblers in Reno tip real heavy."

We stayed on the job. I had no choice because I had brought Phyllis and we had gotten married in Reno. I was out in the world on my own now, and I had to try to make it.

The man who owned the club also owned the restaurant where we ate and the hotel where we stayed. At the end of the week I owed him twenty-one dollars for food and rent against a salary which was still only fifteen dollars. Oh no, that's not quite right; I forgot the tips. When we split the week's take it amounted to $1.60 apiece.

Phyllis and Bob's wife, Georgia, got jobs as clean-up women in a cheap hotel. With the few bucks they managed to save we got out of Reno. One night the four of us packed our stuff, loaded Bob's ancient and decrepit sedan, and slipped out of town.

Count Matthews and my buddy Rudy Jordan went back to California and we were bound for Denver. Why Denver I don't know, but we had to go somewhere. We weren't going home defeated, and, anyhow, Bob said he had relatives in Colorado who would help us get situated.

We must have looked like the *Grapes of Wrath* rolling down the highway: drums and bass fiddle were strapped on the top and cardboard boxes containing our meager belongings were inside. Tied to the front bumper was a spare gas tank we had picked up at a junkyard.

None of us had ever been out of California before and we had the misguided notion that there would not be any gas stations through long stretches of the Western desert. We also had eight or ten of Count Matthews' empty gallon wine jugs full of water with us, to make sure we didn't die of thirst—the way we saw it happen in the movies.

The only purpose the spare gas tank served was to block the air from the radiator, which finally resulted in an overheated and burned-out motor. To make matters worse, the spare tank leaked and we lost our reserve fuel. Consequently, we ran out of money about fifty miles out of Denver.

Somewhere out on the blazing Nevada desert sits a drum hoop, if it hasn't completely disintegrated after twenty-five years of exposure. At dawn, the first day out, the vibration of the moving car worked one of my drum hoops loose and it rolled out into the desert. We pulled up and I got out to retrieve it. Sitting in the middle of the hoop, under a jutting rock, an evil-looking rattlesnake lay coiled, tongue flicking, beady eyes blazing, and tail buzzing away. I hope he enjoyed the hoop, 'cause I gave it to him.

Somewhere in the Rockies, a couple of days (and many hunger pangs) later, we ran out of gas. We were on the downslope and managed to coast into a gas station.

"Now what?" I asked.

"Damned if I know," Bob answered, "but we've got to think of something!"

Bob dreamed up a beautiful lie on the spur of the moment.

"We're on our way to play a gig in Denver," he explained to the station attendant, "and we forgot to bring our money with us."

"Who plays the geetar?" the man asked, spotting a guitar in the car.

"He does," Bob pointed to me.

Bob had bought the guitar in a pawnshop just before we left home. His intention was to learn to play it, but he hadn't learned the first chord yet, and I knew even less.

"Say, how about filling us up with gas and oil and we'll leave the guitar for collateral until we come back by tonight after the job?" Bob asked.

"Okay, by God, that's a deal," the man said, "but on one condition. This boy got to play me 'Red River Valley' on the geetar before ya' leave."

I don't remember how the hell we got out of that bind, but one thing's for sure, I didn't play any "Red River Valley" on the guitar or anything else.

In Denver I got a job at the Rossmore Hotel, washing dishes. On Thursday nights there were jam sessions across the street at Benny Hooper's. I met the local musicians and eventually landed a regular spot in George Morrison's band. With Morrison's band I gained my first experience at playing floor shows.

One night after the job I had a very drastic experience. We were staying in an apartment with some friends next to the Rossonian Hotel. Phyllis had just gone up the steps and I had walked back to the hotel to wait for a couple of musicians when a white fellow walked up to me and said something like:

"Any luck yet, buddy?"

"What do you mean?" I asked.

"You know . . . nigger gals."

I tried to get away from him, but he was half drunk and insistent. He grabbed me by the arm and said, "Don't give me the old brush-off, Mac. I saw you with that nigger gal. How about her?"

I cursed him and pushed him away. He snatched up a piece of two-by-four and swung at me. I slugged him and he went through a plate-glass window. In a panic, I reached through the broken glass and picked him up. His hand was bleeding.

I heard someone holler, "Call the cops!" and I ran into the hotel. I flew up the steps to a little balcony that overlooked the street. I was scared to death. Suppose the guy was cut bad? It was dark on the balcony and no one on the street below could see me, but I could see them.

The cops arrived, a crowd gathered, and a few minutes later

an ambulance pulled up.

The guy refused to get into the ambulance. Finally, one of the ambulance attendants said, "Well, he's not hurt much anyhow."

I almost died of relief.

He kept telling the cops that someone had tried to mug him. The cops kept telling him that's what he got for coming down into this neighborhood. Then they put him in the patrol car and drove off.

I crouched on the balcony, sweating, my heart pounding a mile a minute.

NEITHER Phyllis nor I had ever been to Los Angeles prior to 1943.

World War II, with its stepped-up draft program, had created a shortage of workers in many areas. Music was no exception.

While we were living in Omaha, Nebraska, the Nat "King" Cole Trio played a one-nighter at the Dreamland Hall on 24th Street. At the end of the dance, Nat Cole suggested that I contact Harlan Leonard in Los Angeles because his drummer, Jessie Price, had been drafted and the job was open.

I didn't follow through, but I did wind up with the job sometime later. Back then, Preston Love and I had left Lloyd Hunter and were co-leaders of a combo at the Barrel House Club in Omaha. Jimmy Witherspoon, who was a Pullman porter at the time and who later became a famous blues star, used to drop by the Club to sing a few numbers with the band just for kicks.

"Johnny," he said one night, "Nat Cole told Harlan Leonard about you, and Harlan told me if you come to Los Angeles he'll give you a job with the band."

"When you get to LA," I said, "tell Harlan I'll be there within ten days."

The night before I left Omaha we had a little farewell get-together in a little 24th Street restaurant. The proprietor, sensing that this was some kind of occasion, brought out some Near-Eastern delicacies.

"Here are some nice Greek sweets for your little party, boys," he said. As he spread them out he began to explain what they were called in the native tongue.

Preston Love looked at me and smiled. The old Greek didn't know it, but Preston knew that I could've identified them as well as he. The smells and tastes of the almond-sesame-honey goodies swept me back to when I was a little kid.

"When you get to LA, look up Sonny," Preston said, and he wrote his brother Sonny's address out on a scrap of paper.

Lacking money to buy a ticket, I managed to join a group of people who were driving to California. I was to "pay" my way by helping to drive.

There were six of us. Three elderly ladies, William "Blick" Avant, drummer Dick Hart, and myself. After seeing me behind the wheel for a few miles, Dick and Blick asked me to pull over. I wouldn't have to worry about helping them drive, they informed me.

I got the job as soon as I got to LA, but the war had created a housing shortage and rooms were impossible to find. I spent three weeks sleeping on a pallet on the floor of a little room in the old Clark Hotel on Central Avenue with two roommates: trombonist Harpo and trumpeter James Ross. Finally, I found a room in a crummy little hotel near skid row, and Phyllis came out from Omaha to join me.

When Harlan Leonard's engagement at the Club Alabam came to an end, I joined Bardu Ali's band at the Lincoln Theatre. While playing with Bardu, the late Curtis Mosby, owner of the Club Alabam, asked me to form a group and become house band at the club. I sent for Paul Quinichette, Von Streeter, Curtis Counce, Leonard Enois, and Kent Pope. With these men and the musicians I recruited locally—Teddy Buckner, Arthur Farmer, Kenneth Medlock, Tony Moret, George Washington, John Pettigrew, Lemuel Tally, Lee Wesley Jones, Bob Harris, Leon Beck, Billy Jones, Edward Preston, Howard Martin, and Burney Cobb, I had a full group—and I was in the band business.

The early forties at the Club Alabam were exciting and eventful. War-bloated Los Angeles was full of escape-seeking servicemen and defense workers, and the club was jumping every night in the week. They were the days of full-scale floor shows with top acts, chorus girls, extravagant productions. Producer Patsy Hunter presented shows built around stars like the Peters Sisters, Jackie "Moms" Mabely, the Archie Savage Group, the Norma Miller Dancers, Wynonie Harris, and Marion Abernathy. All the top stars in Negro show business and many of the Hollywood greats would drop in regularly.

I used to idolize Bill "Bojangles" Robinson until one night at the Alabam he called me aside and promised to take me on his upcoming theatre tour if I would fire my musicians and replace them with white boys. It might have been very funny, but he was dead serious.

Another time, agent Joe Glaser and Curtis Mosby instructed me to get under a sun-tan lamp so I wouldn't stick out like a sore thumb on the planned Wynonie Harris Deep South one-nighter tour. The tour never materialized, nor did the tan. I fell asleep under the lamp and damn near burned up.

I finally ran into Sonny Love one day at 43rd and Central. By this time Phyllis and I had managed to get into a little apartment on Washington Boulevard, and Sonny moved into our spare bedroom. During those days there was one period when I couldn't find a gig, and we lived on spaghetti and corn flakes.

I had applied for a job with a number of bands, and I remember waiting for the phone in the hall to ring with news of employment. One evening the phone did ring for me. The voice on the other end of the line said:

"This is Earl Hines at the Plantation Club. Our drummer, Shadow Wilson, became very ill and had to return to New York. I wonder if you would consider joining the band? The job only pays one hundred and fifty dollars a week, but we'll soon be back in New York and at that time the salary goes up."

When I finally got my heart out of my mouth I shouted, "Yes sir, Mr. Hines . . . I sure would like the job!" I was going to play with the great "Fatha" Hines!

The voice on the other end began to giggle. It was my old friend, drummer Ellis Bartee, playing a joke on me. If he could have known how sick we were of spaghetti and corn flakes, he would have realized what a cruel prank he'd pulled.

Two weeks passed. Still no job, still on spaghetti and corn flakes (half rations now), and the phone in the hall rang for me again.

"Hello," the voice on the other end of the line said, "this is Count Basie. Joe Jones is sick and I wonder if you could come out and play the night with us."

I thought it was Bartee and called him every MF in the book and told him he couldn't pull the same stunt on me twice.

But it *was* Count Basie! After an awkward and hasty apology, I jumped into my old 1928 Rockne and rushed out to the Plantation Club in Watts. To this day, when I see Basie, I wonder what kind of nut he secretly thinks I am.

That night after the gig, Phyllis observed, "Well, you've come a long way, from Willard Marsh's Collegians to Count Basie!"

SIX

Where the Spirit Refuses to Yield

"I am a law-abiding citizen, a mother of seven kids, a couple in college, a couple in high school, and a couple in elementary school, but I saw something last night that let me know that this community is on the verge of one of the biggest . . . I don't know what you would call it. And if something isn't done, we can talk nice if we want to . . . we can talk nice, be nice . . . be nice, I believe in being nice. As I say, I'm a law-abiding citizen, but I am afraid if I had of had a weapon I might have been in jail this morning, and I've never committed a crime in my life. But how can you see your boys lying on the street, already hand-cuffed, helpless, and blood is running from their heads on the pavement. If you're a mother and you have a son who is about to go into the army, you can't help but say, 'I'd rather him die here' . . . that's how I felt. And I felt, 'why should he go die for somebody else, why shouldn't he die on the streets of Los Angeles for his people?' and I don't know what can be done, but we must do something. Fighting is not the answer; fighting the policeman is not the answer." — *Woman, interviewed during the Watts riots.*

"Where you been, man?" one Watts man was supposed to have asked a buddy just after the rioting, "I haven't see you for a week."

"Oh, man," the other fellow answered, "they had me runnin' back and forth downtown every day."

"No kiddin'?"

"Yeah . . . they been investigatin' my problems."

"What happened?"

"Well, I went down there Monday because they said they wanted to find out why I was so poor. So they asked me a bunch of questions and they decided I was poor because I didn't have any money. Then the next day they checked me out on *why* I didn't have any money, and they said it was because I didn't have a job."

"Then what happened?"

"Then I had to go back Wednesday so they could see why I didn't have a job, and they said it was because I didn't have enough education."

"Did you go back Thursday?"

"Yeah, because they wanted to know how come I didn't have enough education, see. And they figured out it was because I lived in the Poverty Area."

"Oh. How about Friday?"

"Well, Friday I had a long interview to see why I lived in the Poverty Area and they said it was because I was so poor. . . . I didn't go back any more. I figure we were back where we started, so I hit on a dude for a bean, got me a jug of Sneaky Pete, and got my head tight."

THE California Poll is a periodic opinion survey. On November 23, 1965, it released the results of a study taken to determine what people thought were the causes of the riots. How far apart the white and black communities have grown in thinking is reflected in the findings.

When asked if they felt unemployment was the basic cause of the riots, 47 per cent of the Negroes polled said yes, compared with only 22 per cent of the white people who thought that was the cause. Thirty-two per cent of the Negroes thought living conditions were the cause, but only 15 per cent of the whites agreed. On police mistreatment the score was, Negro 13 per cent, white, 3 per cent.

Then we come to an area where the opinion of California whites and Negroes is reversed. When asked if they felt "outside agitation" was a prime motivating factor in the riots, the results were, 28 percent white who said yes, and 7 per cent Negro. This is to be expected, of course, because blaming it on the Communists is easier on the white conscience than admitting that unemployment, living conditions, or police mistreatment were the causes of the riots. To do so would be to tie the albatross of shame and guilt more tightly around their own necks.

The races have grown so isolated from one another in big urban areas like Los Angeles that it is sheer nonsense to ask the majority what's plaguing the minority. Even if there were any demonstrable evidence upon which to base the belief that whites, in general, harbor concern for Negroes' welfare, it would be impossible for them to have any inkling of what might be bugging the black man way across town with whom he never has social contact and rarely even sees. Asking the white man what ails the black man in America is like a doctor asking a patient, "Where does it hurt?" And rather than accepting the pained reply, he calls a third party, long-distance, and is informed by the faraway stranger that the patient doesn't hurt at all.

There has been much speculation on how big a contributing factor the passage of Proposition 14 may have been in the Watts rioting. Proposition 14, opposed by California Negroes, was passed by a whopping 2 to 1 ratio in the 1964 elections. An analysis of how the various blocs of California voters performed on this issue shows Negroes solidly against and whites strongly in support of a landlord and property owner's "right" to refuse to sell, lease, or rent on the basis of color. The proponents of the notorious "Segregation Amendment" piously denied this, but it was all part of the "Big Lie" technique used so effectively throughout the campaign.

Edward Howden, Head of the State Division of Fair Employment Practices, said he believed that the passage of Proposition 14 "struck minority-group Californians like a smashing blow to the teeth. Negro and other non-white residents," he said, "felt this as a stinging and deeply damaging expression of persistent and implacable racism. No other interpretation of the vote was felt to have any value."

California real estate interests underwrote the campaign and guided it successfully through the murky, political underworld of untruths and fear. Howden attacked the campaign as one "promoted widely and most effectively through the reckless use of the 'Big Lie' technique and all the scare devices in the arsenal of the skilled propagandist." What it actually boiled down to, as Mr. Howden has pointed out, was a campaign "to induce fear."

The old bitter chestnut, "Do you want your daughter to marry a Negro?" was replaced by, "Do you want your family to live next door to Negroes?"

Not everyone, however, felt the passage of Proposition 14 played a vital role in fomenting the disorders. John Buggs, Executive Director of the County Commission on Human Relations, has stated that he doubts if nine-tenths of the rioters even heard of Proposition 14. "If it contributed at all," Buggs said, "it was in a tangential way—in that the Negro leadership group felt all they had been doing was for naught."

Given the same set of circumstances, the riot would have occurred with or without the existence of Proposition 14, but to assume that the participants didn't know about Proposition 14 is incorrect. The people were aware that they had suffered some kind of political defeat that had to do with whites denying Negroes the right to housing, but they were uninterested. They were too preoccupied with more pressing and immediate problems to be concerned with a fight to live in white neighborhoods. Most of them couldn't find a job and many of them were perpetually at grips with the dilemma of where the next meal was coming from. Expecting them to get involved in a campaign about buying houses in white areas was out of the question when they couldn't buy even the bare necessities in the ghetto. They were at least vaguely aware of the Proposition 14 battle. After all, there had been months of ballyhoo about it, in the streets, on radio and TV, in the paper, and on the billboards. And let us keep in mind that the gap between the completely disadvantaged Negroes and the lower-working-class individuals is not so wide that it eliminates contact and interaction.

Howden, testifying before the McCone Commission inquiry into the uprising, scored white Americans by declaring they "built the theatre, set the stage, and wrote most of the script leading to the terrible drama in Los Angeles. It is cruel hypocrisy and dangerous delusion," he said, "when a people proclaiming the quality of man are laggard and insensitive to the harsh realities of imposed inequality, even in the second century after the formal abolition of slavery."

Mr. Howden then proceeded to put his finger right on the prime cause of the blow-up: unemployment. "During the eruption," he said, "the common target of complaint was the police, and immediately afterward the cry was for JOBS." He then called for a series of changes to "toughen and sharpen" the California Fair Employment Practices Act and summed up his testimony with, "We, the white Americans, have written, enforced, and perpetuated the rules of the game. We have established and tolerated the ghetto in housing, the exclusion or subordination in employment and business opportunity, the second-class schooling, the stigma of caste, and the multiple affronts and indignities of Jim Crow. We have been and are in control . . . were we to fail at this late date to face our collective responsibility for racial segregation and inequity in our state and nation, we would be derelict beyond hope."

Every student, amateur or professional, of the present-day scene has his own version of where things are. With recent his-

tory as a backlog and current events constantly supplying points
of controversy, the average armchair philosopher usually man-
ages, within his own frame of reference, to patch together an
opinion or two on the burning issues of the day. And he can be
counted upon to defend his conclusions as vigorously as the most
renowned and respected journalist in the land.

And why not? Surely he has as much right to dream up and
project his ideas as do the "great" pros. In fact, the amateur's
conclusions are no less nonsense than some of the sievelike pro-
fundities that our prestigious opinion-makers would have us
swallow as scientific and correct analysis. At any rate, neither the
vocations nor the avocations of analyzing, theorizing, and forming opinions on what *has* happened and what *is* happening
suffer from a shortage of manpower. But deciding why things
happened and what they mean is one thing; getting at the heart
of what today's events portend is another. That's the real trick!
Trying to figure out where things are heading. What lies up
ahead? And how do we address ourselves to the issues of tomorrow *today*, so that we do not constantly find ourselves scooped
by history and reacting with our drawers down after the fact?

A perfect example of being upstaged by chronology is the
position of the church in America on the race issue. The liberal
church leaders try to get as much mileage as they can out of
their recently acquired militant civil rights posture, but they
don't get much—not in the eyes of the victims of American
racism, anyhow. It's too late, hundreds of years too late, to take
a stand in behalf of black humanity. George Bernard Shaw observed that the trouble with Christianity is that we've never tried
it. So, instead of coming to grips immediately and uncompromis-
ingly, the church—like the Democrats, the Republicans, the
Government, the press, and the opinion-makers—reacts meaningfully only when crisis and pressure won't be denied, and
that's too late. If the church really practiced what it promises,
the clergy marches on Selma, Alabama, would have occurred

one hundred years ago, if not three hundred, and today they would be moving toward new humanitarian goals. In the case of the Government's derelictions, it has been argued that in a democracy the will of the majority prevails. Which is another way of saying that the American majority will treat the American black minority as badly as it can and still get away with it, constitutional legality or moral principle notwithstanding.

The church, however, cannot cop-out on this basis because it proclaims to the world that its laws are not man-made, and that "Love thy neighbor" is neither debatable, deniable, nor dilutable.

When Gandhi said, "There go my people . . . I must catch them, for I am their leader," he understood that being caught in the tide of history was in itself nothing special. After all, everyone is swept along. What really matters, and particularly to a man who presumes to "lead," is to try at all times to know in which direction the winds of change are blowing, and to be in some position to relate to those changes and to try to cope with them when they become reality.

On one hand the Watts riots have been hailed as a "glorious uprising," and on the other they have been denounced as a "subversive, criminal orgy." Between these two extremes lie expressed descriptions that run the gamut of political ideology, official proclamation, editorial policy, and just plain old man-on-the-street reaction. What the riots really mean in terms of the broad sweep of human history only time will tell. That is to say that history, *future* history, will have the last word, and it will depend upon who writes that history, I suppose, whether it will speak "true" or "false." Be that as it may, *past* history always holds certain clues which can help us in our attempts to appraise the present and, hopefully, gain a line on the future.

The McCone report on the riots contains the following: "Nor was the rioting exclusively a projection of the Negro problem. It is part of an American problem which involves Negroes, but which equally concerns other disadvantaged groups. In this report, our major conclusions and recommendations regarding the Negro problem in Los Angeles apply with equal force to the Mexican-Americans."

Some future historian, upon reading that portion of the report, would most certainly conclude that the Negro uprising in Watts had performed a valuable service not only to the Mexican-American community, but to other disadvantaged groups, to the Negro community and, in fact, to the cause of American democracy and freedom itself. Surely it was the riot that dramatized various injustices to the point of prompting the Governor of the state to appoint a blue-ribbon committee which in turn had been moved to urge immediate remedies.

But the next sentence of the report might confuse the hell out of our future historian. It reads: "That the Mexican-American community did not riot is to its credit." Now he's got to figure out whether the Los Angeles Negroes, in burning Watts, had pulled off a patriotic Boston Tea Partyish coup in the finest American revolutionary tradition, or whether they had hit a bad lick. And left equally unclear is the historical position of the Mexican-American community in the overall riot picture. Does the Mexican-American community, in spite of its documented plight, receive points for abstaining? Or does it owe a "thank you" to the Negroes for bringing their common misery to the attention of the world? Was it then indeed, in the broad historical view, to the credit of the Mexican-American community that it did not riot?

I hope that the historians of the future will have more than the McCone report to guide them on the Watts situation. And we can be equally certain that we are not at this time, no matter how hard we ponder, going to foresee accurately what some future generation will conclude about the era we are living in. But we have to try, if we can, to get a peek of what lies up ahead, if for no other reason than to pull the present into some kind of perspective.

Like any other spot on earth whose inhabitants are perpetually locked in mortal combat with poverty and affliction, Watts is shot through with visual evidence of its plight. And even when the blemishes and the squalor cannot be readily picked up by the eye, they can be felt. You can almost cut with a knife the rage that this imposed ugliness generates. In the more densely populated and consequently shabbier neighborhoods, this grim and unlovely emotion pervades the atmosphere like a noxious gas.

But, on the other hand, in Watts, as in any other spot on earth where the human spirit refuses to yield, there is deep and startling beauty. In the heart of Watts one can feel the surging glory of the African character. It continues to endure like some indomitable, indefatigable, will-'o-the-wisp that denies the separation of thousands of miles . . . defies the span of hundreds of years, and tenaciously holds fast. The Afro-American character, uniquely fashioned under duress, battered and bruised, often diluted and diverted by some sociological miracle, survives. It survives in spite of centuries of genocidal onslaughts and white supremacist propaganda. It is surviving and is, in fact, triumphing in the splendor of gospel music, in the creative soulfullness of rhythm and blues and jazz, in the brilliant, bright eyes of a black child who dares to hope even though he is surrounded by an immediate sea of hopelessness, in the ebony, chiseled dignity of an old man who sits amid the rubble of a burnt-out building on 103rd Street, cleaning one hundred bricks a day for a penny apiece.

If the American white views the black man as an entity of value, it is usually a value based on how much cotton the black man can chop, how cheaply his labor can be bought, how good a soldier he will make, or how many home runs, touchdowns, Olympic medals, or hit records he can produce. Dr. W. E. B. DuBois once wrote, "We cannot forget that America was built on Africa. From being a mere stopping place between Europe and Asia, or a chance treasure house of gold, America became, through African labor, the center of the sugar empire and the cotton kingdom and an integral part of that world industry which caused the industrial revolution and the reign of capitalism."

No one can deny that the black man has been valuable to America, as far as menial and manual labor is concerned. But the truly precious gift from the "mother continent" to America was not sweat and muscle. It was the black soul, the African character. This rare cultural quality is there for all to see and feel, but not all see it. If one is preconditioned to believe that the ocean is a frightful, liquid monster that will do one much harm if one looks at it, then there's not much chance of seeing it in all its beauty as it really is. The involuntary African gift to the New World goes largely unaccepted and unappreciated. Oh, white Americans are entertained and perhaps even thrilled by the cultural artistry of the Nat Coles, the Ray Charleses, the Duke Ellingtons, etc. And white teen-agers emulate Negro dances and singing styles, but it's not a free cultural interchange; it's more like remote-control, long-distance theft.

I heard an art student, a painter, make a half-serious suggestion recently: "Let's bring Picasso to America. Get him over here and let him soak up Watts. Since white Americans can't seem to realize the worth of the black man, maybe one of their European kinsmen—a sensitive artist like the great Picasso—can reveal it to them. Bring the old master here before his days run out or before it is too late to reconcile the American dilemma. Let him burn his eagle eye into the misery and the beauty of Watts. Let him wade into the contrasts and contradictions, the hate and the love, the bitter and the sweet, the pain and the ecstasy. Let him get a good, long, close-up look at the rainbow faces of survival, at the descendants of the uprooted and transplanted, at the eyes and limbs of the besieged and condemned

Afro-Americans who refuse to succumb and struggle to prevail! No point in bringing over African sculptors. They've been expressing and depicting the phenomenal black character for centuries. Nobody over here pays any real attention. We put their work on bookshelves and mantelpieces for effect, but we don't really see them or feel them or want to understand them. No, bring Picasso. HIM the Western world pays serious attention to. And dig this: Coming to a pregnant oasis of human strife and soul like Watts will give Picasso in his twilight years the inspirational nourishment for a surge of creativity. He's had his pink and blue periods . . . now let him have his black!"

SEVEN

Hunting, Fishing, and Cards

"And this woman passed by and we wouldn't move off the street and she said, 'Get off the street, nigger,' and I swear to God if I had of caught that lady I would of stomped her face in the ground." — *Young girl, interviewed during the Watts riots.*

SOME OF MY fondest memories are concerned with fishing and hunting experiences. Traveling with bands for so many years gave me an opportunity to enjoy these pastimes in many parts of the country. But here and there, through the years, there were some negative experiences connected with hunting or fishing and my attempts to enjoy these sports.

I remember one day in 1942 when a carload of us were nearing a private lake some miles out of Omaha. We were anticipating a fine time. We had never been to the spot, and didn't know anyone who had, but the ad in the paper said that for a dollar apiece we would enjoy "the fishing experience of a lifetime . . . a lake that has been closed to sportsmen for years . . . teeming with black bass, crappie, and catfish! . . ."

"Hey, Pres, I didn't bring no sinkers . . . damn!"

"I think I've got some in my box, and if not we can buy

some at the lake. The ad said 'tackle, refreshments, rest rooms . . . '"

"Yeah, and I'm gonna get me some beer 'cause it's hot as hell and I'm thirsty as hell."

"Hey, Blick, the sign says 'lake this way.' Turn left at that bend."

"Man, it's nice up here. All the pretty trees and everything."

"Say, man, watch it! You're drivin' too fast. You're knocking all the hooks and stuff on the floor!"

"Get out and walk, mother, if you don't like my drivin'."

"Well, slow down, damn! You act like you ain't never been to a private fishin' lake before."

"I ain't, and you ain't neither, poor boy. Ha-ha!"

"This'll be a relief from Carter Lake and Nathan's Lake. I've never caught anything there but little chinchy bullheads and stunted carp."

"Listen, man, the best thing I ever caught was some crappies at Nathan. I don't think I've ever *seen* a big moth bass outside of a fishin' magazine. Umm, sure will be nice to carry some big bass and fat, juicy catfish back to 24th Street. Nobody'd believe it!"

"You know how come fish are so puny in Carter Lake?"

"How come?"

"BBB?"

"Bare Butt Beach. Too many bare butts. Makes the fish sick. Ha-ha."

"You go to hell!"

"Oh, oh, there she is, right ahead. . . . *Get ready you big black bass and you ugly catfish. Here comes the Izzak Walton of 24th and Lake after you!*"

"See where the man is over there by the building. Pull over there. Not that way, simple, *that way!*"

"Okay, now, let Norman do the talkin' so we don't all be

runnin' our mouth at once."

"No, let Johnny do the talkin'. He'll figure Johnny's white and we'll get better consideration."

"There you go with that Down-South crap! Damn the talkin', man, just give the cat a dollar and let's go *fishin'!*"

"HOLD IT . . . hold that car right there!"

"He said stop, Blick, hold it."

"Okay, I'm holdin' it. Now what the . . ."

"This is a private lake. Private property . . . can't come in here."

"Aw . . . here we go!!!!"

"Can't come in here? Why not?"

"Just can't come in here, that's why. Private property."

"You're open to the public, aren't you?"

"We're open to who we want to be open to."

"You mean we can't come in 'cause we're Colored, that's what you mean?"

"I said you can't come in."

"We're not good enough to come in your funky lake, but it's okay to go to war for you, huh?"

"Now just pull outa here; you're blocking my road. Don't give me no trouble or I'll get the sheriff to take care of you."

"Let's go, Blick."

"Yeah, let's get outa here. The hell with this dump."

"I hope the Russians and the Japs come over and blow your white asses up. And when they do, I'll *help* 'em!"

"Come on, let's go Blick. It's not worth it to get into trouble about this stupid lake. Probably no fish in the dump anyhow."

"Yeah, let's go."

HUNTING AND FISHING were things we enjoyed occasionally, but there was one pastime we engaged in constantly.

"Hit it and take it."

"Busted!"

"How about you, Von?"

"Give me a little one."

"That's good."

"Okay, dealer's gotta hit . . . uh! . . . now I've got a lousy fourteen."

"Give him a ten-spot card!"

"Uh! . . . Now I've got sixteen. Ain't that a bitch!"

"Why don't you wait on sixteen?"

"Why don't you stop talkin' in the game, man, you ain't got a dime at stake!"

"Well, now I might wait on that sixteen at that . . . let's see."

"If you do I'm waitin' on *you* with these two face cards."

"You wish you did have two face cards."

"You wish you didn't have sixteen to hit, that's what."

"Just for that I'm gonna hit it . . . *uh!* . . . Twenty-one, gentlemen. . . . *Just leave the cards and the money on the board. . . .*"

"*Goddam!* That's a lucky cat!"

"Cox, I'm gonna quit playing with you. *Nobody's* supposed to hit up on *that* many twenty-ones. That's some buuuuuull shiiiiiiii . . ."

"Quit cryin', man. You cryin' and I'm sittin' here with twenty . . . and you're sittin' at the end of the line with a cripple-ass fifteen and you cryin'. Why didn't you hit instead of cryin' so much? Play your damn cards right!"

"All right, all right, I ain't gonna make no money listening to arguments. Deal the cards, Cox, and you better not hit up on no more twenty-ones."

"Say, get another candle Buster, this one's gone."

Playing blackjack by candlelight on a piece of plywood in the middle of a sleeper-bus aisle, going down the highway to the next one-nighter gig can be a lot of things. It can be (and it was for me) a way to lose what little money I made playing in a

Midwest-territory band. Or it could be a way to pass the endless hours between gigs. It was a matter of trying to go to sleep, which was hard to do while the game was on, especially if you had the blackjack bug, or of peering out the bus window at the passing telephone poles. For some of us, Von Streeter, Orville Cox, Buster Coates, Lawrence "88" Keyes, and myself, it was a way of life; blackjack every night. For most of the other men, Preston Love, Russell Embry, Wendell Jenkins, and Wendell Turner, it was a casual pastime. They usually had fun kibitzing or hoorahing rather than gambling.

"Do you have to peek over my shoulders at my cards, Preston?"

"Does your mama have to peek over my shoulder, Streeter?"

"All right, Preston, I told you about that!"

"Ha-ha. Oh! I'm sorry. I forgot you don't play like that."

"You're a crazy SOB!"

"Oh, oh, I thought you said you didn't play the dozens, Streeter. You just talked about my mama, didn't you?"

"I didn't mean it like that."

"You said my mama was a B. How come you called my mama a B? I didn't call your mammy a B!"

"Aw, shut up, man. Don't you see me trying to play cards? Hit it, Cox. Damn! Take it, man, I'm busted!! Preston, will you *please quit messin' with me*! Say, Buster, trade seats with me, man, and get this fool out from behind me!"

"Ha-ha."

"That's right, laugh, Johnny. Everything your boy does is funny, ain't it?"

"I wasn't laughing at you, Streeter, I was laughing at this blackjack I just got."

"*I'll buy it from ya*!"

"Nope, I'm gonna deal this one."

"I'll go in partners with you on the deal, okay?"

"I thought you was mad at me, Streeter."

"Aw, man, damn that. Here, put up three bucks apiece. You deal and I'll handle the bank."

"Okay."

"Can I be your partner too, Von Streeter?"

"No, Preston, you be your mama's partner!"

From time to time the melted candle wax would pile up so thick on the board that we'd have to hold up the proceedings while we scraped it off. If the game was hot and heavy, we would ask a non-player to clean off the board while we continued on a suitcase. A number of times, back in those years, the bus would break down or we'd get hung up in a blizzard and we'd be forced to violate the old saying "the show must go on." But no matter what, the game went on.

One day the bus was parked in an empty lot just outside St. Joseph, Missouri. We had a few hours before the dance and the game was on. We had enjoyed a good week's work and there was a lot of money in the game. At that time a *lot* of money was like sixty or seventy dollars, but it looked like sixty or seventy thousand to us then.

It was hot midsummer and we had the trailer door open. Through the opening we saw a white fellow weaving his way through the bushes toward us. As he got nearer, we could see that he was weaving because he was loaded to the gills. The colorful sign that spelled out "LLOYD HUNTER'S ORCHESTRA" on the bus had evidently attracted him.

"What'ch got here, boys, a minstrel show?"

Some of us began to grumble, but one of the older and cooler heads had spotted a fistful of tens and twenties sticking out of the guy's lapel pocket.

"That's right, Cap, we're a minstrel show and we got a good little sociable blackjack game going here, just to pass the time," the "old head" said.

"Get them banjos out and let's have a little jig music. Come on, let's get hot!" the white guy answered.

We started grumbling again, but the old "cool head" gave us young "hot heads" a withering look.

"We're gonna get hot at the show tonight, pal. In fact, we're gonna take you with us. But come on, now, get in the game here and have a little friendly fun."

"I ain't gonna play with that mother . . ."

"*Shut up, fool,*" the cool head hissed, "*don't you see all that money sticking out his pocket? And this peckerwood's drunk, too.* All right now, let's play. What did you say your name was, Cap? Bill Sweeny? Okay, Bill, what's that, five dollars? Okay, how about you, Buster? Johnny? Come on, get down, Streeter. Yessir! We're gonna have some hot banjo strummin' right after the game. Ooops! I've gotta hit!"

Bill Sweeny had a lot of money on him and a lot of whiskey, too. We had endured his stupid cracks in order to relieve him of some of his liquor and all of his money. But it didn't work out quite like that. He kept nipping out of his bottle, never offering us a shot and ignoring anyone who hinted that he would like to have one.

The more he nipped the drunker he got, and the drunker he got, the more he called us "boy" and "George." We gritted our teeth and kept waiting for the moment when his incredible luck would forsake him or when he would get so full of whiskey he'd begin to gamble carelessly. We waited in vain.

After he cleaned us out and polished off the last drop of the whiskey, he staggered out of our lives.

"If you play with a dog he'll lick you in the face," observed sax man Howard Martin. The rest of us were too disgusted to say anything.

EIGHT

The Club Alabam

Recording executive over talk-back speaker to Negro vocal group during recording session in a Hollywood studio:
"All right, come on, boys, give it that ole soul beat . . . more feeling . . . you know, like Elvis Presley!"

IN 1943 THE Club Alabam in the Central Avenue district of Los Angeles was really jumping. Every night was a thrilling experience for me. There had been nothing in my earlier days in Omaha and the Midwest to compare with the big-city life I was now living. The war was still on, jobs were still plentiful, servicemen were everywhere, their pockets full of money, looking for a good time, and the Alabam was just the place to have a ball and get rid of your money.

In addition to the razzle-dazzle of the general scene, I was playing with Harlan Leonard and his Kansas City Rockets! For a Count Basie worshiper like me, this was almost as exciting as being with Basie himself. In the early days, Harlan and Basie had both been in Bennie Moten's band, and when Moten's band split up, some went with Basie and some went with Harlan. And here I was working with musicians who had been part of the early Kansas City scene. Years later, when some young person would ask in awe, "Is that really Pete Lewis?" or "What is Little Esther really like?" I understood because I had had the same feelings about some of my early idols: Joe Jones, Lester Young, Harry Edison, and Jimmy Rushing.

I couldn't wait to get to Los Angeles to get me a zoot suit. I had a pair of drapes but they were too conservative for my countrified taste. As soon as I made my first payday, I started paying on a brown chalkstripe, thirty inches in the knees, with fourteen-inch bottoms and a coat down below my knees. I chose the long intermission between matinee and evening performances one Sunday to spring my new suit on the cats in the band. I was the youngest guy in the band, and in my youthful ignorance I thought my zoot suit was going to make a big hit.

Feeling very Cab Callowayish, I tipped into the Brownskin Cafe next to the Club Alabam, where some of the cats were enjoying Tila's great chili. The first cat to spot me was Merle Anderson, the tenor sax man, and he almost choked on a mouthful of chili. James Keith, the other tenor man in the band, was sitting with him and he was the first to recover.

"You're looking sharp, daddy!" Keith lied. They were both fine fellows and rather than hurt my feelings they tried to act casual and tell me how good I looked, but I felt there was something wrong. In the next booth were trumpet man James Ross and "Jelly" the trombone man Harpo. Standing talking to them was Jessie Price, the great drummer who had been with the band since its early Kansas City days and who was now on his own. He used to call me "Folks" (short for white folks) and in fact, he still does. His nickname was "Country."

"Hey, Country, what's happening?" I said.

"Folks," he started to say, then blinked. "What is that shit you got on?" He took a good look and started carrying on something awful. The cats in the booth didn't mean to be unkind. Neither did Jessie. But I guess I looked like something out of a corny, hepcat movie, and they couldn't help laughing. Merle Anderson took pity on me and pulled me away.

"Don't pay any attention to that simple Jessie Price," he

said.

As I think back, I'm lucky Bardu Ali, whose wife, Tila, owned and operated the Brownskin Cafe, wasn't in at the time, because then I really would've caught hell. Bardu is the world's greatest hooraher.

I walked into the club and back to the kitchen, where producer Patsy Hunter was having a cup of coffee. Patsy had been extremely helpful to me from the day I first joined Harlan's band. I had never played a full-scale floor show before coming to the band. Patsy was always willing to take time to explain things to me, and I held her in great esteem.

As I walked in, Patsy did a double take and immediately pulled me aside and told me like it was. What really got it was when she asked me if I ever saw any of the men in Basie's, Duke's, or Lunceford's bands wearing zoot suits. The way she told me took most of the sting out of the situation. Had she been less tactful and diplomatic it could've been a much more painful and humiliating situation. I quietly slipped back to the empty dressing room and changed back into my band uniform. I took some kidding from the cats in the band, but that soon died out. The last I heard about it, Daddy Sutton, a waiter at the club, was chiding me about my "clown suit" when a thug called Nightlatch came to my defense. "Shut up, motherfucker, leave the kid alone!" Nightlatch was known as a bad cat, and indeed *was* a bad cat, and things got quiet.

I'm not sure exactly how Nightlatch operated in the underworld, but because of his nickname I always assumed it had something to do with burglary. Nightlatch had taken a liking to me when I first joined Harlan Leonard's band. He used to say I sounded like Lunceford's drummer, Jimmy Crawford. This would frustrate me terribly because I wanted to play like Joe Jones. As I think back, I should have been elated at Nightlatch's amateur appraisal because Crawford was a great, great drummer.

It was Nightlatch, the bar-stool philosopher, who first explained white people's sexual sicknesses to me. We were sitting in the Club during intermission one crowded Saturday night, talking about New York, which I had not yet visited. Nightlatch was from Florida and had moved to New York with his family in the late thirties. There he had lived and operated until the war broke out. He had almost gotten busted for smoking pot and had decided to try the West Coast, where he wasn't so hot.

Mr. Levy, the maître d', whispered to me that the well-dressed, prosperous-looking white man with the beautiful woman in the fur at the next table would like to speak to me for a moment. Would I mind joining them?

After some preliminary beating around the bush about how swell the band was and how well he thought I played, the man leaned over and got down to business. He would make it worth my while if I could arrange to have a certain young man join his wife and him in a "party." The young man they wanted was a tall, black kid who worked as a porter around the club, carrying cases of liquor, ice, chairs and tables, and the like.

I had heard about this kind of action but this was my first personal experience. I tried to set things up, but the fellow they wanted was young and nervous and he backed off. The chick was so fine I started to ask the white guy if I could stand in but I knew I wasn't the type they were after.

After that I had a number of similar experiences. I guess they would look around and spot me as a likely contact man. I don't know why . . . maybe because I was the lightest-looking person around.

Nightlatch tried to get me to move him into the deal. I told him I had tried and the white guy didn't go for it. That was a lie. I knew they didn't want Latch. He was almost as light as I, and he was the meanest, most forbidding-looking cat you ever saw. Nightlatch was full of stories about the Savoy, Small's Paradise, and Connie's Inn in New York. He told me about the white freaks who used to come to Harlem to get their "special" kicks. Some of these special kicks were way, way out—like the old society matron who used to pick up young black men every week and pay them fat fees for wiping her face with their underwear. And the guy who paid Negro prostitutes to beat him with a whip and then urinate in his face. I used to think Nightlatch was making some of that stuff up, but as the years went by I talked to many people, prostitutes included, and saw enough myself to know that these things existed.

During my stay with Harlan Leonard's group, a white fellow joined the band for a while. He played well and the cats in the band liked him personally. What I remember about him more than anything else, however, is his unique domestic situation. He was married and his wife was a practicing prostitute. I don't mean that she was his chick or something like that; she was his wife and they had children and a home. In my inexperience, I found it hard then to understand a family, with kids, in which the father was a musician and the mother was a hustler—and I still do.

Because I don't want to embarrass him, I'll call him Jim. He used to laugh at me for being broke all the time. He always had money to spend and he explained that he played music just as a hobby. His wife's income supplied him with all he needed to get along on. He once half-suggested I hit on Phyllis about going to work with his old lady, and I think the look I gave him kept him from ever bringing it up again.

Jim knew I loved to go fishing, so he cooked up a scheme that was designed to turn me on to a hustling chick under the guise of a fishing trip. He explained that he had to drive his wife up to a mining area known as Red Mountain.

"All we have to do," he said, "is drop my old lady in town and then you and I can have a ball fishing on the way back to Los Angeles."

In addition to his wife, Jim had another woman in the car

with him when he picked me up. Just before we left the LA city limits, he stopped for gas. I got out and asked him who the extra chick was and what was happening.

"She's yours if you play your cards right," Jim answered. "Her old man got drafted and he's gone overseas. Now get back in the car and start making your pitch and you won't be broke no more."

The chick had given me a very blasé nod when we were introduced. "Why didn't you tell me about this?" I demanded of Jim. "Anyhow, the chick seems hostile as hell."

"She'll be all right when she gets to know you. She makes a lot of money and she's got nobody to give it to now, so play it cool."

I thought about money, I thought about fishing, about the chick being older than me (she was), about how I could pull such a thing off even if I wanted to (after all, I was married), and most of all I thought about the way the girl looked—fat, stringy-haired, and unkempt. I'll try, I thought. I didn't want to look like a completely foolish square in front of Jim.

When we got back to the car, Jim's wife had set up a new seating arrangement. The chick and I now had the back seat all to ourselves. Within minutes I knew that we weren't going to make it together. First of all, she glared at me like I was a snake, which meant she couldn't stand me at all, and then I noticed that she had a peculiar odor, which killed the deal as far as I was concerned. She smelled sour.

Jim and his wife tried to create a jolly air with their conversation, but the back seat remained deadly silent. Once I shifted in my seat and the chick thought I was making a move in her direction. She reared up like she was going to hit me, but all I was doing was trying to move closer to my window to get some fresh air.

Jim pulled into a roadside motel. I tried to tell him he could forget it, but he had planned all this for my benefit. He explained that the girls couldn't go into Red Mountain until the following day anyhow, because women had to have a health certificate in order to stay in town and the office wasn't open in the evening. So we might as well make a cozy night of it.

I finally convinced him that trying to bring the chick and me together was a lost cause. The girls would sleep in one room and we would sleep in another. Evidently he forgot to explain this to the girl, 'cause she was just waiting for me to act like I thought I was going to sleep with her so she could explode. I was helping Jim carry some of his wife's things into the room the girls were going to share, and as my bad luck would have it, Jim and his wife were back in the car. As I walked into the room I almost bumped into the chick.

"Don't you touch me, you bastard!" she screeched. In the dim light I think she mistakenly thought I was trying to grab her. But I didn't have time to rationalize at the moment. Her scream unhinged me, and all my distaste for her poured out.

"Don't nobody want you, you funky white bitch!" I shouted. "I came up here to go fishin'!"

The next morning, as we approached the town where the girls were going to work, Jim told me that the sheriff of the area was a cat named Red Ryder who didn't allow no pimps in town. We would have to stash somewhere in the outskirts while the girls drove in and had their physical and got their certificates. Then they would pick us up and we would fish during the day. Later, in the cover of night, we would drop the girls in town and head back to LA.

Thinking the girls would only be in town for a short while, Jim decided that we would hide out in a tunnel under the highway nearby. Everything was okay for a while because it was early and relatively cool. But as the hours ground slowly on, the sun became a fiery monster and the heat in the tunnel became unbearable. I began to wish I had a drink of water.

Jim had a theory: "If we get high we won't notice the heat

and the thirst so much." With that, he pulled out a stick of pot and lit up. Now I could just see us getting busted for pimping *and* pot! But the idea that getting high would beat the heat intrigued me. When he passed the stick to me, I didn't hesitate. In about five minutes I was sailing! But the higher I got, the thirstier I became, and what had been a very hot tunnel became Satan's oven! As narcotized as I was, I remember thinking that I must really be a freak for going fishing if I let myself get into this kind of a crack!

I think that even more than the fear of getting busted, what kept me from becoming a regular marijuana user was the fact that it always put me to sleep. I knew better than falling for the "immoral" and "dangerous to health" propaganda that one still hears. From a health standpoint, I wish I had kept on smoking pot and *stopped* smoking cigarettes, which are *really* deadly dangerous. But why take a chance on going to jail for something that was quite expensive and did nothing more, really, than put me to sleep—and I've never had trouble going to sleep. In the tunnel that day, the marijuana soon took its usual effect and I fell asleep. But what a sleep! Full of dreams about steaming deserts and blistering ovens! I really didn't wake up completely until we were halfway back to LA.

NEGRO celebrities, and occasionally white ones, too, were in and out of the Club Alabam regularly. Monday night was celebrity night. I remember how I thrilled at the sight of people like Joe Louis, Lena Horne, Ethel Waters, Lionel Hampton, Billie Holiday, Ella Fitzgerald, and Louis Armstrong. Later I would have my own band and get to work with many of these stars and become good friends, but at first I was just like the proverbial hick gawking at the skyscrapers. One Monday night, a young lady came out of the audience and sang "Stardust." I remember how impressed I was with this relatively unknown singer. She was Pearl Bailey and was destined to become a great star. Though I never had the pleasure of working with her, I later worked with dancer Bill Bailey, her brother.

Not all of the people who performed on the talent-night show became big, nationally-known stars, but in some cases this was just a matter of lucky breaks, because some were really fine. Caroline Harlson sang "Honeysuckle Rose" one night and all the cats in the band were turned on. We had never heard of her at the time, but she was really good. In later years, Caroline and I were to meet again, this time in the civil rights struggle. We became personal friends and our families have been very close ever since.

There were some unhappy events at the Club Alabam, too. One night we got word that Fats Waller had died. And there was the time, just after I had opened at the club with my own band, that my piano player, Fletcher Smith, busted owner Curtis Mosby in the mouth! I thought we had lost our gig for sure, but actually I came closer to getting canned by Curtis over another incident. One night the club was crowded, and a performer—I can't recall his name, but he was a little guy and I remember he was from Detroit—was going through his master-of-ceremonies chores. He had about a five-minute spot in which he had to kill time with a few gags, but a big, red-faced drunk at a ringside table was giving him a hard time. The little fellow paused in his act and very courteously asked the white drunk to give him a break. The drunk jumped up from his seat and lurched toward the little guy, blurting out something about a "damn nigger!" The sight of our meek little MC standing forlornly at the mike and a big, burly six-and-a-half-footer coming toward him set some of us from the band into motion. My drums were placed in the front line and I would've been the first one on the cat, but just as I made a turn onto the dance floor, our band boy, Levi, wrapped his big arms around me and held fast as the other cats were passing me by.

"What are you doing, man?" I said incredulously.

"You ain't going out there, baby," Levi said softly.

The house was in an uproar and I couldn't move! "Turn me loose!" I hollered.

"Oh, no," Levi answered calmly.

Out of the panic, Curtis Mosby leaned over and said, "That's right, Levi, hold him."

Suddenly the uproar was over. The other white people at the drunk's table had grabbed him and hustled him out before anything really happened. I was now madder at Levi than I ever had been at the drunk. I had had a chance to give vent to my pent-up, brutal aggressions about white racists and also act like a hero in front of the chorus girls in the show, and Levi had caused me to blow it.

"I oughta kick your ass!" I roared at Levi.

"You oughta, but you won't," Levi said. "After all, I did you a favor and plus we're suppose to be boys."

"What kind of favor?" I demanded.

"That big cat might've whipped your butt—plus, I tried to keep you from gettin' fired," Levi explained.

At intermission time I was summoned into Curtis Mosby's office. In addition to Mr. Mosby, the assistant manager of the club, a man we knew as Uncle Lou, was there. Uncle Lou looked just like a white man. He was so white-looking he even had white hair. He looked more like Mr. Charlie than ever this evening, sitting there at the desk with a very stern, businesslike look on his face.

"You tell him, Lou, I'm too disgusted," Curtis said.

"Listen, Nat Turner," Lou spit out sarcastically. It was the first time I had ever heard the name Nat Turner. I had no idea what the name and the caustic tone of voice meant. "You are hired to play music, not to chastise naughty white folks. And tell the rest of them spooks in your band we don't need any bouncers and bodyguards—only saxophone players and trumpet players— understand?"

MANY of the people I came in contact with got high on pot. We called it gage then. I had actually lost interest in marijuana years earlier, because, as I have already mentioned, all it did was lull me to sleep—and I needed to go to sleep in those exciting times like I needed a hole in the head. Once, though, I got hold of a special kind of pot that did not put me to sleep.

It was in 1946 and we had just arrived in New York for the first time. We were playing the Apollo Theatre and I was staying at the Braddock Hotel in Harlem. We had finished the last show and I was settling in for the night, when I heard a knock on the door. Outside was a furtive little character I had seen earlier hanging around backstage.

"Let me come in for a minute, JO, I've got something good for you," he whispered.

He slipped in, looked around, saw that we were alone, and proceeded to tell me that he had a trunk for sale, cheap. Now it happened that I needed an extra trunk, but I was worried that this article was hot and we would all wind up in jail.

He kept insisting and swearing that the trunk was his and that he had no use for it and that he was in dire need of some money.

"Just five bucks, man, a fin, and she's all yours. And she's a good one, too," he kept saying.

Finally, as much for the purpose of getting rid of him as anything else, I said okay. He darted out the door, and in a short while was back, pulling at the front end of a worn-looking steamer trunk. At the other end was another furtive-looking little cat.

As I slipped him the five, I asked why it seemed so hard to carry. Both of them were perspiring profusely by the time they had it up the stairs and into my room.

"Is there something in it?" I asked.

"Nothing important," he muttered as he made for the door.

"Hey, it's locked. Have you got the key with you?" I called out.

"I'll bring it right back," he said over his shoulder as he hustled down the steps after his brother.

I waited and waited and then realized he wasn't coming back. I realized, too, that the trunk had probably just been stolen somewhere and that the surreptitious brothers had no more idea than I what was in the thing.

Now my curiosity grew. I wanted to see what was inside. But how could I get into the trunk? I struggled to break the lock. Eventually, I did manage to snap it open with the help of a piece of curtain rod I found in the closet. Expecting the police to break into the room at any moment and arrest me as a fence, I proceeded nervously to empty the contents on the floor. It was full of some kind of lodge paraphernalia: robes, aprons, weird hats, books, even a pair of ceremonial swords. I was so disappointed at not finding any valuable loot that I dumped the remaining stuff out on the floor and put the empty trunk in the closet. Then I climbed into bed and lay staring at the pile of junk, thinking that I would have our band boy dispose of it in the morning. That is, if the cops didn't bust me before then. As I lay there looking, I saw something I hadn't noticed before—a big, brown paper bag, and it seemed to be full. I went over and picked it up. It wasn't very heavy. I sat on the bed and investigated. It was filled with a coarse, dusty substance. I moved over toward the light. A king-sized sack full of pot!!! I kept running my fingers through it and pinching up some to smell. It was a lot finer, almost like heavy dust, than any marijuana I'd ever seen, but it sure smelled like the real McCoy. Now what was I to do? If this *was* pot, I was holding God knows how many thousands of dollars' worth in my hands!

I tried calling various cats in the band. They were all still out. I could hear a radio next door, and I remembered that it was Dinah Washington's room. I telephoned her.

"Say, Dinah, this is Johnny Otis in the next room . . . are you alone?"

"No, I've got a couple of friends with me."

"Well, excuse yourself for a minute and come on over. It's important."

"Okay."

Dinah came in with her usual flamboyant and profane manner. "Okay, now what kind of bullshit are you up to . . . and it better be important, too."

"Ssssshhh! Close the door and be quiet," I whispered. "Tell me what this is in this sack." I held the sack up near the light, so she could see it better. Dinah took up a little handful, smelled it, tasted it, looked at me, looked back at the sack, hefted the sack, and exclaimed: "Ooooooooooooooohhh, baby! Where did you get all this outrageous amount of good shit from?"

I told her the story and she told me to wait a minute. She went back to her room, dismissed her guests, and called me to come over and bring the sack with me.

"We're safer in here than in your room," she said and I agreed. If the cops somehow traced the stolen trunk to my room, it would be better if the pot and I were elsewhere.

"But, Dinah," I said, "whoever owned that trunk owned the pot, too, and they wouldn't call the cops, would they?"

"Damn that," Dinah answered, "we're still safer in here. Hand me the sack and go out and buy some Bull Durham paper."

I knew better than to argue with Dinah. I went next door, dressed, and hit the street, looking for rolling paper. I guess I'd still be looking if I hadn't lucked up on my trombone man, John Pettigrew, coming down 125th Street near Seventh Avenue. I quickly filled him in. He had paper in his room, so we made it back to the Braddock.

Dinah was smiling when we returned. I thought she had been at the stash already, but no, she was just in a jovial mood.

"Wouldn't you know this lucky fucker would come up with something like this!" she almost shouted. "A whole *sack* of shit, whole big sack of pot and a trunk, too, for five bucks!"

Pettigrew was putting his expert eye on the sack. He looked up. "You don't know the half of it, baby," he said in a kind of serious tone. "This is not just everyday shit. This is hash, baby, *hashish!*"

Oh man! Hashish, I thought: It must be worth three, five, maybe ten grand! But I knew I didn't have the nerve to try to peddle it. In fact, I wasn't sure I had the guts to even smoke it. Hashish!

But I did turn on with Dinah and John that night and for once I didn't get sleepy. This really was different. John was right. This stuff kicked me right up through the roof, and I was still wide awake and having a ball when dawn broke. The only trouble was, I couldn't get to sleep and when I finally did get sleepy it was time to go to the theatre. I spent a miserable day trying to stay alert on stage.

I toyed with the idea of trying to turn the sack into money, but I didn't have the stomach for the risk. I wound up giving Dinah and John a third apiece, and when the cats in the band found out about my portion, it didn't last very long.

NINE

Pigeons

"They just trying to prove a point and they can't prove a point, and they tried by talking, and peaceful means of demonstrations and that hasn't helped, so therefore, they have to go out and show them what they mean." — *Woman, interviewed during the Watts riots.*

I SPOTTED THE PIGEON right away. It was half-stuffed into the young guy's jacket but there was still enough showing to tell me what it was. A kid with a pigeon under his coat was the last thing I expected to encounter at the stage door of the Apollo Theatre in New York, but there he was. He was part of a group of fans waiting for autographs. Louis Jordan came out and scribbled a few, right quick. He wisecracked at one of the kids in the crowd something like, "Ain't you Aunt Julie's boy?" The kids howled with delight and Aunt Julie's boy blushed, recovered, and tried to crack back, but Louis was in his car and gone.

A sudden movement frightened the pigeon. It gave the pigeon panic-hoot and tried to wriggle out of the kid's grasp. The familiar grunt-coo that pigeons emit when startled flashed me back to Mr. Williams' coop. He was the old man on my paper route who fed me such unscientific bits of pigeon lore as "The hen gives the baby his size and strength and the cock gives him his color and shape." He was a very kindly old fellow, who tried to answer every question a kid with the pigeon fever could con-

jure up, even if some of the answers were way this side of
Mendel or Darwin.

"Please, Pa, please Pa . . . Mr. Williams says I can have
'em if you say okay!" Something about Mr. Williams' health demanded that he move to Arizona. The pigeons were mine, fantails, satinettes, homers; all I needed was my father's permission.
Papa grumbled and fussed. "In the middle of a Depression he
wants to feed pigeons," but even as he grumbled he was building the coop on top of our garage.

"You gonna pay for the feed from your paper route," Papa
declared in a loud voice. Then he added almost under his
breath, "I sell it to you wholesale from the store." I went
through the motions of paying for the feed but Papa wouldn't
take the money. He loved to holler and admonish but he was all
bark. "No, dolling, you don't have to pay . . . what kind father
am I to make my son pay for chicken feed?"

I couldn't keep the various breeds isolated as Mr. Williams
had. With only one wire enclosure they were all in there together—fantails, satinettes, and homers—a democratic conglom-
eration of feathered integration. Pigeons breed for life, I reasoned, so why worry. The first generation at least will breed true
to type, and by the time the babies get old enough to start looking good to each other I'll have more coops. The mated pairs
lived true to one another, fantail to fantail, satinette to satinette,
and homer to homer. But Mr. Williams must have given me
some uncommitted individuals. Either that, or the trip across
town had shaken their fidelity, because before I knew it, I had a
gang of mixed marriages on my hands. Mr. Williams would've
been outraged I know, but the hell with that. I wanted to raise
birds, and I wouldn't care if one of 'em mated with a seagull, as
long as they laid eggs and hatched 'em! Come on, you guys, I
used to think, let's get to layin' eggs. One week passed, two
weeks . . . no eggs. Finally, a fantail hen that had mated to a
satinette cock came through. This seemed to trigger the whole

colony off. Now there were eggs in the next boxes, on the ledges, and on the floor.

"Hey, Rudy, look at that one, he's half-and-half."

"Half-and-half what?"

"Half one kind and half another kind."

"He's still a funky little somebitch like the rest of 'em."

"Oh, man, why don't you learn to appreciate pigeons. They're great."

"Well, if they're so great let's have some squab for dinner."

THREE thousand miles from home, and the sight of a pigeon's head peeping out from under a kid's jacket had melted the years like butter. The kid wanted to talk about my band and I wanted to talk about the bird in his bosom.

"I used to raise pigeons. What kind is that?"

"A flight. . . . What's your saxophone player's name who sounds like Lester Young? Is he Pres' son?"

"Paul Quinichette. He's not Pres' son. What are those kind of pigeons used for?"

"They fly a long time, way up high. Is the other tenor man Von Streeter?"

"Yeah. Do you have more birds than that one?"

"Yeah, I got a gang of 'em. Do these two guys dislike each other?"

"What two guys? Streeter and Paul?"

"Yeah."

"No, man, they're boys."

"Well, I heard Lester and Herschal hated each other. . . . Is that true?"

"I don't know, I never saw Herschal."

"Didn't you make some records with Lester?"

"Yeah."

"Did he ever talk about Herschal?"

"I didn't see him that much." No point in trying to explain

that Lester talked a special language that he had invented himself and that following his conversation was a job for a decoding
expert. Come to think of it, maybe Lester had talked to me about
Herschal. Most of what he said was a mystery anyhow. "Where
do you keep your birds?"

"A couple of blocks from here, where I live."

"I'd sure like to see them."

"Okay. Hey, is that chick with your trombone man his
wife?"

Yeah, one of 'em, I thought, and we moved down the street
toward where he kept his pigeons. We had an hour and a half
between shows and I was about to see my first rat-and-roach-
infested Harlem tenement apartment building from the inside.
On the way to the roof we stopped on the third floor to say hello
to his mother.

"Mama's home because she fell in the subway and hurt her
hip, or else she'd be at work."

The trash and garbage boxes stacked in the hall produced a
darting cat that gave us a baleful back-glance for disturbing his
operations. As we passed the trash mountain, the kid kicked one
of the boxes out of the way and the thump blasted a gang of
roaches out of the heap. They streaked up the stained and
plaster-cracked wall in a starburst design. People live here, I
thought. *People* . . . people live here!

"Is that you, Marcus?" A woman's voice echoed out from the
other room.

"Yeah, a man wants to see my pigeons. He's a bandleader
from the Apollo. Can we come in and say hello?"

"So you from California, huh, son? How 'bout this boy of
mine? Can you make somethin' of him? He tootin' on that ole
horn enough, he oughta be a expert by now."

A battered C Melody sax was propped on the mantelpiece.
Three tired chairs leaned toward an ancient table that had troubles of its own. Sometime during the wars against the dinner-

time armies it had lost one of its legs. A length of two-by-two
cut a trifle too long kept it standing. Four of Marcus' brothers
and sisters, all younger than he, were in the room with the
mother, who was propped up in the bed in the corner. On the
mantel next to the sax stood a picture of a Negro Mary with
brownskinned Jesus in her arms. Little black Jesus' piercing eyes
seemed to follow me around the room.

"This is my horn," Marcus said as we walked over to the
mantel. Little Jesus kept looking right at me from the mantel.
This cat's gonna probably pick that horn up and sound like
Charlie Parker, I thought. He honked and squeaked while I lost
any idealistic notions I may have had. I had hoped he would be
a great talent and I could take him in the band. He could then
take his mother and the kids out of this roach trap. But two toots
and a squeak and that dream vanished.

"We're going up and see the pigeons now," Marcus said.

I tripped on a massive hole in the carpet. "Watch it, son,
don't hurt yourself now," Marcus' mother said. Little black Jesus'
eyes followed me as I picked myself up off the floor. I could feel
them burning into my back as we went out.

"This coop was already here when we moved here," Marcus
explained. "These ain't all my birds; a bunch of us keep our birds
here and we chip in for the feed."

"Lemme see the babies," Marcus' little sister implored.

"Ain't no babies," Marcus answered.

"Yes it is, you showed 'em to Cissy. Lemme see 'em, lemme
see 'em!" she begged.

"After a while. Now get back out of the way." Marcus was
waving a long pole with cloth streamers on it to keep the flock
up in the air. Every time they dipped toward the roof as if to
land, he would shoo them up again.

"You know something," Marcus said, "people don't know it
but there's hawks right here in the city. They lay up in them tall
buildings and wait for a juicy pigeon to come by. Do you have

pigeon hawks in California?"

"Uh, yeah," I answered. But the truth was I had never seen one because I had never let my birds out for fear that they would make it across town to Mr. Williams' house and never come back.

"I'll tell you what's worse then hawks, though, man. Rats. There's some rats up here big as me! They're bold, man. They come right in the house at night. One night after we was all in bed I saw a great big one climbing around in the baby's bed. Man, it like to scared me to death. There was a baby down the street had some candy on his mouth and a rat chewed the baby's lips off, man! I took an old chair leg and beat that mother fucker to death. And dig this, that rat stood up on his hind legs like a natural man . . . and what'd he do that for?"

"Marcus kill 'at rat. Guess what, Marcus kill 'at rat with a stick. And Mama say Marcus a goooood boy for that, too," the little girl said. Her eyes were wide as teacups. Where had I seen those eyes? Oh, yeah, downstairs on the mantelpiece.

After giving Marcus his hero credit, the little girl begged again to see the baby pigeons. I took a good look at her as Marcus went in to get a couple of squabs. She was all the heartrending waifs I'd ever seen on posters wrapped up into one. A pathetic little ragamuffin standing chalky-kneed and scraggleheaded in a frayed and faded dress, silhouetted against the Harlem twilight.

Her eyes lit up like diamonds as Marcus handed her the baby birds. "That one his brother and that one his sister," she purred as she snuggled them close.

On the way down I met Marcus' father, who had just come in. He was a West Indian immigrant with a fierce sense of nationalistic pride.

"The blahck mahn is sleeping now, mon, but he will not doze forever. Soon the blahck mahn will rise again. It won't be long either, I tell you that. When the blahck mahn awaken, things will not be the same. No more short end of de stick. De whole ting will be changed. No more exploitation, no more humiliation, no more roaches and rats, I tell you that!"

On the way back to the theatre, we passed a storefront with big portraits of black generals and tribal chieftains. The place was covered with signs and slogans heralding the greatness and the awakening of the black man. A man standing on a platform talking to a group of people assembled on the sidewalk.

"The blahck mahn will not sleep forever . . ."

"That's the place where my father always goes," Marcus said. "They're always talkin' about the 'blahck mahn' is going to kick the shit out of the white man and all that kinda stuff. He's always making me go with him to meetings and my mama's always making me go to church . . . damn! You're lucky you don't have to go through all that stuff. I'll be glad when I get my horn straight so I can split."

I took him backstage where he met Streeter and Paul. It was almost time for the next show. We exchanged addresses. I noticed his middle initial. "What's the G stand for, Marcus?"

"Garvey, man, that was my old man's idea."

TEN

The Negro Wars

"If you wish to possess the white man's things you must begin anew and put away the wisdom of your fathers. You must lay up food and forget the hungry. When your house is built and your storeroom filled, then look around for a neighbor whom you can take advantage of and seize all he has." — *Chief Red Cloud, Oglala Sioux.*

I'VE HEARD IT OFTEN ENOUGH to be convinced that no matter how long and hard you squeeze a turnip, you'll get no blood. People, on the other hand, give up blood when squeezed hard enough. The only catch is, and history proves it, that if you squeeze people hard enough and long enough you'll come up with blood. But sooner or later some of it is bound to be your own.

Three hundred years of racial strife in America has produced an appalling amount of bloodshed, but so far it has been flowing only one way—*from* the black man. The bloodletting that has continued down through the centuries can be measured by more than the armies of charred, black bodies hanging like Spanish moss from southern (and northern) trees. It doesn't end with the ghosts of numberless Negro inmates worked, beaten, and starved to death on chain gangs, or gobbled up by a capital-punishment monster with a penchant for dark flesh, with nightly sacrifices served up to the gory high priests of sadism in the nation's police precincts. There are other less sensational and more effective ways of squeezing the blood out. One of them is to eliminate the person before he or she is born, or as soon thereafter as possible.

Poverty, being such a notorious life span shortener, serves as one of the most effective murder weapons yet discovered. The correlation between poor health and low (or *no*) income is well documented. A newborn Negro baby has less chance of survival than a white. A Negro baby will have its life ended seven years sooner. This is not some biological phenomenon linked to skin color, like sickle cell anemia; this is a national crime, linked to a white-supremacist way of life and compounded by indifference.

On December the first, 1955, in Montgomery, Alabama, Mrs. Rosa Parks decided she had "had" it with Alabama white folks and Jim Crow bus-seating arrangements. Mrs. Parks had no way of knowing it at the time, and the rest of America surely wasn't aware of it, but when "Mister Charlie" pointed to the "white only" sign and she, in effect, told him to "shove it," the world stood still for a quick second while old "Yassa, boss" got off and young, "Screw you, white folks!" got on.

Mrs. Parks' act was not violent or bloody. It was simply a point of departure, the end of one long and dismal era and the dawn of a new day. Whether the button that Rosa Parks pressed will mark the beginning of a long, bloody struggle depends entirely upon how squeeze-minded the anti-Negro forces remain in the face of the new ground rules.

Because the American black man has been preempted, the Negro woman has been forced to assume the impossible role of both mother and father, breadwinner and homemaker. The entire world of womanhood stands taller and prouder as a result of the American Negro woman's historically supreme job of holding her race together with her bare hands. In the finest tradition of womanhood, Rosa Parks struck the spark that lighted fires in twenty million hearts, and started an emotional surge that transcended mere survival. Her defiant act plucked a responsive chord not only in other Negro women's bosoms, but even more important, it breathed militant life into millions of black men who had heretofore been bludgeoned and brainwashed into an impotent, Lazarus-like submission.

Considerably dimmed and obscured by time and the many racial events that succeeded it, the Rosa Parks incident, nevertheless, was the touchstone—the catalyst which helped bring forth a myriad of forceful men, women, and organizations, and helped spur into more positive postures such traditionally quiet and conservative groups as the NAACP, the Urban League, and the Negro Church.

This is not to say that there had not been a prolonged and dedicated effort in the racial arena long before the Rosa Parks incident. But nothing had occurred previously to bring the Negro to his feet in such an angry and militant mood and on such a massive, national scale. True, the new army was made up for the most part of relatively advantaged Negroes, middle class generally, but the fact that the real victim (the overwhelming mass at the bottom of the ladder) was not attracted to the civil rights movement, or at least did not participate to any degree, does not mean that he wasn't interested in his own destiny. It simply was not his cup of tea. When he got ready to get in a lick, he did it *his* way, in Watts. And who is to say that he didn't know the best way to approach a problem that was, after all, more intimately *his* than his more privileged kinsman's?

All that transpired in the American racial scene in the ten years that passed after Rosa Parks refused to give up her bus seat can be described as Phase 1. Phase 2 was ushered in in Watts in mid-August, 1965, with a wild celebration that featured fireworks and free goodies.

From the first day of the rebellion it was evident that this was a turning point in American history, because the Watts riots were not and are not a Los Angeles, California, or even a Negro problem. The Watts situation is an American problem and there are potential Wattses all over the nation. Even if Watts was one of a kind it would still be an American problem. But Watts is not unique as American ghettos go.

"For crissakes! you got all the civil rights laws and Supreme Court decisions you need, what do you want now?" a fellow moaned to me after a recent panel debate. I thought fleetingly of an answer: I want the same life expectancy and birth survival rate for Negro children that whites enjoy, and job opportunities and quality education on an equal basis, or . . . but what the hell, that kind of discussion would take all night.

Perhaps the best answer to the question is that the average black person in America wants a full, unadulterated position in this society, an equal, uncut share of America. This is mostly what all the marching, picketing, exhorting, demanding, requesting, pushing, shouting, struggling (and more recently, burning) has been all about. That's all. No more, no less. To date the door remains slammed shut. I heard a visiting Englishman describe as "excruciatingly droll" the fact that every time a Negro individual or group makes any waves there is an immediate charge of "Communist influence." Isn't it strange that a black man can't even get full credit for conducting his own protest? And isn't it even stranger that a white man can enjoy the full privileges of citizenship and is lauded as a "fine patriot" for supporting the "free enterprise system," but a Negro is branded a Communist or a Communist dupe if he asks or demands to be let in?

I remember in the thirties we used to go to dances in Oakland sponsored by Communist and Communist-front groups. We went to eat the free food and get to the very democratic and "charitable" chicks who always seemed to be around. What it was all about politically we knew not and cared less. There are Communists working to get something going here and there, just as there are Democrats, Republicans, Anarchists, Socialists, and Fascists.

Along with the cry, Communist, we now hear the cry, Muslim. But in the case of the Muslim there is every possibility that a Negro may be a member, and if he is he will identify himself with fierce pride. In spite of the growth of the Muslim faith, the vast majority of American Negroes remain uncommitted to and uninterested in new, exotic religious societies.

The Britisher who thought it was "excruciatingly droll" for Negroes to be branded Communists because they wanted to be part of the capitalist system, also stated that he thought it was phenomenal that American Negroes, in view of all the ill-treatment and denial received in America, had not begun to be at least very curious about socialism and communism.

"It would seem," he observed, "that just the old idea of 'my enemy is your enemy' would have created among the American Colored people a strong affinity for the idea of Socialism, not to mention the fact that almost without exception the newly emergent African states have been socialist to the core. But I suppose they see the white majority living well, and they like what they see and simply want a slice of the pie, as it were."

To assume that there is not at least intellectual curiosity about socialism among American Negroes, and particularly the young students, is quite an assumption. And to assume that all American Negroes will continue to be forced into second-class citizenship without undermining their commitment to the American economic system or eroding their loyalty, is perhaps the most presumptuous thought of all.

The college Peace Movement, which grew out of the general civil rights activity on American campuses, contains, within its core, inquisitive and highly militant young Negro students who are equipped to articulate the burning issues of the day from the viewpoint of black America. For the first time, Negro students are to be found among the intellectual "bearded" revolutionaries who are challenging the defenders of the status quo in domestic and international matters. They bring a a new perspective and fresh vitality to the American academic society, or at least to that part of it in the vanguard of the search for twentieth-century answers to current questions.

It is interesting to note the almost unanimous, although individually arrived at, feeling of new-found *Negro* identity expressed by the young people of this class. A Rhodes scholar from Watts, Stanley Saunders, typifies this reaction when he points out that the Watts riots seemed to reconfirm his identity as a black man.

The effect of the riots is also evident within the ranks of the civil rights leadership. Among this middle-class-oriented group we find evidence of a reevaluation of its past approaches and a search for ways to more effectively reach and "get with" the people. Here, too, in the wake of the shock of the uprising, there is an obvious wave of new pride in being black.

But it is among the masses of the folk (from whence the riot participants actually sprang) that the reaction is most impressive and profound. In the heart of "Soulville," in the streets and in the poorer homes among the people, one can almost reach out and touch the aura of exhilaration, the feeling of rebirth, of dignity, of manhood.

The "New Negro" has been a long time in the making, and many groups and factors contributed to his final form. Molded by a hostile and often genocidal white majority, prodded by the civil rights movement of the past ten years, the "New Negro" burst into full being Phoenix-like, from the flames of 103rd Street.

His birth ushered in a different era in the ongoing drama of the American dilemma. This newborn babe has experienced a three-hundred-year gestation period in which, unlike a fetus, he has seen, heard, felt, and remembered everything that has happened to him, and therefore he cannot be dealt with as an infant.

Whether he is dealt with in the person of a college student, a black nationalist, a civil rights leader, or one of the unemployed on the streets of Watts, he can no longer be viewed against a backdrop of slavery as in the Reconstruction and post-Reconstruction era, against a backdrop of nonviolent marches and demonstrations as in more recent years; today he must be considered against a background of burning and rioting.

It has been pointed out many times that either good or bad can come out of the events of August, 1965. The statement in itself is meaningless unless one attempts to dig into what "good" and what "bad" can come of the riots.

Obviously, a "good" that could emerge from the situation would be white society taking the cue and reacting in a positive and humanistic manner. It would be very "good" if the riots served to open the majority's eyes to the misery and suffering that led to the frightening explosion. A truly meaningful effort to relieve the misery of the masses and thereby remove the causes of the uprising would necessarily have to involve not only economic progress but must also be framed in a broader effort to effect racial brotherhood. Here's where the question of "good" coming out of the riots gets bogged down. Because no matter how much progress could be made where comparative economics is concerned, the evils of the color-caste system would continue to erode relations between the races, and a confrontation would be inevitable. I cannot agree with a theory that says the almighty dollar solves all. Racism is a cancer that ignores wealth, academic achievement, science, or reason.

The fact is that the Watts riots have hardened the attitudes of the white majority. The road took a sharp turn in August, 1965. The question is: Where will it lead? If society moves according to the will of the majority, we must know what the will of the majority is as far as Negro Americans are concerned. Can white Americans adapt to or accept the uncompromising demands of today's Negro movement? Or will the traditional resistance prevail, leading to an even more drastic polarization of the races?

The often-drawn analogy between Germany's pre-Hitler Jews and America's present-day Negroes is not as far-fetched as some naïve and over-optimistic observers would hope for. The question is: How many burning Watts' would it take to establish the idea of Negroes as an intolerable menace in the minds of the majority of white Americans?

Today's sociopolitical thinkers tend to shy away from this question and its ramifications. There is little, if any, dialogue along this line. But the question must be dealt with as an imminent possibility . . . because it is imminent.

Negroes must also become acutely aware of the danger of the tide of majority opinion turning all sour. This must be anticipated not in terms of tempering the tone of the movement, but in terms of how to best protect the group, should the struggle for equality produce ever-increasing violence and a genocidal race war.

If one cannot relate the plight of the Jew in Europe to the Negro's struggle in America, then consider the history and the fate of the American Indian.

Tempering the tone of a people's revolt, particularly one that takes on a desperate, spontaneous nature is an impossible task. When a movement contains certain deep-rooted ingredients, moderate leaders dare not call for a slowdown. And if they do they are either ignored or denounced. This was borne out in the Watts riots.

My opinion does not stem from any notion that Negroes are more prone to violence than others, but rather from the knowledge that black people are just as apt to turn to violence as a last resort as anyone else. The real danger for the future, however, grows not out of the Negro community's struggle for justice, but out of the white community's historical and continuing rejection of these demands.

The most that has come out of the struggle to date are a few legal reforms. And, in the pure sense of the word, most of these were already guaranteed constitutionally. The fact that well-defined rights have to be reconfirmed by new legislation is evidence of the general reluctance to extend them to all citizens.

Out of the Watts riots came a sudden search for civil rights measures to ease the situation. The realization that California already had most of the necessary laws on the books was driven home with frustrating impact.

I am not suggesting that the effort to strengthen and pass new civil rights laws be abandoned. I am simply pointing out that *with* all the civil rights laws in existence, there is still job discrimination against Negroes, which results in an appalling unemployment rate, still de-facto school segregation and unequal educational opportunities, still miles of sub-standard housing. Negroes in the disadvantaged parts of the California ghettos are often as oppressed and discriminated against as those in the ghettos of states lacking civil rights laws and agencies.

What is so stupidly misunderstood (when it *is* actually misunderstood and not simply distorted) is the *racial* tone of the movement, the *nationalistic* character, as against the political or economic. Because often even when an expression sounds political it is in fact racial or nationalistic.

For instance, a friend described to me how he shook up the owner of a plush, segregated housing project situated in a beautiful California valley. He was part of a group of Negro bartenders and waiters brought in from Los Angeles to serve at the grand opening. At the end of the affair, the owner, full of good cheer and enthusiasm for his enterprise, put his arm around my friend and said, "What does it make you think of when you look at those beautiful rolling hills over there?"

My friend started to answer that it made him think of the many Negroes who were barred from enjoying them, but he answered instead, "It makes me think how a quarter of a million Chinese will look coming over the top of those hills."

I'm sure the owner immediately pegged my friend as some kind of Communist.

The whites who make an almost hysterical attempt to equate or relate the Negro movement to Communism completely miss the true nationalistic flavor of the revolt. One wonders when the "Karl Marx of race" will come forth. It is not at all unlikely that such an individual will emerge, if not in America, then maybe in Africa. The battles lines have long been drawn in the policial and economic sense. It might be an idea now to examine the entire world in terms of white and non-white.

To reject this idea as inflammatory or fantastic is to ignore the effect that white supremacy, colonialism, and imperialism have had upon the non-white majority of the world's population. They are the majority, and without exception they are moving toward self-determination, industrialization, and military might.

America seems more inclined than most Western nations to view "uncommitted" nations (practically all of whom are non-white) as Capitalist-economy "friends" or Socialist-leaning "unfriends," rather than as members of the vast global family of non-whites.

Non-white nations everywhere, regardless of their political or economic systems, have one sure basis for unity. It is their fear of, and their hatred for, white supremacy. It is backed up by centuries of hard, cruel history and forms the basis for at least one firm concurrence, even among nations or men who are otherwise at each other's throats.

Africans, Arabs, Asians, and non-white South Americans have all, in one way or another, experienced the white man's racism. They may not be able to agree on many things, but on the subject of white supremacy there is tacit solidarity.

The "Indian Problem" in the United States was not considered solved until the entire native population was either run into Mexico or Canada, starved out, deposited securely in reservations, or killed off. The "Final Solution" of the Indian problem is a bloody and disgraceful blot on American history, but the passing years, aided by tempering propaganda, have dimmed the national memory to the shame of genocide and theft which brought on what our history books record as the Indian Wars.

Scholars have tried to present the true facts of the era but Hollywood has long since appropriated the field as the popular authority and the accepted historian on the subject. An unending succession of Western film epics showing fair-minded John Waynes and Gary Coopers stoutheartedly, and in the finest American tradition, defending their Indian "brothers" against small cliques of profit-seeking white cutthroats have served to both assuage the national conscience and inflate the Anglo-Saxon ego. And then there's usually a lovely Indian maiden, played by a toned-down white actress, whose father, the great Sioux chief, and whose brother, the angry young brave, go "Ugh!" enthusiastically enough but are somewhat diluted in their attempts to portray the noble Red Man because their blue eyes show through the brown makeup.

What was being written by white settlers in America during the seventeenth century sheds some light on what was done to the indigenous populace. The following lines are reputed to be the earliest-known piece of American verse to be printed in England:

> *Stout Master George Sandys upon a night,*
>   *did bravely venture forth;*
> *And mong'st the savage murtherers,*
>   *did form a deed of worth,*
> *For finding many by a fire,*
>   *to death their lives they pay:*
> *Set fire of a Towne of theires,*
>   *And brevely came away.*

Virginia colonist Edward Waterhouse paints us a vivid picture of the order of the day as he sets down certain guidelines to be followed by early Americans in their dutiful labors to rid the land of Godless heathens:

"Victorie of them may bee gained many waies; by force, by suprize, by famine in burning their Corne, by breaking their fishing Weares . . . by pursuing and chasing them with our horses and blood Hounds to draw after them, and Mastifs to tear them . . ."

HERE's a chilling thought: The Negro Wars. And to add to the draft, a very imaginative friend of mine recently recounted a dream which he claimed he had had on the subject:

"You know how some dreams are," he began, "so real you can't shake 'em off for days? Well, this one was like that. It was way up in the future, see, and George Orwell had missed his prediction a mile because the world had been blown up by nuclear war and there were only two big primitive tribes left in America, one black and one white. Incidentally, Johnny, you got killed in the dream when your son mistook you for a white enemy one night and shot you through the neck with a bow and arrow."

"Thanks a lot," I said.

"But I'm ahead of the story. These were the Negro Wars, see, and 'they' occupied the East and 'we' held the West, got it?"

"Yeah, go on."

"Well, we've got us a great leader, see? He's a real *old* man named Joe Black. We call him 'Chief Joseph.' Now, Old Joe is a military genius. He learned how to make Molotov cocktails as a kid, way back in the Watts Uprising. When the odds are anywhere near even, we beat the shit out of the 'Gowsters.' Oh, yeah, I forgot to give you the drawin's on the names. We're the 'Gowsters' and they're the 'Brookses' see? Incidentally, some of the Brookses are black, but we can tell they're white because they wear the Brooks Grey. You know, with three buttons on the flannel jacket and a Texas ten-gallon hat and like that. Anyhow, we're having a hell of a time because there are ten times as many of them as there are us, and they keep raiding our villages at night, raping our chicks when we ain't looking, and burning down our tepees!"

"You're just a damn liar," I interrupted. "You didn't dream all that stuff!"

"The hell I didn't!" he exclaimed. He shifted on the bar stool. "You don't have to hear it if you don't want to."

"No, no, go ahead, I'm listening," I said. I wanted to hear more about the Brookses and the Gowsters. This was more interesting than the Chicago version. And since I had been accidentally killed by Shuggie earlier, in my friend's dream, I couldn't know how the Negro Wars turned out, could I?

He took a lingering sip of his whiskey sour, fixed me with a steely gaze, and continued. "Now listen close, 'cause this part is something else. Whenever the Brookses would capture some of our people, they would ship them off to an area Down South which was roughly five states in size. This was because these five states had been so severely contaminated by radiation that nobody wanted to live there. And besides, it was easier than having to feed the prisoners or putting them in ovens. Now word got back that a young brave named Ex had organized the people Down South and instead of dying off like they was supposed to, they were making out okay in the forbidden land. Only thing was, the radiation in the ground produced some kind of mutation effect that turned the people green and caused them to grow twenty feet tall!"

"Aw, man, why don't you stop making up all that stuff . . ."

"Wait! You ain't heard the rest yet." He had really warmed to the task and wild horses couldn't stop him now. "Now pick up, a Medicine Man in our tribe named Martin Luther Gandhi gets to bendin' Old Black Joe's ear and next thing you know, we're all on a new kick. Now we're all going on a mass, nonviolent march to the Brookses' capital city to demonstrate for 'Gowster Rights' and to end the fighting so we can live in democratic brotherhood and stuff."

At this point he paused for breath and gazed leisurely into the mirror behind the bar. He was taking a moment off to dream up some more bull shit, I figured.

"Well, come on, man, don't stop now. Or have you run out of material?" I asked.

"Wait a minute," he answered. "Say, bartender, fill this glass up while I'm gone, will you, baby? I gotta go to the little boys' room for a minute."

"Okay, but don't be gone all night," the bartender countered. "I want to hear the rest of that jive." By now the bartender and everyone else in the joint was gathered around, picking up like mad. While our storyteller was gone, an argument flared as to whether he actually had dreamed the story or was cooking it all up on the spur of the moment.

"I'll bet the cat really dreamt it. You know ain't nobody gonna make all that stuff up as he goes along," a fat guy wearing a cap ventured.

"Are you outa your mind, man? That cat is puttin' us all on. But it's all right 'cause the stud's got a hell of an imagination!" the bartender replied.

"I think he's a ssshtone nut!" a slightly intoxicated chick at the end of the bar declared.

The dream-story resumed when my friend returned and the bartender called for attention: "OKAY! Hold it, everybody. Proceed, man."

"Where was I?"

"You wash taking all them spooks to Washington to sshee the . . . hic . . . GRRRRREAT White Father . . . ha . . . ha . . . haaaaaa!" the drunken chick offered.

"Shut up, baby!" the bartender shouted, forgetting, in his anxiety to hear the rest of the story, that he was supposed to be courteous to the paying customers. "Don't mind her, man. Continue."

"Oh yeah, the march. Well, as I was saying, we marched to the Brookses' capital and a lot of interesting things come out of it. First we had plenty of conferences and negotiations. Then we had a blue-ribbon commission investigation and finally it was agreed we could have 'Gowster Rights,' which included things like the right to sit next to a Brooks in a hot-dog stand, the right to serve in the Brooks army, and a lot of stuff. But what happened next was really a cold shot. You see, the people Down South, who now called themselves 'Truebloods,' had been joined by a big mass of cats from overseas known as the 'Origionals' and the 'Semi-Origionals' . . . and by the way, these dudes had also been eating radioactive vegetables, so they were green and twenty feet tall, too. Now here's what happened—and wouldn't you know that we spooks would have some bad luck! Not only did we never get our hard-earned 'Gowster Rights,' but just as the Brookses' president, 'Chief Goldenwater,' was about to sign the 'Gowster Rights Bill,' a whole slew of them green, twenty-foot-tall, granny dodgers showed up on the scene and wasted everybody in sight! . . . NOW . . . what do you think the moral of that dream is?"

"What?"

"Don't mess with the Jolly Green Giant!"

"Say, bartender," the drunk chick mumbled, "pour this out and give me a double shot of hundred-and-forty-proof rum."

ELEVEN

Mister Charlie

"I don't blame them for doing it, I really don't, not at all. Because we are getting tired of being pushed around by the white man, that's all. We're tired of it. We can't do this and we can't do that . . . why? Simply because we're Negro. I mean, all men were created equal. We're just as good as they are. Sure, maybe some of them have more money than we do, but, I mean, we're as good as they are. They want to spend millions and millions of dollars going to Russia and to Mars and to the moon. Why don't they help the people on Earth first, before they try to find out the conditions in space?" — *Woman, interviewed during the Watts riots.*

SOME YEARS AGO, three Negro jazz musicians attended a stage play. They were watching the performance, and everything was calm until it came to a part where one of the actors recited a rhyme that went, "Who told you a nigger don't steal? . . . I caught three in my cornfield."

There are times when minor irritations are shed with a minimum of effort, but this was not one of those times in the life of Bill, the sax-playing member of the group. He had come to the theatre that night seething with rage anyhow, what with just having come off a southern band tour during which, for the first time in his life, he had personally tasted the humiliation of Dixie racism. He had hoped that going to the show and perhaps relaxing a little would help ease his anguish, but the vulgar little poem had the opposite effect.

The actor had hardly finished the phrase when Bill leaped to his feet and in a burst of frustration shouted, "Ain't that a bitch! . . . Not one nigger, but *three!*" He kept repeating it at the top of his voice. The performance ground to a shocked standstill, and Bill's flabbergasted buddies were obliged to lead him out of the theatre, where he fell into a fit of tearful sobbing. People passing on the street wondered what this full-grown Negro was doing, crying like a baby in public while one of the other men cradled him in his arms and murmured, "That's all right, baby, that's all right."

There was a big uproar in the papers a while back about Negro writer LeRoi Jones' Black Arts Repertory Theatre. The fact that this Harlem drama project had received a cash grant under the antipoverty program created a blast of reaction because the money was allegedly being used to produce plays like Jones' *Jello,* a takeoff on the old Jack Benny radio show in which Rochester winds up killing all the whites in the cast, including Jack Benny.

One daily-press writer described the play as "seething with rage against 'Whitey.'" The headlines read, "TAXPAYERS' DOLLARS FINANCE HATE SCHOOL" and "FEDERAL AID FOR HATEMONGERING." One might ask, Where does hate start? Does it start on a theatre stage in a make-believe performance, or does it rise out of the real-life world? Does the author of the work that contained the "nigger verse" enjoy a special poetic license privilege that does not extend to Mr. Jones?

As long as the white majority treats the black minority hatefully, there will be an emotional reaction. And as long as the Negro continues to suffer the ravages of mass unemployment, inferior educational opportunities, miserable ghetto housing, and concentrated anti-Negro attitudes, there are bound to be expressions of displeasure, whether they be acted out in LeRoi Jones' theatre or spontaneously spawned in the streets of Watts.

MANY TIMES during the years that I toured with my band I promised my wife that one day I'd take her with me on a southern tour so that she could see the "land o' cotton" with her own eyes. Phyllis, born and raised in California, had been with me on several trips to the Midwest and the East, but had only hearsay evidence, books, and eyewitness reports to go on about the South. Finally, but with some misgivings, I agreed that she would accompany me on our fall tour, which was to include most of the states below the Magnolia Curtain. I would have honored that promise, too, had it not been for an incident that occurred during our summer one-nighters.

The bandstand in this particular Texas nightclub had been enlarged with a rope barrier to accommodate the larger-than-usual number of musicians and entertainers we carried in our company. Before a dance actually starts, audiences usually hang back and don't move up around the bandstand until the music begins. This humid night was typical in this respect except that a young Negro girl walked up to the bandstand to ask us to play a certain tune she liked. While talking, she leaned against the rope barrier. This brought a white cop out of the shadows of the dimly-lit room, who snarled, "Keep offa that goddam rope, and I don't wanna have to tell you again. Heah, gal!"

The girl gave the cop a quick, apprehensive glance and fled.

"Say, that's no way to talk to a person . . ." I started to say, but he snorted and strode away. A little bell rung in the back of my mind. What if that had been Phyllis? I thought. Oh well, I'll keep her with me up on the bandstand and that way we won't have any trouble. But even then, Phyllis' chances of seeing the South had been considerably weakened.

"'Mister Charlie's' in rare form tonight, isn't he, man?" one of the cats in the band observed.

"Yeah, the dirty bastard. I wish I had him in Watts!" another growled.

The evening wore on, and as the rhythm and blues music worked its magic on both audience and performers, the ugly incident was all but forgotten. I got a glimpse of the girl a couple of times during the first set. She was wearing a bright red dress and was easy to spot because of it. Seemingly undaunted by the harsh treatment she had been forced to endure earlier, she and her lanky young boyfriend were pouncing upon the 90-millimeter-cannon-shot-blues-beats we were rolling out to the dancers. The hostile, real world was forgotten momentarily by the crowd as it pulsed in a rhythmic ecstasy that transcended mean white cops and gave birth to a dazzling succession of graceful, creative, effortless writhings and weavings—the kind that flow so beautifully and freely from Afro-Americans when they are primed by the right combination of beat and sound, and which are picked up by white kids years later and touted as the latest dance crazes.

But the sweet-abandon mood of the rhythm and blues celebration was shattered violently at intermission. We had just finished the set. I announced the break and the crowd had begun to fade back, when another young woman walked up to the bandstand and leaned on the rope. She didn't resemble the first girl at all but she too wore a red dress. The cop rushed up and slugged her in the face.

"You black bitch! I told you not to lean on that rope!" he bellowed as he drew his pistol. He fixed the audience with a baleful eye that seemed to say, "I hope one of you act like you don't like it so I can blow your brains out!"

For a crazy, white-hot second I thought of reaching in my drum case for the big pistol I kept stashed there. Hundreds of people stood like frozen zombies. The men—all of us—had been reduced to dogs. To less than dogs. We were dirt!

The cop put his gun in his holster and walked away with his hand at-ready on the butt. A tall black man walked woodenly to the fallen and bleeding woman, picked her up, and walked out. Suddenly I had to vomit. I barely made it out the back door behind the bandstand. As I knelt in the Texas dirt, retching, I realized that one of my bandsmen was standing next to me, crying his heart out.

Phyllis never saw the South. If that had been Phyllis, I kept trying to reassure my gutless self, I would've blown that cop's head off . . . and Jack Benny, Santa Claus, Donald Duck, and any other white MF.

TWELVE

A Week at Mama Lou's

"It's the only way to get these people to realize that the Negroes are tired of being oppressed. They have been oppressed. They have been oppressed for a hundred and fifty years and more. And like a hundred and fifty years ago we were supposed to be free, but we're not free, and I think it's a shame." — *Young girl, interviewed during the Watts riots.*

IT WAS 1946 OR PERHAPS EARLY '47. The entire troupe—musicians, singer, dancers, and comedians—numbered more than thirty people. Finding lodging in the Midwestern town for a one-week stand was a problem. The few Negro families in town absorbed most of our group, but six of us were unable to find a place to stay. Our attempts to check into white hotels and motels were subtly frustrated, but we finally got a lead.

"Try Mama Lou's house," we were told by a local resident. "Mama Lou" turned out to be a plump, good-humored, and very businesslike individual who maintained a rambling old mansion on the outskirts of town where she catered to the more earthy whims and pleasures of various males of the area. Most of her customers were railroad men, and while her "ladies" ran the gamut of human hues from Caucasian pinks to oriental tans to African bronzes, her customers were limited to, and admitted according to, strict policy: white only.

On the way out to her place, the phrase "Mama Lou's

house" kept me wondering: if the guy had said "Mama Lou's Cafe," or "Mama Lou's Club" . . . but "house?"

A little middle-aged lady in a nurse's uniform admitted us.

"This looks like an old folks' home or a hospital," one of the fellows murmured.

"Yeah," another agreed, and I could feel a wave of disappointment flit through the group. But the mood soon brightened. There on the velvet papered wall hung an embroidered sign that proclaimed: "IT TAKES A HEAP OF LOVIN' TO MAKE A HOME A HOUSE." The true message got through.

"This ain't no sanatorium, baby," Jimmy, the sax man, observed with relief.

It wasn't a hospital or a home for the aged . . . but we probably would've stood more chance getting rooms if it had been. Even if the owner had a surplus of available rooms, I couldn't see her renting them to six horny-looking young musicians. I was right. Mama Lou, it developed, was a groovy person, very warm and friendly, but to rent rooms for more than an hour or two at a crack tickled her funny bone, and to rent them to young Negro musicians for a week was unthinkable.

"Sweethearts," she purred, "you got to be kiddin'. I can't let you have rooms for a week. This isn't a rooming house."

At the far end of the hall, nymphlike creatures flitted about behind semi-transparent curtains. This activity had a very disquieting effect on our group.

"But Mrs. Lou . . ." one of the cats pleaded.

"Just call me Mama Lou, sugar," the proprietress cut in.

"But Mama Lou," he went on, "you can't just throw us out in the streets. All the rooms in the Colored homes are taken and the white hotels gave us the shoe."

"But, sugar baby, I've got a business to run here. I can't do it, not possibly, honey. What do you boys do? Play ball?"

"No," I answered. "We're with the show opening at the theatre tomorrow. We're part of the band."

"Band players!" she chirped. She fell into a sudden burst of laughter that built to such a crescendo that it brought on a coughing fit. She collapsed into a chair as the little maid rushed up with a glass of water.

"Now, sugars," she said as she regained her composure, "I'm not laughing at your music. Oh no. My Bill was a piano player, God rest his soul. I'm laughing at the idea of bringing all you cats into my place, and for a *whole week*. Musicians! *Lord have mercy!*" And she started chuckling again. But she stopped short, as if something vital had occurred to her.

"Do any of you play the piano?" she asked.

Our piano man was not with us. But I had always plunked away at the blues. What could we lose?

"I do," I stated.

"That's right, he do. I mean he does," Sack, the trombonist, quickly added, with one eye on Mama Lou and the other cocked furtively on the magic curtain at the end of the hall.

"Can you play the blues, sugar?"

Oh happy day! Maybe we had a chance after all.

"The Okies and Arkies that come here at night to see my ladies like all that okey-doke jive, but Mama Lou likes the blues. Come on in here, baby, and let me hear you play me something."

As we moved into the plush, Victorian-style parlor, a flock of "ladies," who had evidently been peeking and listening, rushed out amid a swirl of silk and a chorus of giggles.

In the middle of the room sat a formidable and very ornate full-sized Steinway grand. Oooh! What if she called for an intricate ballad or show tune? But Mama Lou wanted to hear the blues, period. Fortunately, one the cats was a good blues singer and between us we moved Mama Lou to send for a bottle. I declined a drink because I don't like bourbon, although my trembling fingers could probably have used some.

"Play 'C.C. Rider' again, sugar, just like my baby Bill used to. Come on, you can't play on an empty stomach, baby. Have a little taste."

"Have you got any wine?" I asked the question as softly as possible, but one of the guys heard me.

"Wine!" he hooted. "You can take 'em out of Watts, but you can't take Watts out of 'em!"

But Mama Lou knew what I had in mind. "Lord, just like my Bill! Emmy, get the wine out of my closet. The big bottle with the black label on it."

After a glass of imported burgundy, the grand piano lost its awesome character and we got down to some serious blues business. But one thing threatened our progress: Sack kept trying to slip into the part of the house where the chicks had disappeared.

"Get back in here, fool, there'll be plenty of time for that after we get in here," one of the cats hissed at him, loud enough for everyone, including Mama Lou, to hear. I missed a couple of notes, but Mama Lou didn't hear him, or if she did she didn't seem to care.

Finally, Mama Lou took me aside and proposed a deal. It seemed that her piano player had disappeared and she had been unable to get a replacement.

"It's bad for business, see, sugar. These Okies expect to hear the piano, and this damn fool has got lost somewhere. Now, you and the boy that sings the blues, you two can stay here—free room and meals and drinks—all you gotta do is play a couple of hours at night."

"We don't get off at the theatre till eleven thirty, though."

"That's okay, sugar. We don't get real busy around here till after midnight anyhow."

"But I can't leave the other guys out in the street."

"Well, baby, what do you expect me to do? You know what I've got here. I can't keep 'em here, either."

We argued back and forth and finally she agreed to put us

all up in the building behind the big house. It was a converted garage where Pierre, her "man of the house," lived. The "man of the house" was a tall, muscular but very effeminate bouncer who dressed in Mandarin silks and kept the "Okie" customers in line. Pierre was enthusiastic about the arrangement, but it didn't sit too well with the fellows, who had built their hopes up for a week of good times in the harem atmosphere of the big house.

We solved the problem of the songs the customers preferred by bringing our regular piano man into the deal. He was more than happy to leave his room in town when we described the scene at Mama Lou's. We decided that he would play for the customers and I would play for Mama Lou!

We went over so good the first night that Mama Lou got full of her juice and decided that her two piano players deserved to live in the big house. She gave us Bill's old room. We had a big double bed and a cot, a private bath and balcony, but we also had Emmy, the maid, to contend with. Once the festivities were over for the night and everyone had retired, Emmy kept her eagle-eye on us unrelentingly. Mama Lou had decreed that there would be no fraternizing between the girls and the musicians, and Emmy was the watchdog. During business hours we saw the girls often enough, but when the joint closed down for the night, we were blocked by Emmy's room and by Emmy's dedication to her task.

The guys in the back house saw the girls regularly, however. The girls would slip out of the side door of the house to Pierre's pad without Emmy being aware of it. Mama Lou was always loaded to the gills by three o'clock, anyhow, and a few dollars kept Pierre quiet.

We tried to move back to the garage but the guys screamed "overcrowded." Besides, Mama Lou wouldn't hear of it.

"Nothing's too good for my boys," she said. "Those common horn tooters stay in the garage, but my piano players stay with Mama Lou in style!"

The food was great. We ate with Mama Lou; it was like eating at the captain's table. Everything was nice, except for those hours late at night when everything got quiet and we could hear faint sounds of music and laughter floating up to us from the party going on in the garage.

Mama Lou began to brag about how she had rescued us after we had been discriminated against by the white hotels. To hear her tell it, she was a civil rights and Negro-cause champion. But in all honesty, she did come through like a champ on one occasion that involved a racial altercation.

That particular night a big, burly, drunken customer became very abusive.

"Wassa matter with ya, goddamit! I shaid 'The Sain Looey Blues,' boy," he slurred. "I'm a white man! When I shay play 'Sain Looey Blues,' I mean play it right now! Understand, Sambo?"

Pierre rushed up. We thought he was going to straighten the drunk out, but he just wanted to make sure that we didn't do anything rash while he went to get Mama Lou.

"Now hold it," he said. "Mama Lou likes to take care of these situations personally. Keep cool while I get her in here."

Mama Lou burst through the curtains doing fifty miles an hour, the cape on her gown flying up behind her like wings, looking like a fat, tropical bird on the warpath. She got to the room just in time to hear the drunk use the word "nigger."

She chastised him in a very loud and angry voice and in a few minutes had the guy half sobered-up and apologizing. Her lecture had a positive effect on the other customers, too. They chimed in and gave the guy hell, and things settled back to normal.

"You see, sugar," she explained to me later, "I used to let Bill try to handle that kind of mess, but I learned early in the game that that would only make matters worse. Sooner or later Bill would knock the crap outa one of them crackers and that would start a race riot because the rest of them would take it personally and they would proceed to tear the joint up. You notice when I do it the rest of them help me, and the jerk who messed-up acts like a bad boy who's been scolded by his mama, and it's all over with, no sweat."

During our week with Mama Lou a very touchy and somewhat touching situation developed. One of Mama Lou's regular girls had her younger sister staying with her. She had come from the Deep South with her newborn baby. Her husband had died from a beating he had received in a Mississippi jail. Mama Lou had given the older girl permission to send for her sister and the baby, and to care for them at the house.

A hell of a place for a young widow and her infant child, one might feel, but it was better than the streets of Mississippi.

Mama Lou, upon seeing the young sister for the first time, must have made secret, future plans, because the girl was a stunning beauty. From time to time, customers would get a glimpse of the girl, whom we'll call Mary, and would put in a bid. Mama Lou would explain that Mary was not available, but one could almost see her rubbing her hands in greedy anticipation of the days and dollars that lay ahead. This scene was not unnoticed by the older sister, whom we'll call Dolly, and she was distressed because she loved Mary and didn't want her to wind up hustling.

Dolly brought Mary to the theatre on opening day to see the show. They came backstage and Mary met one of my musicians. We'll call him Jack. Jack invited Mary to lunch, and while they were out eating, Dolly told me her sister's tragic story.

"I'm surprised she accepted the invitation to go to lunch with your guy, but I'm glad she did 'cause all she does is sit and cry all the time. I had an awful time even getting her to come out of the house today."

"How did her husband get killed?" I asked.

"He was arrested in Mississippi on suspicion of stealing

something, and while they had him in jail they beat him unmercifully. Then they found out someone else had done it and they let him go. But he was hurt too bad; he died two days later. That was six months ago. Now sis just sits and cries and keeps saying, 'He didn't even get to see his son . . . he didn't even get to see his boy!' "

After they left the theatre I asked Jack if Mary had told him the story. She hadn't. As I told him about it he listened very quietly.

"You know, Johnny," he finally said, "I want to tell you something. My father was killed before I was born, too, only it didn't happen quite the same way. My old man was shot down in a southern swamp by a gang of Ku Klux Klanners who claimed he had 'insulted' a white woman. My mother never remarried. We moved to Watts and she worked her life away in white folks' kitchens trying to raise us up. I never did see a father."

Jack fell silent again. I couldn't think of a thing to say. What could I say? That I had had a sweet old man who lavished love and kisses on me? It was true but it had no place in this conversation. This was the kind of thing that I didn't know about, and I couldn't come up with anything. This man Jack, who wasn't too young—about in his mid-thirties—had always seemed a little wistful and lonely. Now I knew why.

"You know something? I asked that girl to lunch because she's so fine-looking and everything. Nothing serious. But now I'm glad you told me about her husband and the baby because that baby is going to have a father if I can help it. If that girl will have me I'm going to have me a family, and the baby's going to have him a father, and a good one. You know I can go back to the post office, and I'll do it, too."

I thought at the time that it was a very noble and touching sentiment. I thought Jack was just temporarily carried away by the emotion of the moment and that would be the end of it.

With Dolly's help, Mary slipped out of the house with the rest of the girls at night, but instead of going to the after-hours party in the back house, she and Jack would go over and sit in the band bus that was parked in an empty lot down the street, and they'd talk till dawn.

The evening before we closed out our engagement, Jack asked me if I'd join them that night in their after-hours rendezvous. The weather had turned cold and I found them huddled together in one of the bus seats with Jack's overcoat over their shoulders. I expected Jack to ask me if it was okay if Mary came along on the tour. I had received many such requests in the past. But there was more to it than just that.

"Johnny, we got a marriage license today," Jack stated with an almost pathetic tone of finality.

"Hey, that's great!"

"Yeah, we intend to get married tomorrow. Mary and the baby are leaving with me, but we've got a problem."

"What's that?"

"Well, Mama Lou advanced Dolly the money to send for Mary and the baby, and then the room and board has been building up since they've been here. But that's not the impossible part. You see, we don't want to make it tough on Dolly, who has to get along with Mama Lou after we're gone. Mama Lou has plans for Mary, you know that. We've talked about it. Nothing out in the open, you understand, but it's obvious from every move Mama Lou makes where Mary's concerned."

"I know what you mean."

"In some ways Mama Lou's an all-right old chick, but on the other hand, she's a money-grabbin' old madam and she's got high hopes of making Mary her top money-earner."

Jack was leading up to a point and I could tell by the look on Mary's face that I had been nominated for something. But what?

"Look, John," Jack continued, and from the tone of his voice

I knew the punch line was coming, "I want to ask you to do me a favor. See if you can get the old biddy to look at the situation like a human being. Now I could tell the bitch to go to hell and punch that Pierre faggot in the mouth if necessary, but I don't want to create a strain for Dolly."

"What time do you plan to get married tomorrow?"

"Tomorrow night after the show. We've got a little jackleg preacher lined up."

"Okay," I said. "I'll try to appeal to the nobler side of her nature tomorrow morning."

The following morning Emmy informed me that the fellows in the back house had some mail for me, so I decided to go back and check it out before Mama Lou and I had our little heart-to-heart talk.

The guys in the back house were having a good laugh about a letter that Pierre had received. Pierre Touché's real name, it seemed, was Willie Carver Johnson and Emmy had confirmed it.

"Yes," Emmy had told the guys, "that sissy's name is Willie Johnson. That Pierre Touché part is a lot of jive."

"Look at this, man," Sack was waving a letter with a Georgia postmark around his head. "A letter from home for our sweet Pierre. The cat's real name is Willie. . . . Wait till I see that swish. Hey, Willie, baby, here's a letter for ya' . . . ha-ha!"

I looked my mail over and was about to start back when I heard a commotion up in the big house. Then Pierre rushed in, all upset.

"Well, children," he sopranoed, "it done hit the fan, and it's all your fault, Sack!"

"What the hell you talkin' about, it's my fault? What's my fault?"

"You and that slut Eula Belle, that's what. You couldn't be satisfied with just her, could you? Oh, no, you had to hit on Pearl, and Eula Belle found out about it and went into a jealous fit and spilled the beans to Mama Lou 'bout us partying back here every night!"

"Oh, shitty, diddy, widdy, I'm glad the week's over now!" Sack said.

"Yeah, the week's over and you're glad 'cause you can leave now that the damage is done. But I just got fired, and all the broads are in the doghouse!" Pierre's falsetto went up an octave.

"Where is Mama Lou now?" I asked, because I couldn't think of anything else to say.

"Up in the parlor, but ain't no use in tryin' to talk to her now. She's pitchin' a bitch!"

On the way to the big house I met Mary standing on the back porch with the baby in her arms, crying. She explained that Eula Belle had told all to Mama Lou about her and Jack, even the part about them getting married, although she couldn't imagine how she found out about that. Well, that saves me the pain of having to talk to Mama Lou about it as I had promised Jack I would, I thought. I detoured around the house and kept going straight to the theatre.

That Friday marked the most disturbed and unrelaxed five shows that I ever tried to play. The guys were all upset and nothing went right. Between shows Jack and Sack almost got into a fight when Jack called him a stupid idiot for causing the trouble. The curtain finally fell on the last act and it was time to go to the house and face Mama Lou. We had three days off coming up, but spending them in this town seemed out of the question now. I wondered if Mama Lou was going to expect us to entertain her customers that night.

When we got to the house the lights were burning on the front porch and a group of people were gathered on the sidewalk. They must have really had it while we were gone, I thought. Maybe there had been a fight or something. But it wasn't anything like that. Mary's baby had become very ill and an ambulance had taken Mary, the baby, and Mama Lou to the hospital.

"Mama Lou's been screamin' and cussin' all day long!" Pierre explained. "She had us all in the parlor a little while ago and she was giving Mary holy hell. 'What do you mean it's a chance to give your child a good father? Ain't I been like a mother to you? Don't you think you owe me something, goddamit?' Just then the baby started throwing up in Mary's arms. He was gaspin' and chokin' somethin' awful, and he started turnin' a funny color."

Dolly took the story up where Pierre left off. "Then Mama Lou started hollering 'Oh my God! Call the ambulance. Quick! That's the same color my Bill turned when he . . . oh, God . . . CALL THE AMBULANCE!'"

"Then what happened?" I asked.

"Mama Lou kept crying and wailing and the baby looked worse and worse. When the ambulance got here they thought she was the patient, she was carrying on so. They tried to keep her out of the ambulance, but she kicked up such a fuss they let her in and took off."

"How long ago was that?" Jack asked.

"Just a few minutes ago," Pierre answered.

"Call me a cab, Pierre," Jack said. "I'm going to the hospital."

The rest of us sat around the parlor and waited for word. After about two hours the phone rang.

"It was Mama Lou," Pierre announced. "The baby's all right. It wasn't anything serious!" We all cheered.

Sack jumped up and did a little dance.

"Sit down, bastard!" Dude Love growled. "You're the one who caused all this shit!"

Pierre called for quiet. "Johnny," he said, "Mama Lou wants you to come with me in the car to pick them up."

At the hospital, Pierre, looking very dap in his chauffeur's cap, held the door open while we helped Mary and the baby into the big limousine.

"Give me a little taste, Pierre," Mama Lou said.

Pierre produced a silver flask from the glove compartment and Mama Lou took a long, healthy slug. Now she began a mournful song of repentance that lasted till we got home.

"God was trying to punish me for being a mean, evil, old bitch," she moaned. "Help me, Jesus. Forgive me, Lord! Johnny, son, God don't love ugly. You know that, don't you, sugar? He was punishing me for messin' over this child and her baby. Ooooh . . . God help me! God help me!"

Sunday afternoon Jack and Mary had a swell church wedding. All the chicks from the house were there and so were the people from the show. But Mama Lou was the star of the occasion. She was decked out in her furs, a giant flowered hat, and dripped with diamonds. The preacher was a very staid Methodist. Much to his chagrin, Mama Lou chose this occasion to revert back to the Baptist lore of her childhood.

"Thank you, Jesus!" she shouted after his every phrase. "Yes! . . . Yessss, Lord! . . . THAT'S ALL RIGHT NOW! . . . AAAAAMEN!!!"

But her greatest line of the afternoon was, "Oh, my baby, my little innocent baby!"

Any stranger in the church would've laid you 10 to 1 that she was Mary's natural-born mother.

But if the wedding was a winner, the reception at Mama Lou's that evening was a double-barreled gas. She closed up shop for the night, but her customers had no way of knowing this and trickled in all evening. As they came in they joined what was probably the most democratic wing-ding that little town had ever seen.

The last I saw of Mama Lou that night, she was deep in her cups and even deeper in Pierre's unwilling arms. Her whiskey kept telling her that Pierre was her dearly departed Bill, and Pierre wasn't for it at all.

"Kiss me, Bill, baby," she gushed at Pierre.

"Every time she gets to this stage she thinks I'm Bill," Pierre complained. "I gotta get a few more slugs under her belt so she'll go to sleep before she tries to start something silly!"

THIRTEEN

"White" Negroes

"I feel as though the riots were, in a way, necessary because the white man is strictly causing confusion. The blue-eyed devils should move away. We as a race, we will soon become strong, because before our people realize what really is happening to us it will take a lot of us away. The Negro is a weak race, because he has listened to what the white man has taught him already. The white man has brainwashed him in many ways, but the Honorable Elijah Muhammad teaches us every day that the blue-eyed devil cannot surpass the dark man. The dark man shall overcome, like the man came the other day and shot up our temple for no reason at all. It wasn't necessary. He did it because he had the authority, the power, but yet and still, we're coming back, we'll meet him on his terms. The white man is already scared, he's nervous of what's happening today, because the Negro has revolted. The Negro has brought a big change, right here, in front of his face. We'll all see each other face to face in the street." — *Man, interviewed during the Watts riots.*

IN THE TOTALLY Negro community we find a segment striving to "live white." On the other hand, among whites we find many, usually the young, who aspire to successful careers in popular music, imitating the culture, the patois, the "sounds" of the Negro folk, while the black bourgeois puts on the manners and airs of upper-class whites.

In their effort to act and sound "Colored," the white kids of the rock and roll set project an artificial and contrived, often ludicrous, picture, much like the impression created by the straining Negro upper set. The difference is, however, that the

Negroes who strain to live and act "white" pay heavily for their expensive society balls and their burdensome hillside mansions and luxury cars, while many of the white performers who "borrow" from Negro folk culture make thousands or millions of dollars.

The term "folk music," it seems to me, has been twisted and distorted out of reality. The dictionary defines the word "folk" as follows:

> In a people bound together by ties of race, language, religion, etc., that great proportion of its number which determines the group character and tends to preserve its civilization, customs, etc., unchanged.

Under "folk music" and "folk dance," the dictionary says:

> Of or pertaining to the folk; designating songs, dances, etc., originated or used among the common folk.

In America, the music originating from the common folk, and therefore, the true "folk music," would be the rhythm and blues music of the black folk and the country and Western music of the white folk, and the gospel music of both groups. It is not the highly stylized and artificial rock and roll, nor is it the carefully contrived product of the professional "folk music" specialist.

Jazz, an outgrowth of the Negro blues-gospel fountainhead, is, in its pure and basic sense, also a true folk form, but it has tended to lose its indigenous identity through the onslaughts of two groups: white musicians who enter the field with a mathematical and "intellectual" approach, rather than an emotional and cultural one, and numbers of Negro "jazzmen" who, in the past twenty years or so, have been so influenced and frustrated by white musicians and white society that they have become tangled and lost in an almost neurotic, never-never land of academic, super-cool, "three-button," way, way-out experiments.

I agree with the black nationalists, who place the great Negro creative innovators—Charlie Parker, Dizzy Gillespie, Max Roach, Duke Ellington, Charles Mingus, Jimmy Smith, Count Basie, Cannonball Adderley, Lester Young, Miles Davis, Ramsey Lewis—in the rhythm and blues category and leave the term "jazz" to the white imitators and the Negro imitators of the imitators.

I am not suggesting that the imitators on both sides have no right to lift and artificially contrive their hybrid products. I am insisting, however, that the true "folk" music of America is produced by such people and groups as Ray Charles, Aretha Franklin, Muddy Waters, B. B. King, James Cleveland, The Caravans, The Staple Singers, and Fats Domino in the Negro world, and by the Johnny Cashes, Hank Williamses, Merle Travises, Eddy Arnolds, the Statesman Quartet, and the Blackwood Brothers of the white world.

Negro rhythm and blues and white country and Western music have something in common: they're both soulful and honest, and they truly spring from the "folk."

FOURTEEN

Baby Jitters

"Well, it's kind of hard, you know. You work hard for your money and then you go to buy. Say you got four children to clothe. I go to buy clothes. I can't buy school clothing and pay cash for them all at one time, so I have to buy them on credit. I go to buy them on credit. I pay twelve dollars for a cotton dress for my daughter to go to school in, where if I was able to pay cash for it . . . six dollars, you know. . . . You buy a living-room set that you could buy, if you were . . . well, I guess if you wasn't Colored, you could pay, $299. But if you buy it on credit, it costs $599. See? I know what I'm talking about. . . ." — *Man, interviewed during the Watts riots.*

BACK IN 1947, when our firstborn, Janice, was just a few weeks old, I remember going through what might be described as the "first child jitters."

"Why did you get up and go over to the crib?" Phyllis asked.

"I thought the baby wasn't covered up."

As I answered I knew I had picked the wrong explanation. The weather was hot, too hot to worry about the blanket being on the baby. Phyllis didn't comment but I could feel her mind clicking in the dark. The truth was that I would lie in the dark and imagine the baby had stopped breathing. Nonsense, I would tell myself, but the thought would overpower me. I couldn't hear a sound . . . something was wrong . . . she wasn't breathing! Finally, I'd get up and touch Janice to make sure she was alive.

What kind of silly neurosis is this? I'd say to myself, but the next night I was apt to do it again.

Years later Phyllis told me she had suspected what I was doing because she had experienced the same fears. I was even more relieved to learn that this happens to many people with their first baby. Recently, my daughter Laura and her husband confessed to similar midnight creeps to the crib with their new baby.

Looking at Janice today it's hard to imagine the spindly little creature she was then. She looked so frail and sickly she had me fearfully taking her pulse every other night. The fact that Phyllis and the doctor had labored two full days to get her into the world, and then with forceps that left marks on her forehead, doubled my sense of insecurity. The marks on her forehead eventually disappeared and within a few months she lost that wrinkled, little-wet-mouse look. But until that time, I guarded her from the prying eyes of friends and relatives whenever possible. I was so sure we had an imperfect little weakling.

"No, you can't see the baby. I'm sorry, she's sleeping."

"She is not," Phyllis would say.

"She is, too!" I'd retort, much to the amazement of our well-wishing friends.

I was determined that they weren't going to stand around and stare at our poor, unfortunate child. I didn't discuss it with Phyllis, but in my mind I had prepared myself for a lifetime of protecting our kid from the cruel eyes of the world. I felt tragic as hell. Later I learned that most babies look like small wrinkled gargoyles at birth. The newborn babies I had seen in the movies were probably two or three months old.

We had been married for six years before Janice was born. We had stopped making plans and talking about the children we wanted to have. It had become a painful subject and we avoided it.

Phyllis often accused me of not really paying attention when people were trying to tell me something, and one night she proved it to me. We were in New York, playing the Apollo Theatre and staying at the Hotel Theresa in Harlem.

"I guess we'd better start thinking about me going to San Francisco to be with my mother. The last few months will be here before we know it," Phyllis said.

"Um hum," I answered. The bulb in the bedside lamp was orange and I was having trouble copying some music in the dim light. I considered getting up and getting dressed and going down to get a bright white bulb. I had called twice for room service, but so far no luck, and I was getting more PO'd by the minute. What had she said about San Francisco?

"What last months? Something wrong with your mother?"

"No, nothing's wrong with my mother. See, you don't listen when people tell you something. You don't even know what I'm talking about."

I set the music aside and sat straight up in bed. "What in the world *are* you talking about?" She's hot about something, I thought. Wonder what I did? Going home to Mother and all that. . . .

"I'm talking about having a baby. Do you mean you haven't understood what I've been telling you all these weeks!"

WE played in New York for a while and then the doctor decreed that Phyllis get to California so that her mother could care for her when the time came. Not being with her was going to be a drag, but our tour with the Ink Spots was starting and I had no choice. The same day she boarded the train heading for California, the band embarked on the annual Ink Spots tour. A few days later an amazing coincidence occurred.

The doctor, it seemed, has misjudged Phyllis' time and as the train approached Omaha, Nebraska, she became ill. During the layover in Omaha, Phyllis asked a porter to phone Preston's mother, Mexie Love. Mrs. Love picked her up and took her to the hospital. And that night we arrived in Omaha for a one-night stand, so I was going to be there when Janice was born.

The following day Phyllis was still in labor. The doctor advised us it would be some time yet, so Mrs. Love and I took a walk. Mexie Love is a legend among the old-timers in Omaha. Her husband, Deb, had died during a flu epidemic, and she had raised eight children by herself during the Depression years. Her sons Preston, Sonny, and Dude and I had become very close friends. Coming back to Omaha was like a family reunion for me.

It was a sparkling May morning, and as we walked through a park Mrs. Love reminisced about the old days when there were very few Negro families in Omaha, and all about her early days with Deb.

"The reason I wanted to walk through the park is because it holds some very fond memories for me," she said. "Can you believe it, Johnny, right on this spot was the little ramshackle house where we lived. And over there, by that bed of daffodils, my first baby is buried."

"Really, Mex?"

"Yes," she said. "It was different in those days. You talk about poverty; we really had it. It wasn't that Deb didn't have jobs. He had plenty of them. For a while he was a mechanic with Barney Oldfield, but Deb couldn't resist the cards and dice. You've got to understand that Dude, although he doesn't gamble, is so much like his daddy—handsome, dashing, full of life. Payday would roll around and I'd wait in that little shack, praying that he would come right home so we could buy some food and pay the rent. The night would roll on and I'd know that he had messed up again. Around dawn he would crack the door open and throw his hat in. I'd be ready to kill him, but you couldn't stay mad at Deb. Just like Dude, he was a child of the wind. He'd blow hither and yon, and you just had to blow along too."

"Say, Mex, what happened? Your first baby died?"

"I started not to mention that at this time. I know you're worried about Phyllis and all, but don't you worry. Things are different now. Hospital care and everything. No, my first baby didn't have a chance. It was so pathetic. He never saw the light of day, and we just buried him near the house. Nothing else we could do. But Phyllis has all the modern care. I'll bet you'll be the proud pappy of a baby boy when we get back."

She missed on one small detail. It was a girl.

LAURA was born in Watts during the time that I had the chicken ranch and The Barrelhouse Club. One Saturday night in 1949, just as the band had begun to cook and the people were having a good time, Phyllis called to say it was time to get to the hospital. Mario Delagarde, my bass player, and I rushed home and drove her there. It was a close call. Nothing like the long, drawn-out labor when Janice was born. We had hardly settled down to wait when we heard Laura squall to the world that she was here.

Later that year I almost lost three fingers of my right hand in a power-saw accident while I was building chicken coops. Being unable to play at night, I decided to visit some of the spots around town. I dropped into the Largo Theatre on 103rd Street in Watts to pick up on the talent show.

I was impressed by a kid who sang like Dinah Washington.

I leaned over to Mario and said, "Man, that little girl's got a great feeling."

Someone behind me overheard what I said.

"That's my sister," she proudly proclaimed.

Her name was Esther Mae Jones. I wrote some blues songs and Esther Mae sang them and soon we had a string of hit records. Little Esther became the hottest attraction in the rhythm and blues field. By surrounding Esther with the talent we found at The Barrelhouse—Mel Walker, Lady Dee Williams, Redd Lyte, Don Johnson, Lorenzo Holden, Lee Graves, Pete

Lewis, Kansas City Bell, Walter Henry—I formed the Rhythm & Blues Caravan. This unit was the first R & B "package" to tour the nation.

Early in 1950, with Dude Love as my "assistant road manager," we left Watts and hit the road. The last time I had toured it had been with my large swing-jazz band. This time it was with a blues band and R & B singers. It was different in another way, too, because we had two baby girls now and Phyllis had to stay home and care for them.

FIFTEEN

The Barrelhouse

"I'd rather be living in Texas than in California. Down there I know where we stand with the Caucasian. Out here, I don't know where I stand." — *Man, interviewed during the Watts riots.*

I WONDER what it would cost to open a nightclub in Watts today. In 1948, four of us opened what was to become the first night spot to feature exclusively rhythm and blues music and entertainment. We called it The Barrelhouse. We put up one hundred dollars apiece and on opening night we still had twenty bucks of the initial investment left in the kitty.

Located on Wilmington at 107th Street, The Barrelhouse was in the heart of a section of Watts that had at one time been a Mexican-American community. Today the spot is best identified as "one block from the Watts Towers." Until we renamed it The Barrelhouse, the spot had been a Mexican beer joint. Negroes had moved in, Mexicans out, and this was one of the reasons we got into the place so inexpensively. We had a license to serve beer, soft drinks, wine, and food. A hard-liquor license was thousands of dollars beyond our financial reach, but as it developed we did all right without it.

One day I was helping my partner, Bardu Ali, dispose of the previous night's whiskey bottles. Although the law forbade hard liquor in the club because we had no license, it was almost impossible to discourage our customers from slipping bottles in, so every night dozens of dead soldiers littered the floor. The following day we'd take them out back and break 'em in the trash receptacle.

While we were popping bottles into the can, Bardu was reminiscing about his early days in show business as front man with the Chick Webb band. I never tired of hearing about the day he discovered Ella Fitzgerald.

"This was January of 1935," Bardu was saying. "We had just played the first opening day show at the old Harlem Opera House Theatre and I was the last one to leave the stage. I spotted a little skinny girl, standing in the shadow of the wings. I had heard her singing the night before on this same stage with Tiny Bradshaw's band. It had been amateur night and she won first prize. I said, 'Say, little girl, I told Mr. Webb about how nice you sang last night and he'd like to hear you.' I'll never forget what she was wearing: brown, low-cut boys' shoes and a raggedy dress with some cat fur around the collar. Ella was only fifteen at the time, and I didn't know it then, but she had run away from an orphanage up on the Hudson River and was just existing in Harlem. I took her up to the big band room where most of the cats, including Chick, were playing cards. A couple of the guys looked up, and I guess they were wondering what I was doing with the waif. I introduced her to Chick, and John Truehart got his guitar. The cats were making a hell of a racket with their card game, but by the time Ella got through three or four bars of the old song 'Judy,' you could hear a mouse pissin' on cotton!"

I plopped an empty pint of I. W. Harper into the can.

"Funny how people would rather sneak a bottle in than buy the stuff by the drink," I said. "I mean, even if we had a liquor license people would still slip a jug in."

"Sure, man, I don't blame 'em," Bardu said. "You can go

broke quick buying this stuff by the drink in a joint, but you can nurse a jug for a long time. And what the hell, we sell 'em Cokes and that's money right on."

The guy who really made the money, though, was the white man who owned the liquor store across the street. (I thought about that store when the riot broke out. The Barrelhouse, now a church, still stands, but the liquor store was burned to the ground.)

"We oughta own the liquor store," Bardu used to say, "and then we'd really get straight!"

"Right," I'd answer.

In those days, Phyllis and I lived right down the street on 118th off Wilmington. We had two acres which I had loaded with hundreds of chickens, ducks, geese, rabbits, and pigeons. Mario Delagarde lived with us, and we had a little partnership in the poultry business going. We had an old ice-cream truck and he'd drive through Watts peddling chickens and eggs while I built coops and fed, watered, and dressed the fryers and broilers.

Once a week I would appear on Hunter Hancock's R & B disc-jockey show to plug The Barrelhouse. That past Thursday I had mentioned that I raised and sold chickens and by the time I got back to Watts there was a line of people waiting to buy chickens. They kept coming and by Saturday we were sold out.

I told Bardu about it. He thought for a moment and said, "You know, people are funny. They can buy poultry anywhere, but they're curious to see what the hell an entertainer is doing raising and selling chickens. It's like a gimmick. It can't hurt you, though, 'cause everything that helps build your name in show business is good . . . even chickens. Maybe you'll be known as Johnny Otis and his Chicken-Shit Blues Band."

"Very funny, Bardu," I said. "But I'll tell you something, I might go for that, too, if some steady employment came out of it."

"Name is everything in show business." Bardu was leading up to another story of the old days.

"That's right," I answered.

"Chick Webb used to say, 'If we can get the name built up we got it made.' We had a funny thing happen once in the Deep South, which proves that what may be a big name to one person can be meaningless to another. We were going through a little town in Georgia and I was driving. Chick was laying on the back seat under a blanket, and him being so tiny you could hardly see him. I pulled into a gas station to fill up. When I drove up, the attendant was waiting on another car. The guy glanced over at me but instead of waiting on me next, he kept waiting on everyone else who drove in. Finally, there were no more cars coming in so he decided to come over and wait on me. I was so mad I forgot I was in Georgia and said, 'Well, I guess if white people had kept driving in here all day you would've kept me waiting all day!'

" 'That's right,' he said.

"I was so frustrated I shouted, 'You act like you don't know who I am. DO YOU KNOW WHO I AM?'

"The cat drawled, 'No, by God, I don't. Who are you?'

"Now I had to come up with something and all I could think of was, 'I'm Duke Ellington, that's who!'

"The cracker thought a minute, spit some tobacco juice on the ground, and said, 'Shit, nigger, never heard of ya!'

"I was praying that Chick was asleep and hadn't heard this. I'd never hear the end of it if he did. For a while it looked like he'd slept through it, but after we'd driven out of town a ways, I heard Chick's little voice saying, 'Say, man, for all the good it did you, you might as well have said you was Chick Webb!' "

We were through breaking bottles now and about to go back in the club when the man who lived behind The Barrelhouse poked his head over the fence and called me. I think his name was Mr. Garcia. He and his family were moving out of the area, and he had some chickens he wanted to sell. I climbed up on the fence and told him I didn't need any more chickens. While I was looking over the fence, I spotted three little baby goats.

"Mama goat had three babies last week. They very nice. You want to buy 'em?"

I needed goats like I needed a hole in the head. Our two acres were loaded with barnyard creatures already. Phyllis would kill me. *But they sure were cute!* I bought 'em. There were two males and a female. Bardu named them Bert Williams, Pigmeat, and Florence Mills.

I meant to sneak the kids into the back without Phyllis seeing me, but Mario spotted me a half a block away and I heard him yelp, "Oh Christ! Here he comes again, Phyllis, looking like Noah with a sackful of goats this time!"

Phyllis didn't say anything. She just stood there with Janice in her arms, looking me right in the eye. I stumbled by with the goats pulling in three different directions on three tangled ropes. I muttered something about keeping them for a couple of days for a friend. I didn't dare look back. Mario strolled back to where I was preparing a little enclosure for the kids.

"Who is this friend you're keeping the goats a few days for?" he asked.

"A guy named Williams," I improvised.

"Buuuuuull shit!" was his only comment.

SIXTEEN

Privately Owned Animals

"The things that are happening now were supposed to of happened a long time ago. The white man's no good, and I don't blame 'em for burning up the places actually." — *Young man, interviewed during the Watts riots*

IN THE FALL OF 1952 we phoned a Northern California hunting club and made reservations to hunt pheasants the following morning.

Three of us, Kansas City Bell, R. T. Witherspoon, and I, arrived bright and early, anxious to get into the fields.

The conversation at the gate went something like this:

"Sorry, gentlemen, this club operates on a strict reservation basis and we're filled up for the week."

"But I called yesterday and made reservations!"

"Well, now, there must be some mistake. We've always had this policy. This time of the year, you know."

"Yeah, we know. Never mind."

A half hour and some fifteen miles later we were at another "open to the public" shooting preserve.

"No, boys, I can't do that. If you don't have trained bird dogs we can't let you hunt here. Rules, you know."

"How about those dogs over there in the kennels? Sign says 'dogs for lease.' We'll be glad to pay."

"Those are all privately owned animals, belong to some of

the members. We used to have dogs for rent. Ain't got 'em anymore. Too expensive to keep. Gonna have to take that sign
down, too."

Five minutes and five miles later:

"Look at that pheasant sitting there just behind the 'PRIVATE
CLUB' posted fence sign. Look at him, he's saying, 'Ha-ha, you
niggers can't shoot me! . . . only white folks can shoot me!
Ha-ha!' "

"If it wasn't against the law I'd blast him."

"Hand me my shotgun."

"Don't be no fool!"

"Roll the window down"

"Don't do it!"

BLAMM!!!

WEEKS LATER, as the band bus approached Little Rock, Arkansas, the subject of hunting came up again.

"Say, Johnny," my drummer, Bell, said, "let's go hunting
while we're in Arkansas. A cat told me there's a lot of quail and
cottontails here."

"Okay, I'm for it."

"Arthur, where's a good place to hunt around Little Rock?"

"I don't know nothin' about hunting," Little Arthur answered.

"You know what happened to us in California," Bell observed, "and this is the South, so let's not build up any big hopes
about finding a good place to go hunting."

"I don't know about hunting," Arthur said, "but Jim Crow
works in California as much as it works in Arkansas. They just
use different excuses. In the North they refuse you politely.
Down here they don't make no bones about it. All over the
country they pull the same stuff, only in different ways. Hell, all
the cities are alike. They even *look* the same, when you come to
think about it."

The bus rolled into the outskirts of Little Rock. Amazing, I thought, how look-alike many American cities are, especially the larger ones. Little Arthur was so right. The same gas stations, identical shopping centers; look at the buildings. Could be Des Moines, or Pasadena, or Trenton, or Portland, or Atlanta.

During the early fifties we were traveling a lot. Our phonograph records with Little Esther and Mel Walker were hot and this kept us constantly on the one-night trail. During 1950–1953, we averaged about five thousand miles a month. City after city, night after night . . . no wonder they all began to look alike. But, no, there was a sameness, a monotony. Even the people. Aren't these the same people we saw yesterday in St. Louis, or last week in Denver? Some nights on the bandstand I'd get the eerie feeling that this was the exact same audience that we played to the night before, like it was all some incredible science-fiction joke. Our bus driver must be part of this weird conspiracy! He's riding us in big circles every night, round and round and right back to the same town! The illusion was most overpowering when we played a town we had never visited before. On return engagements, however, sooner or later during the dance I'd spot someone I knew from the previous date, and I knew this was really Little Rock or Buffalo. . . .

We hadn't played Little Rock since last year. I hoped the disc jockeys had been laying on our records. We might pick up a nice piece of percentage tonight.

We stopped for a traffic light alongside a bus-stop bench full of people. They were all white. They did an eyes-left-to-right tennis crowd maneuver in unison. Now they all went for themselves, peering here and there, trying to pull some understanding out of the dark faces staring back at them from behind the windows of this big sign on wheels, which proclaimed to the world in red and green two-foot tall letters that it was the "RHYTHM AND BLUES CARAVAN."

"Hello, white folks, you can't figure out what we are, can

you?"

"He knows what we are. He just don't know what we're doing."

"He thinks we're a Colored sideshow from some carnival."

"Or a minstrel show."

"Say, Arthur, this is your home town. Are the ofays bad here?"

"They're rough, daddy, rough."

"Bad as Mississippi?"

"Hell, no, man. Ain't nothin' as bad as Mississippi."

"Where exactly did you live here in Little Rock?"

"We didn't live in Little Rock. I was raised in Fordyce. That's a few miles out of here. Then we moved to Watts."

"Do you think integration will ever happen here?"

"Not if 'Charlie' can help it! Not in Watts either, if 'Charlie' can help it."

The integration movement hit Little Rock like a ton of bricks a few years later, and Little Arthur was right. He knew "Charlie."

As we unloaded the bus, someone introduced me to a Mrs. Daisy Bates. Her office (she was the head of the local NAACP branch) was below the little hotel that we were checking into. We agreed to present a check to the local NAACP and Mrs. Bates had a photographer take a picture.

A few years passed and the Supreme Court decision of 1954 and the ensuing events made a national figure and a civil rights symbol of Daisy Bates. You should have seen me dig that old picture out of my scrapbook and slap it on the mantelpiece for everyone to see!

Later that day while we were having lunch, Dude had us falling out laughing as he jokingly predicted that the money we had contributed to the NAACP would be used to desegregate quail hunting in Arkansas.

SEVENTEEN

Dude, the Dentist, and Prince Kahoolee

"Like you're going down the street in your car and turn around and the police be staring at you and you turn around and stare at them and the first thing you know, pull over and ask you 'What's so funny?' I mean, I've had that happen to me one morning on the way to work. They want to look under your seat, open up your trunk, push you around. This is all the time, and I think the people just got tired of it. They just built up inside. The night was hot. You know, it was just the right time at the right place and people just blew up all over town." — *Man, interviewed during the Watts riots.*

LOOKED LIKE every time we played Baltimore I wound up in a doctor's office. It had been me the first time around, with what June Richmond had described as the "one-nighter flux," then Little Esther, the last time we had played here, with stomach cramps, and now in 1951, Dude with a toothache.

An M.D. shared the waiting room with the dentist who was pulling Dude's tooth in the next room. There were patients everywhere, most of them in bandages and casts, waiting forlornly to see the doctor. The astringent hospital smell hung heavily in the room, although this was far from a hospital. It was just a converted house, serving the two medical men. We were seated in what had once been a single-dwelling living room. The all-night trip in the band bus had been a rough one for Dude, who had suffered as stoically as his effusive nature would permit. Traveling through the Deep South in the Sunday dawn hours was a very inopportune time and place to develop a severe toothache. From the time we left Florida until the moment we pulled into Baltimore, we found only one dentist who had his office in his home, and *he* reneged when the fact that we were black penetrated his sleep-shrouded Dixie brain.

Two young girls struggled in, helping an older woman with a plaster cast on her leg as big as the youngsters themselves. Three of us got up to give them our seats. The waiting room was overloaded with aches, pains, and broken bones now, and was getting more crowded as the morning wore on. What is more depressing than a doctor's waiting room in an impoverished neighborhood? Nothing, that's what. I wondered what was ailing the sweating fat man who sat Buddha-like, puffing on a cigar stub in the corner. I knew what was wrong with the little kid wheezing in his mama's lap. I knew what he was going through, too. I had paid those asthma dues once upon a time myself. Maybe he'll outgrow his, too, I hoped.

"Go in there like I told you, girl," a woman suddenly shouted at her young daughter. "Don't stand there! Tell him I can't wait all day; I'm too sick. She told me nine o'clock. I was here on time, tell him. *Go ahead!*"

The little girl hung back in awkward embarrassment. She was rescued by an angular nurse who had heard the conversation and had poked her head around the door.

"Yes, Mrs. Wilson, the doctor will be with you shortly. Sorry, but an emergency detained him at the hospital this morning. . . ."

"Well, tell him I'm too sick to sit here all day. I'm an emergency, myself, hear?"

The complaining woman's daughter was suffering the self-conscious misery that indiscreet parents sometimes publicly inflict upon shy children. The little girl seemed torn between concern for her ailing mother and embarrassment at the shattering display of disdain for public amenities, an attitude not rare among the very poor, and her mother's disregard for the feelings of others, a personality trait peculiar to the very ill.

Suddenly I developed a kind of mental-emotional triangle. The three corners were named empathy, sympathy, and zero. My heart was bleeding for the little asthmatic cat who was gasping for breath: empathy. The woman with the big swelling behind her ear (my fast amateur diagnosis: goiter), I know she was going through weird changes with that fearful knot on her neck: sympathy. But the crass hypochondriac who had jarred the scene and mortified her little girl: zero. I started to study the other cases in the room: Dr. Otis' instant diagnoses. I got as far as the teen-age girl with the deliriously burning eyes set in the hollow, cadaverous skull, and I had to stop because the mood was beginning to strangle me.

I grabbed a pamphlet off the table and began to read. "JESUS SAVES . . . Judgment Day Is Nigh! . . . Are You Ready? . . . Only The Saved Shall Survive!" . . . Damn! Everything I saw spelled death! Next week we were due to record in New York. I hadn't written the songs yet. I'd better get on them right away if I was going to be ready. Any more of the kind of stimulus I was receiving today and I'd probably wind up writing new versions of "Gloomy Sunday" and "Strange Fruit." As it turned out, one of the songs we recorded became a bestseller for Little Esther. It was titled "Misery."

The woman with the goiter had the *Life* magazine. I kept hoping she'd finish up so I'd get a crack at it, but she was slowly soaking up every page, and I was stuck with the "Jesus Saves" pamphlet. When I was a kid I thought "Jesus Saves" meant that He was thrifty. Driving from Berkeley to Sacramento in my father's old Model T, I used to see the words painted on rocks and on signs. I never understood how anyone could secure permission to use Jesus' name in an advertising campaign, but I was sure that the signs were part of a bank or savings and loan promotion. The pamphlet reminded me of a dream I had had in which I met Jesus on the street:

"Hello, Jesus, how are you?"

"Oh, I ain't doin' no good, son. So many of my children havin' it tough."

Funny how dreams can be. And Mr. Muhammad was right. Jesus WAS black—dark brown, in fact. At least *this* Jesus was. But actually he was Mr. Williams—and I hadn't seen Mr. Williams for years. Old as he was the last time I'd seen him, he might be dead and gone by now. Mr. Williams always presented himself as a preacher, but we never had any evidence that he actually preached anywhere.

"The Reverend J. C. Williams, at your service, sir," he used to say. The J.C. stood for "Justice Child." He had a cross hanging from his watch chain, and the way he dressed and everything he certainly looked like a preacher. If you said, "Hello, how you feelin' Reverend Williams?" he would usually answer, "Oh, I ain't doin' no good. My children havin' it awful rough!"

I was snapped out of my reverie and back into the waiting room by a loud "UEEEEEEEEEEOW!" It was Dude, hollering in the dentist's chair in the next room. This dentist was evidently *not* related to Painless Parker. The howl jarred the people in the waiting room. The few soft conversations that had been in progress before the holler, ended abruptly. The people in the room exchanged quick, wide-eyed glances. I could have sworn that the kid with asthma had stopped wheezing. Two young men got up and sailed out the door without a backward glance. I know that Dude's yelp cost the dentist some customers. Aside from the guys who lit out of there, I'm sure the other witnesses did the dentist's reputation little good as they passed the word about the scream around town. And you can be sure that they passed the word around because it had been an agonized beaut.

Later, Dude denied that he uttered it, but we'll get to that.

Finally, Dude came out. You'd think that having a tooth pulled would slow his talking down a bit. But if you'd think that, then you didn't know Thomas "Dude" Love. He backed out of the dentist's surgery, holding a little ice pack to his jaw and gabbing away a mile a minute, his voice a little muffled by cotton and ice pack, but unfazed, man, unfazed.

"Okay, Doc, good show, good show! Don't forget, when you're in Los Angeles, look me up. You got my address. That's Hobart Avenue, right? If you lose it, don't worry. Just go to the corner of Adams and Western, see? Ask anybody where's Tommy Love. You can always ask the newspaper man there on the corner. Nick. He'll tell you. He's a great guy, you'll love him. I live right around the corner there. Come on out. You'd be great in California, great! We'll have a round of golf, right? Right!"

I don't think Dude ever played a round of golf in his life, but that didn't matter because if the dentist ever made it out to Los Angeles and looked Dude up and called him on the round of golf, you can rest assured that Dude would've accommodated him, experience or no. He would probably convince the guy that he was temporarily indisposed with a bad back or something, but otherwise was a skilled golfer. And should the man get wise to Dude's bull, you can bet that it would not keep him from joining an army of Dude Love admirers whose motto was: "That Tommy is a great guy!"

As he left the dentist's surgery, Dude turned on his heel and gave everybody in the waiting room a sweeping, "Hello folks!" Then, with the exuberant air of a TV emcee warming up a quiz-show audience, he threw a hearty handshake and a "Good to see you . . . you're looking great!" to a couple of dazed patients who had never seen Dude before that moment and who had probably never looked worse. And now, with a final kiss blown from his fingertips in the finest French cavalier fashion and intended for the patients, the doctor, the people of Baltimore, the universe and beyond, we were out the door and into the street.

"How do you feel, Dude?"

"Great! But this son-of-a-gun does ache a little, though."

"Well, maybe you better not talk too much then."

"Oh, I don't intend to do no whole lot of talking now."

"It must have really hurt bad for you to scream out like you did. We could all hear you in the next room. Two cats waiting for the dentist jumped up and split when they heard you."

"Scream? *Scream?* Are you kiddin'? That wasn't me. You know better than that!"

"Who was it then?"

"Who was it? Listen, you think I'm telling a damn lie, but that spook dropped a big stainless-steel instrument on his foot. That was *him* hollered."

"Him who?"

"The doctor, fool, THE DOCTOR!"

"Oh, you mean the dentist."

"Yeah, the dentist."

"Don't you think I know your voice when I hear it?"

"All right, you don't believe *me,* ask the nurse tonight."

"What nurse tonight, man?"

"The doctor's nurse, of course. You couldn't see her; she was in the other room. Gorgeous bitch. She's coming to the show tonight, and then we're going over to her apartment for dinner. I would invite you, too, but you wouldn't go for it."

"Why?"

" 'Cause her roommate's a sissy. It's her cousin. They're from Louisiana."

I know it sounds unlikely as hell—a guy in a dentist's chair, while the dentist works on him, finding it possible to make a date with the nurse (which theoretically, at least, is not easy with the doctor present), and picking up all that incidental information, to boot. But I had learned long ago that such inconsequential obstacles could never deter Dude. True to his style, that night after the show he brought his pretty nurse backstage. She was, it developed as we chatted, from Louisiana, and she indeed had a homosexual cousin. She had brought him along and he was flaming all over the place. Just before they left the theatre I asked the nurse to tell me who had let out the scream in the dentist's office earlier in the day, but Dude yanked her away before she could confirm what I already would've bet my life on.

When Tommy Love came into a room he lit it up like a Christmas tree. Not everybody had the mental stamina required to put up with his perpetual-motion personality and effervescence; still, not even the sourest individual could find it in his heart to dislike him. He was an untiring dynamo of theatrical exuberance and good humor, exasperating at times and very hammy, but never boring or petty, and there was never a dull moment when Dude was around.

In Los Angeles, in late 1959, Dude succumbed to an untimely heart attack, and I drew the forlorn duty of taking his body back home to Omaha for burial.

Well, Prince, I mused, as the train droned through the lonely Midwestern countryside, we've made many a tour together but this is one I would have liked to miss.

The nickname "Prince" was an inside joke we shared. It stemmed from a Jim Crow predicament we had barely gotten out of some years back.

Although back in the thirties Dude had played alto sax professionally, he was not a performer with our band. He was our assistant road manager, and his job was to stand at the door during dance dates and collect tickets as customers filed through from the box office. Our regular road manager, Papa Joe Hess, used to raise hell with him all the time for striking up conversations with the young chicks as they came in and neglecting to collect tickets, which threw the count off. But Papa Hess had to tolerate Dude's derelictions because he knew that I wasn't going to fire my bosom buddy, no matter how many chicks he hit on and regardless of the people who slipped by him without paying, while he was trying to score.

"Zay, lizzen, loook," Papa Hess used to admonish me, "zat Tommy Luf iss gonna put you ztraight in ze poorhouse. Tonight, again, at least two hundred freebeez . . . zzzooop! Right in, while he iss playing ze great Casanoffah wiz a little skinny baby."

"Now that's a damn lie!" Dude would retort. "I was watching that door like a hawk, like I always do. Joe, you're just mad 'cause you want some of that young stuff yourself!"

"Me?" Papa Hess would say. "I'm an old man."

"That ain't what the hotel maid in Portland told me!"

"Zay, lizzen, loook, Luf, you should be ashamed."

THE chair car was about half-full. The seat next to mine was empty. The seat next to me in the band bus was going to be empty from now on, too. How many thousands of miles had we traveled together through the years? And how about the many, many hours—hours that would've been so empty without Dude to liven them up.

One of the things that Dude *couldn't* do was sing, but you couldn't tell *him* that. And he'd pick the damndest times to yodel the 1930 hit parade at the top of his voice in "poor man's" Nelson Eddy tones.

"Raaaaahmoanaaaah . . . I hear the mission bells aboooove . . . Raaaahmoanaaah . . . they're ringin' out a song of loooooove . . . la da dee doo dee la la la dee doooooo . . ."

"Shut up that cornball yelping, Dude. I'm trying to get some sleep!"

"The trouble with you, nigger, is you don't have an appreciation for real music. Now, if I went, YAAAAH BABY! We gonna rock and rooooool tonight . . . wop, wop, diddy-wop . . . you'd think it was great, wouldn't you?"

"A person can't get a minute's rest on this bus with that loudmouth going all the time. Listen, Johnny, if you want somebody to be able to play tomorrow night you better quiet that damn fool down so we can sleep!" the guys in the band used to complain.

THE conductor came down the line punching tickets. He had to be at least seventy years old if he was a day. Now why couldn't Dude have lived to be that old? The cats in the band wouldn't have to worry about quieting Dude down anymore. He'd be still a long time now. Suddenly I remembered one of the few times I had seen Dude quiet. It was the incident that produced the nickname "Prince."

It was a bright summer afternoon and we had just arrived in Birmingham, Alabama. The band bus pulled up to a gas station, and Dude and I jumped out and caught a cab that was gassing up at the next pump.

"Drive around town, we want to see what's playing at the movies," I told the driver.

He was so busy watching the musicians and singers get off the brightly painted bus that he didn't hear me. But the fascination finally wore off and he pulled away.

When we got to the movie house, the cab driver followed us in to get cigarettes out of the machine in the lobby. I remember his watching us as we walked into the orchestra of the theatre. That should've been a warning, but Dude and I had "passed" so often in the segregated South and we had gotten into the habit of going where we pleased whenever it served our purpose. Years before we had experimented gingerly and appprehensively with the process, but by now we were used to it and didn't give it a second thought. What we hadn't taken into account, though, was the nosy cab driver who had seen us get off the bus and had heard us talking on the way to the theatre. He had decided to exercise his prerogative as a true son of the South and see to it that the downstairs was kept pure.

A flashlight kept flicking in our faces from the side of the theatre. "What the hell does that fool keep flashing that light over here for?" Dude whispered.

"I don't know," I answered. But I hope it ain't what I think it is, I thought.

Nothing more happened, and after a while I banished all worrisome thoughts and settled back to try to figure out what Humphrey Bogart was doing counting out money in a Hong Kong nightclub. Just as I got good and relaxed, I felt a tap on my shoulder. It was a young kid in an usher's uniform, and he looked nervous.

"Pardon me, sir," he said softly, "the manager told me to ask you a question."

What the hell? I wondered. "Yeah, what?"

"Uh . . . er . . . Are you Negroes?" he blurted out.

Oh, oh, here it is! Visions of a funky Alabama jail cell floated before my eyes.

"Let's go!" Dude whispered in my ear. But that would be a a dead giveaway, and I had decided long ago that if we ever got caught in this kind of cramp I was going to bluff our way through, or die trying.

"WHAT!" I said, loudly enough to turn the heads of half the audience. "What do you mean by saying such a thing?"

"Oh . . . I . . . I . . . I'm sorry," the kid stammered, and he hurried away.

"Oh, Jesus, we're gonna get it now!" Dude moaned. "Let's go!"

"Shut up and let me think."

"Man, I'm nervous as a sissy in the YMCA. Let's get outa here!"

"Okay, but let me do the talking."

"You got it, but let's make it."

I walked toward the little fat man in the tuxedo. He had to

be the manager. He was having a conference with the usher at the end of the lobby. The cab driver had evidently done his good deed for the day and split. I had to grab Dude to keep him from flying out the door. I hoped the little fat bastard hadn't called the cops yet.

"Sir, are you the manager of this theatre?" I demanded in a loud voice that belied the butterflies in my guts and the palsy in my knees. He took so long to answer I almost weakened and took Dude's cue to flee the scene. Well, anyhow, I thought, when the cops get through beating the piss out of us and fining us every dollar we can get our hands on, at least we'll be able to say we put up a good front while it lasted.

"Yeeeeees, I'm the manager of this theatre," he answered as he kept peering at us through a pair of thick, milk-bottle glasses. He looked just like Syd Nathan. Maybe he'd turn out to be Syd's brother and we'd all have a good laugh. But that wasn't about to happen, and the time had come to take my best shot or get off the pot.

"Well, sir, I hope you realize that your usher has insulted Prince Kahoolee." (I wished Dude would stop looking around for Prince Kahoolee like that.) "And as a member of the State Department, I can assure you that this outrage could have grave repercussions."

"Prince Kahoolee?" the fat man echoed. I had him. It was incredible, but the look on his face told me he was my meat.

"Yes, Prince Kahoolee of the Hawaiian Islands, visiting our country as a guest of the United States Government. The Prince had lunch with the Mayor. I showed him a Colored minstrel show. Everyone has been very nice, and now this—this unwarranted humiliation!"

"Well, my God! A stupid-assed cab driver! Oh, gentlemen, please, please accept my apology . . . I had no idea . . ."

I turned to the Prince and rattled off quickly in Greek, *"Na mu fas ta skata?"*

"Umgawa," he answered.

Oh, oh, I goofed. What if this cat understood Greek? Well, it was too late now. If he missed *that*, he damn sure wouldn't understand "Umgawa."

The manager bowed and scraped and Dude matched his every dip. They carried on like a couple of Japanese noblemen meeting in Parliament. The manager kept apologizing and, thank God, for once in his life Dude didn't utter a mumbling word. At last, after the manager loaded us up with theatre passes and shook our hands for the umpteenth time, we escaped.

We hadn't gone a block before Dude's mouth began to resume operations in true form.

"Say, that was a close one. Hey, give me those passes, I can use 'em tonight. Goddam, couldn't you think of a better lie than that? Suppose the cat had been to Hawaii on a vacation or something and asked me about some beach or other? Prince K—*who*—ee? Oh, yeah, Prince Kahoolee. Ain't that a bitch! I'm Prince Kahoolee! Man, you're something else. You sure can get us outa more binds. . . ."

BUT now the train carrying Dude, up there in his box, and me back in the coach, rolled on toward Omaha.

EIGHTEEN

Second Letter to Griff

"Sure I throwed rocks. Sure, I stuck with my brothers because I felt they was right, and anytime I feel that I'm right, I'm going to go on and do what I want to do.

"The whole thing from the get-go, everybody else been rioting and everything, I mean, in them other states. What was Watts doing? Nothin', they was just bein' cool, they was tryin' to give the white man a break to see what he was goin' to do for us, and they come to a boiling point; if somebody do you wrong for a long period of time, you'll stand for it for a while, but if it get down, you gonna have to come out, and it just exploded."—*Man, interviewed during the Watts riots.*

DEAR GRIFF: *September 5, 1965*

Please thank Jasmine for the wonderful letter. I appreciate the invitation to come visit, too, but let's face it, I can't make it. I don't have the loot or the inclination. I stopped looking long ago for a place where brothers and sisters abide in love and harmony. I'm sure some places come closer than others, but I ain't comin' . . . I'm staying home. I don't expect it anymore, therefore, I am no longer frustrated by any search for Utopia and equality. My concern, and it is frustrating enough, is to loosen the chains that bind us over here. As for America, I'm convinced that full justice or equality for the American black man, if it is forthcoming at all, is in the hazy future (barring any phenomenal, happy accident), and I am resigned to addressing myself to the job of helping to find ways and means of lessening the immediate misery and improving the situation as much as is possible. This is a part-time activity for most of us because there is the whole problem of paying the rent and feeding and clothing the family, which comes first. This necessity knocks thousands of potential contributors out of the fray because they don't have anything left after eight or ten hours of scufflin' for a living.

Nor do I have any profound, cut-and-dried, sociopolitical long- or short-range solutions. We just play it by ear and hope for the best. That old jive about you shouldn't gripe and protest unless you have a comprehensive "something better" to offer is a fallacy. This enemy we face is a complex and well-rooted national disease. We just have to resist and attack from now on, and in the meantime, try to figure the best way out. But I'm not going to sit down and try to get it all worked out on paper and *then* start fighting it. That's like doing something that needs to be done "when you can afford it," which means never. And don't tell me there are two sides to every question. That's another damn lie. Some questions have only *one* side. Water is necessary for life, for instance. Likewise, people yearn for, and have a right to, dignity, freedom from hunger, protection against tyranny.

Your early enthusiasm for life in Jamaica, then Italy, and now France, are to me reflections of your deep desire to discover a spot on earth where the spirit of brotherhood is real and established. You're not the only one, Griff. I hope you find it, but I suspect you won't. For myself, having abandoned the hope of ever finding that Utopia, I'll try to make the best of life here at home. I can take this approach because I still have hope that in spite of the odds constantly working against us, some meaningful improvements can be made. If I didn't hold out that left-field hope I would be on the next plane to Oslo, Provence, Rio, Ghana, Cairo, Jamaica, or somewhere. Without that hope I wouldn't have a reason to try.

I'm impressed with your description of the multiracial society of Provence. I would like to see it, sure. But not so much that I would be inclined to take the time to actually make the trip. Anyhow, I see it in your letters, and that's a very nice experience in itself.

I'm not lulled into false illusions by examples of political expediency. The fact that de Gaulle took certain positions in the Algerian question does not indicate that the French heart beats compassionately for the North Africans. Thank God, of course, for political expediency when the pressure gets too strong, because that is one of the main things that we have going for us over here. But I never mistake a practical concession on the part of white society as an act out of the goodness of its heart. We make what advances we make because it becomes too painful or too costly for the Establishment to maintain the status quo. The point I'm trying to make is that the pieces may be molded in different geographical and cultural outlines but it's the same old chessboard, be it French or American. The Frenchman is hung up on a past and present as it relates to Algerians and the American is hung up on American Negroes.

And another thing: there is a feeling among many that this may be our last chance over here. A statement the other day by an old man brought the point painfully home. "I hope," he said, "that this revolutionary activity and the present state of mind of our people brings some irrevocable advances. I hope that we make progress and that we are able to secure and defend the gains because there is the dreadful possibility of winding up back in chains!"

The burning of Watts and the guerilla-type warfare that exploded and enfolded has hardened white public opinion tremendously. A minority of whites have been shocked into the realization that conditions were more desperate for Negroes in Los Angeles than they had ever imagined. But the average white is outraged and intimidated. The total effect is one of more polarity. The communities have never been as far apart as they are in the wake of the riots. The average white now has a certified license to express aloud what had become unfashionable to even whisper in recent years. Various governmental agencies are involved in the "blue ribbon" committee hearings and investigations to determine the causes of the flare-up. The answers, of course, are already known and have been for years. But the formal Establishment has to go through the motions. The average white "man on the street" though, is relieved. Full of righteous indignation and fear, but relieved. Now he can pour out his long pent-up venom. Now he can give them goddam niggers hell, and the guy next door will be listening and agreeing, if not wailing louder than he.

The civil rights movement, or Negro revolt, heretofore staged by the middle- and upper-class intelligentsia in behalf of the dispossessed, had not (until Watts) had the unique experience (or the advantage) of the victims' personal participation. There was no preplanning, no preparatory meetings conducted with parliamentary decorum, no executive board decisions, no pious prayer to kick it off. Just BAM! And away we go! This one was different. This one came from the victims, from the *victims in person*. This one was where it was *really* at. No picket captains. In fact, no pickets. What the hell for? No singing of "We Shall Overcome." This was way beyond all that. This was indeed, *something else*. The man who had inspired all the nonviolent protests and demonstrations had finally shown up on the scene and got in a lick in his own behalf. And what a lick.

It was such a whopping lick that it set off investigations and inquiries that should have been held just after World War II, or a hundred years before that.

"We've got to look into the community to find the causes," they say.

"You're the cause, 'Whitey.' *You're* the cause," answers the ghetto.

"The people must become more responsible to their own community," says the downtown power structure. But if the people of Watts and other similar ghettos are going to be held responsible for the communities they are forced to live in, these will have to be made truly their own communities. One way would be for all others to get back and let the people of the ghetto govern themselves—their own mayor, their own city council, their own police and fire departments, tax-levying systems, Board of Education, Department of Public Works, etc., etc. Then the residents of the area *could* be held responsible for the community. In the meantime, the responsibility is upon the most irresponsible members of the cast in this classic tragedy: the politicians, the white absentee landlords, the white merchants, all of whom suck the blood out of the community, but few, if any, of whom are around when the community needs an emergency transfusion.

Just because the improverished Negro is forced to live in the ghetto does not mean that the ghetto is *his*. Can you see the residents of Brentwood burning their area down? You don't burn down or destroy what you feel possessive about. People of the Watts area feel IDENTIFIED with Watts, but until the riot it was not a feeling of pride. It was more like a trap, or a social stigma, a curse.

Negroes in the nicer sections of the Westside would not burn their areas, either, but more than one middle-class Negro expressed a feeling of exhilaration at the sight of Watts getting it on TV.

Some of us move great distances only to find, sooner or later, that home is back there where you thought you were escaping from. James Baldwin went to Paris, you went to Jamaica, then Europe. I only moved across town, from Watts to the Westside, but that was a long way too. "Go West, young man," I thought I heard a voice say, and I did. That was over ten years ago. And so did almost every other Negro family or individual

who could. Some of us moved to the Westside, some to the nicer
areas of Compton and the Southwestern side of town. But for
the comparatively few who got out, thousands from out of state
(mostly Deep South) poured in. Watts is bulging, cracking at
the seams. Unemployment is rampant. The very atmosphere
reeks of despair. A deep and sullen rage lies just below the surface. The explosion had to occur sooner or later; it was just a
matter of time. The riot has had the effect of a temporary escape
valve. These are times of reaction and assessment and fear on the
part of the white community and times of exhilaration and new-
found power in the ghetto. But this is just a passing phase, a lull
in the wake. Unemployment is still here. So are the hovels. The
rage is still smoldering even if 103rd Street has stopped. Thousands are in jail, many on a hummer, you can be sure. What
possibly could happen in the future if meaningful relief is not
soon forthcoming is anybody's guess.

Immediately after the riots, food went on sale in Watts.
Only Negro women were allowed to shop. Men were barred.
Aha! Does that have a familiar ring? There are more ways than
one (hundred) to cut out a black man's manhood. The ashes
hadn't cooled good yet, but the emasculator's blade was back at
work. So many families in Watts are already without a father
image . . . or a father . . . and here in one fell swoop, one day
after the fiery protest, what fathers did exist were shot down
officially and publicly.

I may have told you a while back that our old house on the
Westside became an impractical burden. The neighborhood had
been rezoned, taxes were way up. So were apartment houses,
which were going up all around us. The forty-year-old plumbing,
electrical system, furnace, etc., were constantly in disrepair. It
was a matter of selling, investing in apartment units, or leasing. I
went after the apartment-house myth. We went as far as having
plans drawn for a twelve-unit building. We were one month
away from demolition of the old house when I got cold feet. I

began to notice that the other new units in the area were full of vacancies. I backed off.

The big house on Harvard Boulevard became a bigger drag as time went by. With Phyllis working as a secretary at the local UN office and the girls in school, the place became impossible to keep up. Finally, the big, hotel-type furnace in the basement conked out and the bill came to over $400! That did it! Good-bye "Sugar Hill." I leased the place to a lady who runs it now as an old folks' home. All the great big bedrooms and the big yard were made to order for her business. My problems weren't over, though. I had to find a four-bedroom house that wouldn't take me to the cleaners financially. Two bedrooms, even three bedrooms, we learned, are not too difficult to find, but try to find a four-bedroom house in LA without getting into the telephone-figure class. Finally, we found a nice place. It was located in the south end of the ghetto, just on the perimeter of the Watts area. How about that? We had come back home.

Four months after we moved back to the south end the riots broke out. I came back too late, I thought. What a presumptuous and preposterous thought! What the hell could I have done? But maybe if all the others hadn't run away? But that was as stupid as the first thought.

As I watched the street blaze up from the foot of 103rd, I thought, burn, you son of a bitch, burn! Not that I enjoyed seeing people lose their businesses, but that's not what I'm talking about. I meant, burn down, symbol of deprivation and human misery, burn down you raggedy, funky image of Watts. Nostalgic memories were going up in smoke, too, but it didn't matter. Yes, it bothered me a little to see the feed store where Mario and I used to get supplies for our chickens and the Largo Theatre where I first saw Little Esther on the talent show, go up in smoke. But burn anyhow, DAMMIT, BURN!

NINETEEN

Black Cannon Fodder

"Cops handcuffed the boy, the boy said something to him, he slapped him. While the cuffs was on him. Well, this is unfair. Now, he was being punished for being black, not for the crime that he committed, and this is worse. It's bad enough being born black, but to be punished for being black is even worse than anything God could ever create altogether."
                                        —*Man, interviewed during the Watts riots.*

THE WAR IN VIETNAM, it has been suggested, is affording new opportunities to young Negro draftees and recruits inasmuch as it rescues them from the streets and give them the benefit of various G.I. programs (forty per cent of the U.S. noncommissioned officers serving in Vietnam are Negro). It also makes for black cannon fodder, I'd like to add, and the more black young men there are who go to Vietnam, the fewer there are to protest and riot at home. Since very few Negro students make it to college, the academic deferment tests also take on special significance.

During World War II there was plenty of pride within the Negro community concerning the accomplishments of Negro servicemen in the war against Fascism. Today there are voices in the community calling for an end to Negro help in "Whitey's" war against their Asian brothers and sisters of Vietnam. This war is *for* Fascism, they say, and they cite General Ky as an example of what they mean.

The stark racist overtones of the United States involvement in Vietnam are further pointed up when one considers the mass carnage visited upon the Vietnamese people—women, children, farmers—with the use of napalm, defoliation, the Lazy Dog bomb (thousands of slivers of razor-sharp metal), gas, and all the rest. This kind of indescribable horror and murder of innocent civilians would never be applied against a white nation.

The President, nettled by the handful of Americans who have an insight on what is really happening and the guts to protest, calls them Nervous Nellies, and the average citizen, preconditioned by a shoot-'em-up cowboys and Indians culture and an anti-intellectual "white is right" mentality, goes along self-righteously, piously, super-patriotically . . . and blindly.

John Lennon, of the famed British Beatles, says that in his opinion Christianity is on the way out, and right away the American press and much of the broadcast industry is outraged. But American foreign policy is killing thousands of human beings (both American and Vietnamese) in Southeast Asia, and many Christian institutions in the United States don't utter a mumbling word! Can John Lennon's prediction be that far off if a so-called Christian nation can support an immoral, illegal, and murderous government policy? I have always heard that it is "Christian" to tell the truth, but the American public doesn't seem to be unduly bothered when its government keeps lying and double-talking about the Vietnamese involvement.

Former Assistant Secretary of Defense Arthur Sylvester told a group of reporters in Vietnam: "Look, if you think any American official is going to tell you the truth, then you're stupid. Did you hear that, stupid." Mr. Sylvester's point is well taken, especially when one recalls Secretary of Defense McNamara's statement that our men would be home by 1965.

We are told that we are in Vietnam because the Vietnamese people asked us to come and protect their freedom. But that's bull shit, because if that were true, why hasn't the United States

Government responded with guns and armies rather than token support to protect the freedom of the black people in America— in Mississippi, for instance, where the black people have asked for help? Or how about the freedom of the people in Angola, South-West Africa, Rhodesia, South Africa, or Haiti? I'm sure they would welcome some United States help.

The reason for United States aggression in Southeast Asia was clearly spelled out by President Eisenhower in 1953, when he said: "Now let us assume we lost Indochina. If Indochina goes, the tin and tungsten we so greatly value would cease coming. We are after the cheapest way to prevent the occurrence of something terrible . . . the loss of our ability to get what we want from the riches of the Indochinese territory and from Southeast Asia."

What many Americans are not aware of (in addition to what President Eisenhower may or may not have said—because Americans don't read) is the great wealth of natural resources in Southeast Asia. *The New York Times* has reported: "Indochina is a prize worth a large gamble. In the north are exportable tin, tungsten, manganese, coal, lumber, and rice; rubber, tea, pepper, and hides." A United States government advisor has observed that "We have only partially exploited Southeast Asian resources. Nevertheless, Southeast Asia supplied 90% of the world's crude rubber, 60% of its tin, and 80% of its copra and coconut oil."

Another little item that seems to escape the average American consciousness is the fact that the United States subsidized the bloody French colonialist fourteen-year war against the Vietnamese people to the tune of eighty per cent of its cost. The United States is not interested in the freedom of the Vietnamese people. If it were, our Government would not have underwritten the French war against the Vietnamese. The United States is not interested in democracy for Vietnam. If it were, it would not impose a corrupt and oppressive government headed by a succession of fascist-minded tyrants upon the people of South Vietnam. The United States Government is not interested in peace for Vietnam because the climate for negotiations or peace is not created by bombing and killing.

The war in Vietnam and the civil rights demonstrations and riots are affecting white youth in America in a very powerful way. First of all we see the familiar, well-scrubbed, white Anglo-Saxon Protestant type reacting in good old all-American fashion, attending "sing outs," Christian Crusades, and joining right-wing causes. On the other hand, there is a sizable group of young white people who wouldn't be caught dead in this kind of activity. In various degrees, they are rebelling against the hypocritical philosophy and way of life surrounding them. They range from the student who is involved in liberal causes, through the white kids who work with CORE and SNCC, to the rather recently-emergent group of way-out, freakishly dressed, pot-smoking, trip-taking youngsters who are apt to say, "I'm through marching and demonstrating. I think everybody should just turn on and make out." This is a direct quote from a young member of the "freak out" set, who had never marched or demonstrated a day in her life, any more than most of these kids have, but it is interesting that she tied the social troubles of the day in with the LSD-marijuana-sex-wild-clothes-psychedelic lights and distorted, pseudo rhythm and blues music of the "in crowd" she is part of. To attempt to dismiss or disparage the kids involved in this latest way of life as "come freaks" or "pot heads" would be not only unfair but inaccurate, because there are too many people moving in that direction to justify such a pat and simple evaluation. As wild and scary as these young people may appear to others, they are products of the age we live in. They're trying to say something or, perhaps more accurately, trying to *do* something. The something they're trying to do may be an attempt to turn in on themselves and shut the real and very disturbing world out. To a young person who feels trapped in a society of lying and bigoted parents, of double-talking, hypocritical religious leaders, public officials, newspapers, TVs and movies full of violence, materialistic poison, and inane "family shows," and a world ever-vibrating with the threat of nuclear holocaust, "in" may seem to be the only way to turn.

Dr. Timothy Leary, who gained national notice with his LSD experiments at Harvard University, sees the movement as a new religion. He attaches profound importance to the conscious-ness-expanding, hallucogenic, acid way of life. He is convinced that the people involved with LSD are going to "build a new civilization . . . whether you like it or not."

In all due respect to Dr. Leary—and I am very much in favor of his freedom to conduct his scientific experiments—I can't see "Suzy Creamcheese" (a mythical character in Freak-Out lore) as a future Vice President of the United States, even though I agree she couldn't do any worse than what we've got. And I cannot help but notice that Dr. Leary is thinking like a typical white man when he says that these kids are going to build a new civilization. The psychedelic movement is almost purely lily-white, and the sweep of history does not seem to me to be moving in that direction in the past few decades. That is, I don't think, all things being equal, that the white man is going to be center stage building new civilizations. He might, if he's a good boy and if there is to be any future civilization, be allowed to participate as an equal, but the day of the white man running the entire show is about over, and that includes Dr. Leary's acid heads.

The psychedelic movement has spawned a batch of new bands that are based on the two-guitar, bass, drums, and organ format of the recent past. But they are even more hysterical, ponderous, contrived, and grotesque-sounding than anything that has preceded them in the rock and roll field.

In the heart of San Francisco's ghetto area, the Fillmore District, is a dance hall called the Fillmore Auditorium. For years it had supplied Negro R & B bands with one-nighter or weekend stands. We played there many times in the past. In recent years, attendance had fallen off so drastically that the promoter, the late Charles Sullivan, dropped his lease and the place stood dark. It came spectacularly back to life in 1966 when an enterprising young man began promoting psychedelic dances in the ballroom. With fantastic shapes and colors, old-time movies, stroboscopic and ultraviolet effects projected upon the walls, and white rock and roll bands bombarding the youthful, costumed audience with a blasting cacophony of hard rockabilly twangs, East-Indianisms, and pseudo blues, attendance skyrocketed.

The local fuzz, ever uneasy and hostile toward anything they can't understand, began to harass everyone in sight. The fact that these were white kids in the heart of the Negro community was more a factor in the police rousts than the outlandish costumes and the drug overtones. One particular evening, while the police were busy protecting white womanhood by getting the white kids out of the black neighborhood and making the world safe for decent and moral people by harassing and busting the "dope fiends," a well-known and much-respected writer for a large San Francisco daily happened upon the scene. Columnist Ralph Gleason, seeing what was going on, covered the situation in an article. The heat raised up.

Although it was right in their own backyards, Negro youngsters did not react to the psychedelic bag. Except for a ring of young Negro men outside the ballroom, watching the hippie-looking whites arrive, very few attended.

One youthful Negro man, who was obviously a spectator rather than a participant at a way-out psychedelic affair, told me he thought that the main reason Negro kids shunned the action was probably the music.

"Let's face it, while the young whites today use the words 'soul' and 'groovy' a lot, few have a true understanding of the terms. And because of the strong nationalistic feelings being developed among Negroes, we hear this music, which was lifted from us and distorted, as the sound of the enemy."

I mentioned to this young man (he was seventeen years old) that I had noticed a few Negro teen-agers enthusiastically reacting to white rock and roll band on the Sunset Strip. His explanation was that most of these kids would be the upper-middle-class, Baldwin Hills-type Negro youngsters who were conditioned by their parents and had lost their perception for true "soul."

"I mean," he said, "why should Negro kids attach themselves to this bag when they can enjoy James Brown and Ray Charles? Now look at that," he pointed to a lone Negro kid in the crowd of costumed whites. The kid was wearing an outlandish get-up typical of the hippie group. "That's what I call the Wanna Be Syndrome."

"What do you mean, the Wanna Be Syndrome?" I asked.

"I mean he wants to be white so bad he can taste it. He's willing to wear their clothes, talk their talk, and listen to their music. But he's not really welcome among these kids, no matter what they might say about freedom and civil rights. He makes them uncomfortable. After all, he might try to make it with one of the chicks, and that sets up tension. But as long as he performs as a kind of court jester and doesn't strain the situation too much, he can tag along. I am not a member of any groups, either civil rights or nationalist, but I am nationalistic, and I know I must think black if I am to have any chance for survival. I'm young and I might change some of my views some day, but I doubt it."

This chance encounter with such an articulate and nationalistic young man reminded me that while most black youngsters were uninterested in, or unaware or, sociopolitical matters, a growing number were moving in that direction. I saw the same young man again some months later, and we exchanged ideas on the phrase "black power," which had, at the time, been worked over pretty well by the press. He said he felt that black power was an attractive thought, but that because Negroes were so grossly outnumbered by whites, the best way to approach the political power question was to operate within the Democratic or Republican parties.

Now, I used to think that way, too. At least, that's what I thought I thought. What I did was kid myself into believing that real political power could be vested in the Negro community by working through the liberal elements of the Democratic Party to elect Negro representation. What I learned eventually was that Negroes were elected either with party-machine power or white-liberal money. Either way they did not belong to the black people who voted them in and they would not, and *could* not, truly represent the Negro community. What has taken me many years to learn and understand has come early in life to certain young Negroes in America. Stokely Carmichael and the people of SNCC who are advocating black power understand this political fact of life. They are able to qualify and articulate it also, but the American press and the Establishment will not permit this. These have attempted to smear the movement as a racist and negative manifestation, and to a great degree, particularly among white people, they have succeeded. But that won't really stop anything. As the saying goes, "Nothing is as strong as an idea whose time has come," and in the concept of black-based, conceived, and executed political power, we may have exactly that.

In the heart of the SNCC leadership there are the field secretaries and other dedicated souls who stayed in the rural Deep South and continued to work with their enslaved brothers and sisters long after the "summer soldiers" had departed. This unique and profound experience has given these men and women a deep insight into how severely enslaved their brethren are, and what kind of radical approaches are necessary to begin to loosen the chains. They can see also, as even many of us older individuals have come to realize, that in the large urban areas, North and South, where Negroes have gained office and political power under the existing political structures, black people, by and large, are as entrapped as ever.

When Malcolm X spoke, the Negro community perked up and listened. While most were not moved to join the Muslim religious group (the Baptist churches are still full on Sunday mornings), his exhortations, "Respect yourself! Honor your women! Know and be proud of your great history! Glory in your blackness!" did not fall upon deaf ears. "Brother" Malcolm, as he is referred to by many people within the community, whether they be black nationalists or no, kindled a spark of pride and confidence that has flamed in many directions.

In 1962 there was a mass community meeting in Los Angeles' Second Baptist Church to protest the police killings at the local Muslim mosque. It was not Black Muslims who filled the big building to overflowing that afternoon. It was the entire Negro community. Every person of any stature spoke that day, and when they were through the crowd began to chant, "We want Malcolm!"

Malcolm X, who was seated with a small group of his followers, including one paralyzed young victim of the police shooting in a wheelchair, stood and spoke. When he was through, it was not Black Muslims or Black Nationalists who exploded into an emotional frenzy—hugging one another, cheering, tears flowing—it was *all* of us. The people did not become Muslims as a result of that profoundly inspirational experience, but many of us, I'm sure, have never been quite the same either.

Since his assassination, Malcolm X has become a martyr symbol in the ghetto. What he said about not trusting the "man" and his "do it yourself" philosophy is echoing and re-echoing, especially among the young. I am convinced that Malcolm's nationalist movement would eventually have become a strong political organization, had he not been killed.

Just as I could hear the white liberals moaning earlier, I now hear the Negro upper middle class cussing me out. But they think freedom means money, and I'm talking about the human dignity and total future of the great mass of impoverished and dehumanized black people.

The white man, whether he will admit it or not, knows that what I say about his national racism is true. So does the average Negro of the ghetto. But the middle-class Negro cannot bring himself to swallow this bitter pill, because to do this he would have to painfully regurgitate all he has swallowed from the white man about money, industriousness, fair play, patience, morality, education, responsibleness, etc., and the reward all this will bring some happy, but very distant, day. Very distant indeed!

I reject the idea that the complete basis of the racial problem is economic. Surely here in America there is more to it than just that. Now, the thing to keep in mind when examining this idea is not the pitifully few right-thinking whites in the country, but the millions of farmers in the Midwest, the factory workers in the urban areas, the rural southerners, the white people who live in all the small towns between New York and Los Angeles, and from Biloxi, Mississippi, to Fargo, North Dakota, and everywhere else. This is the white man I'm talking about. He is anti-black, prejudiced to the core. The myth of American fair play and morality explodes in the black man's face. It's not all economics. It's deeper-rooted than just that. It goes back centuries. And the way the white man claws and kicks and soft-soaps and deceives the Negro for fear that some black man will get next to his old lady or sister, it will last a long, long time yet.

I do not for a moment discount the tremendous impact capitalist economics has on the situation. The white worker fears the competition of the black man, and while they are at each other's throats, the fat cats upstairs are taking them both to the cleaners. These are the "free enterprise" facts of life in America, and the black man, as usual, gets the worst of it. But again, there is more to American racism than mere economics. To begin to grasp it one must also approach it from a sociological, even an anthropological, standpoint.

In the same sense, American aggression in Vietnam is two-faceted: racial and economic. The reason American troops are killing people in Vietnam—and all that nonsense about "the Vietnamese asked America to protect their freedom" aside—is the American industrialist's lust for the wealth of Southeast Asia. And the reason American forces can proceed against innocent villagers with such mindless inhumanity is because the people are non-white.

Just as the American black man is beginning to develop strong nationalistic attitudes, the Vietnamese have been nationalistic for a long time. To understand the reasons behind Vietnamese nationalism (so strong that it moved even Madame Nhu to declare herself a nationalist!) one must recall certain historical facts. Vietnam has a diverse population of Vietnamese (Northern and Southern), Cambodians, Chinese, Thais, and others. The Bhuddist religion is dominant, though there are many Catholics.

The Japanese occupied the country during World War II, the French held it as a protectorate for eighty years (hence the Catholic influence), and before that the Chinese ruled for a thousand years.

President Roosevelt, at the Yalta Conference, suggested that Indochina (Vietnam was then one of the three associated states) be put under a trusteeship. In the power struggles of the post-war era, with Roosevelt dead, the idea of a trusteeship for Indochina was smothered in a cloud of colonial maneuvers in which France was able to install ex-Emperor Bao Dai as head of state and circumvent national hero Ho Chi Minh and other Communist leaders. Under the banner of anti-Communism, the French were able to regain their colonial grip on the economy of the country.

In the resultant war of liberation, barrels of money and blood were used in a vain attempt to hold Vietnam as a French colony. Between 1950 and 1954, the United States sent $2.6 billion worth of military and economic aid to the French in Vietnam. Why, then, did the French lose the war? In his book, *Mandate for Change,** President Eisenhower sheds some light on the subject:

"The enemy had much popular sympathy, and many civilians aided them by providing both shelter and information. The French still had sufficient forces to win if they could induce the regular Vietnamese soldiers to fight vigorously with them and the populace to support them. But guerilla warfare cannot work two ways; normally only one side can enjoy reliable citizen help."

Senator William Fulbright of Arkansas, a bit of a nationalist (white) himself, manifest in his consistent resistance to civil rights legislation, has stated that he, as a Southerner, can understand why the people of North Vietnam have fought back so tenaciously.

"They've been set upon," the Senator explains.

The black man in America has been set upon, too. Set upon many long years ago by a relentless slave master who, in spite of emancipation proclamations and civil rights acts, refuses to let up. In recent years we have seen the beginning of a militant and demanding attitude growing out of the Negro community, and we have arrived at a crossroads. What has all the effort, the marching, the demonstrating, the rioting, actually been about, or for? Is it, as the middle-class, "responsible" leadership insists, a struggle to integrate? To become part of white society? Or is it, as the young radical nationalists point out, a power struggle with the aim of self-determination as the final goal?

* Eisenhower, Dwight D., *Mandate for Change, 1953–1956.* Garden City, N.Y., Doubleday & Co., Inc., 1963.

Actually, the conservative leadership's goal is easier to define. It is quite simply to "advance" integration. The only thing wrong with it is that it is impossible to put into practice because of the prevailing and pervading white racism in America.

On the other hand, the various groups which reject integration as impractical, impossible, or repugnant, range from absolute separatist programs (the Black Muslims: "Give us our own sovereign territory") to the "black power" concepts of the young Turks of the movement who advocate political and economic control of the ghettos of the North and the rural areas of the South where black folk are forced to live.

The latter have instructed their white followers and supporters to go back to their own communities and work to enlighten their own people to the true facts of the situation. If anyone ever had a difficult task, this is it! But in spite of how much these whites would like to be "where the action is," they can best serve the struggle by working among the bigots who create the problem, and leave the leadership with black people where it belongs. Black people themselves are the only ones qualified and the only ones who can be trusted to do the job.

These radical commitments are not easy to embrace because they rend asunder all the dreams of the past (and present) for a utopian, multiracial nation living in love and harmony. In my secret heart I (and many others, too, I'm sure) long for and dream about brotherhood and love between black and white in America, but as much as I would yearn for it, it is only a dream. A sweet dream, true, but preoccupation with it, because it is unattainable, can only contribute to naïve, costly, and incorrect attitudes and actions that tend to perpetuate the nightmare reality of the American way of life.

Integration, in my opinion, is presently impossible to attain because of white society's almost unanimous opposition. I do not think it is impossible in the distant future, but in view of how whites have performed over the past three hundred years, I feel integration in America in the foreseeable future is highly improbable.

The important thing, then, is to press for the attainable—economic equality. If the existing gap between the races could be closed in the areas of job opportunities, education, housing, and political power, perhaps some day it would be possible to begin to think about an integrated society. But again, white society's refusal to do the right thing by its black fellow Americans throws a monkey wrench into the picture. In view of the traditional attitudes of white America, and now with the hardening process brought on by the riot backlash, I despair when I think of what the chances are of America spending the massive sums of money that would be necessary to even begin to close the economic gap . . . let alone entertain the idea of social integration.

TWENTY

The New Bag

"So, I think they just trying to get back. That's all I can see. They destroys a whole lot. They destroyed property that belonged to my mother . . . but it was in the way . . . it was in the way." — *Man, interiewed during the Watts riots.*

THE RECORDING BUSINESS is a gamble. One may have years of experience and know the contemporary "sounds" and recording techniques, and still not come up with a winner. On the other hand, a green high school dropout might come up with an idea that results in a smash-hit record and a huge cash profit. The seasoned and capable producers, by and large, however, are the ones who maintain the most consistent "batting averages." Through the years these "major leaguers" account for the bulk of the hit records, but lady luck still plays an exasperating role.

An Elvis Presley or a Ray Charles can walk into an A & R man's office, and six months later everybody's making it to the bank. Or a talent scout might spot four amateurs in need of haircuts, and the show world (and the *whole* world) will never be the same!

I remember one afternoon in late 1966. I was working as a record producer at Eldo Records in Hollywood. In walked four guys with guitars. Four of them had on leather jackets and one was wearing a tired little sweater. Four were blond brutes with storm-trooper frowns, and one was a slight little fellow with soulful eyes. The little guy was named David Rosen. He was the lead singer. The violent, electronic jangling of the "Hitler Youth Strings" sounded incongruous against David's soft, sensitive, folk-style vocal, but who was I to say what or who can make it in this crazy business! I watched them as they left.

The four bearded young lions strapped their guitar to their motorcycles and roared off. David walked to Hollywood and Vine and sat on the bench at the corner, apparently waiting for a bus.

I felt for a quick minute that I was watching a kind of socio-fiction horror movie. Hollywood and Vine suddenly became the ancient Colosseum. The growling motorcycles with the tawny manes were hungry lions. If they spot David, I fantasized, they'll consume him on the spot!

The sound of a jazz record playing somewhere down the hall broke the spell and brought me back to reality. It was an alto sax solo that reminded me of Howard Martin, except that Howard had been playing like that twenty years ago. If a leaky gas heater in a dingy Chicago hotel room hadn't done him in prematurely years ago, he might still be around playing his horn and writing music. Howard wore a goatee, which prompted bandleader Lloyd Hunter to nickname him "Oglethorpe." The name stuck. Lloyd explained that Howard's beard reminded him of a picture of a guy named Oglethorpe he had seen in a school book. I don't remember that book, but one of the things I remember best about my school books was not what was in them but what was *not* in them.

For instance, the American black man. He was not in there when I was a kid, and he's *still* not in there. Anyone who doubts this can verify it by talking to some school kids. One of the bitter frustrations facing Negro parents is the struggle to try to fill in the blank spots that are part of a white-supremacist education.

"Who was Frederick Douglass, son?"

"Huh?"

"Ever heard of Nat Turner, Billy?"

"Who?"

'What have you learned about Crispus Attucks in school, Junior?"

"Er . . . what?"

"Who was the first Negro Assemblyman in California, kid?"

"You mean like someone who works at Lockheed or Douglas?"

This is part of the pattern that sets up a deep-rooted inferiority complex. "If history doesn't record any Negro achievements, then evidently we are not much," a black youngster might deduce. If a Negro youngster is convinced by what he is taught (or is *not* taught) at school, that whites did everything worth doing in the world and that Negroes did practically nothing, then self-hate can't be far away.

Learned men have examined and discussed the self-hate complex as it relates to the "white is right" propaganda of a society that foists it upon its people (black and white), from the cradle to the grave. This poison is responsible for the lack of confidence in Negro doctors, lawyers, merchants, and so on. It is the virus of the disease that infects black children (and adults) with anti-Negro color bias. It is not uncommon, even today, for Negro men to shun dark women strictly on the basis of color, and vice versa.

"Hey, Johnny," one of my band members whispered once, "look over on the other side of the stage at the 'Jungle Bunny' that Pete is talking to." I walked around the curtain and there was Pete, and there she stood. If she hadn't blinked I might have mistaken her for a life-sized African sculpture. As black and beautiful as an ebony goddess. But my band member thought of her as a "Jungle Bunny." She was very dark and therefore unattractive to him. He was a victim of the white man's brainwashing, and the girl was a victim of his attitude. And the curiously pathetic part of it was that the musician who was ridiculing the lovely girl because she was dark was a couple of shades darker than she!

It's hard to imagine anything more tragic or brutal than what a racist standard of beauty-excellence-human-worth-propaganda can do to people. It took the dynamic exhortations of Malcolm X to begin to make a dent in this cancer. Still, many continue to downgrade or evaluate on the degree of an individual's "Negroness."

"Take me to your losers," I once heard a foreign visitor remark after watching the Miss Universe finals on television. The real losers, of course, never even made the preliminary eliminations. The arbitrary standard of beauty in America is first of all based upon degrees of whiteness. This is the unwritten rule of thumb that governs American ideas of beauty, and depending upon what section of the country we're talking about, it need not be unwritten.

In the process of selling and reselling the myth that "white is right" and that those who possess fair skin, blond hair, and blue eyes are the most beautiful of all human types, the propagandists for white supremacy attempt to convince not only the white population but all others that this is a natural and aesthetic fact. There is certainly no harm in having an honest preference or opinion on the subject of beauty. One may say, "I think yellow roses are the prettiest," or "black horses are the most attractive to me." One may even say, "I think fair-skinned blonds are the prettiest, or brownskinned Polynesians are the most beautiful." The honest personal appraisal of beauty in people, flowers, paintings is one thing, but this is not *all* that the propagandists mean. We are told in a thousand ways, from the cradle on, that the whitest is not only the rightest aesthetically, but that white is intellecutally and morally superior to boot.

The movie heroes are the fair-haired, all-American image;

the bad guys almost always are darker and therefore more "sinister." In the case of good guys and bad guys in movie and TV stories, the Negro is neither. To portray the black man even as the bad guy would be to give him full human status, which is more than the Establishment is willing to concede. In theory, yes, and in political pronouncements, particularly in times of elections or national crises, yes, but in practice, *no*. And to depict the hero as non-white is unthinkable. You know that if you can't be the bad guy, you damn sure ain't gonna be the hero.

You see an occasional Negro singer, dancer, maid, or butler in the movies and TV, and recently non-whites have been seen occasionally on TV commercials. A few Negro feature actors can be seen from time to time on TV and movies. A Negro actor appears as a secret agent on a popular TV series. He and his white partner go through fantastic and exciting weekly adventures as they go after the enemies of America. But even in this show the Negro co-star comes off as only half a man. He's never going to be *all* there. All there like James Bond, I mean. He'll be all there when it comes to shooting Communists and beating up smugglers and leaping from roof to roof, but he's *not* going to make it with any of the little white sex kittens who are so much a part of the secret-agent plots. His partner will, but *he* won't. Negro heroes are shown as a breed of good guys with plenty of savvy and plenty of heart but with nothing between their legs.

Everybody in the Negro community, every young person and every old battle-scarred veteran of the ghetto, knows that when the black man is shown at all he is carefully castrated. From the "all guts and no nuts" sepia secret agent to the black soldier whose legs become paralyzed because his white buddy called him a nigger in the movie *Home of the Brave,* it's the same . . . he can be brave, patriotic, tragic, comic, pathetic, or servile, but he can't be a sexual man.

The Negro woman, on the other hand, is portrayed occasionally as a desirable female, but this is all right as it does not threaten white masculinity. She is permitted to be sexy, as opposed to the Negro man who must be shown sexless, but she is not projected as the kind of girl one would really love or marry.

The white standard of beauty tends to rule the Western world. This concept is reflected everywhere, including in the Negro press, with its emphasis on light-brown, straight-haired, skin-bleached images, and is prevalent among the Negro upper classes, who still think in terms of "good hair." The subjects of E. Franklin Frazier's book, *The Black Bourgeoisie,*° have swallowed this brainwashing to the point where they strive to emulate the so-called "all-American image" not only in physical appearance, but in speech, manner, attire, point of view, and attitude as well. Trapped in a society that almost always reserves its juiciest material rewards for the fairest-skinned of all, it is no wonder that we find a Negro privileged class striving and straining to make it by out-white-folksing the white folks.

The foreigner who wanted to see the losers of the beauty contest asked, "Where are the American black women and the brown women?" Someone tried to explain to him that if there were indeed any black girls in the contest they didn't get beyond the early culling. A more qualified answer may have been that black girls were categorically disqualified from any natural chance of winning a national beauty contest the day they were born black in a white-supremacist land.

In spite of the American point of view which insists that superiority is wrapped in a white skin, there is strong and persistent evidence that whites are not themselves totally sold on this idea, at least not in the physical sense, and surely not at night. If this is not so, then why the nightly mass-pilgrimage to worship at the warm, sweet shrine of the black ghetto? That which is forbidden in the broad sunlight pulls an army of

° Frazier, E. Franklin, *The Black Bourgeoise.* New York, Free Press, 1957.

whites, in spite of the risk of ostracism and fear of mugging and rolling, into a thousand American Harlems after dark. We must conclude, then, that one *can* tell the difference when the sun goes down.

And when the sun goes down in the ghetto, the white chicks are often found inside the clubs with a Negro fellow with whom they have already struck up a relationship, or are waiting and hoping to be nominated before the festivities cease for the night. The white guys are more apt to be outside as the crowd lets out, lurking in the shadows or milling around the blocks in cars, necks craning, eyeballs bugging, and horns tooting, hoping to make a pick-up. I used to get the impression that the horny guys in the shadows were all waiting for me so they could furtively ask, "Hey, Mac, where can we get some Colored girls?" I wish I had a dollar for every time a hard-up white guy spotted me and figured I was the safest one to ask. When I was a youngster this would frustrate and infuriate me so that I would either blow up in the guy's face or walk away. Finally, I would answer, "I don't know, man. Where can we get some white girls?" This didn't have the desired effect. All it usually got me was a confused, blank stare. I solved the problem by calling my drummer over when I was approached for "Colored girls." Kansas City Bell was his name, and he could not be mistaken for white.

I would repeat the question to Bell, and if the guy was still around, *Bell* would ask him where we could find the white girls. This got it.

The incredible inconsistencies that abound in a racist society are pointed up when one thinks of how, on one hand, "Negroness" or "Negritude" is put down as undesirable, while on the other it is worshiped, emulated, and exploited. American popular music is almost always based on Negro creations. Today, various forms of rock and roll are the rage. All of these rhythm and blues derivatives, like almost all American popular music styles, evolved from the Negro blues-gospel-jazz fountainhead.

The sudden flurry of social-message songs that have become hit records brings up some very provocative questions. Are the masses of American white kids who are buying millions of these records listening to the words? If so, do they have any understanding of the social message? And if they do, will it affect their attitudes, behaviors, and approaches as adults? Is it the teen-rock flavored musical background, the total, overall "sound" that accounts for the present popularity, or do songs like "Eve of Destruction" and "Blowin' in the Wind" hold meaningful food for thought for the present crop of young record buyers?

Are the various American campus revolts indicative of a real social awakening of great masses of American white youth? And are the few young boys and girls who courageously and idealistically lay their lives on the line to travel to the Deep South to help in the Negro struggle in any way typical of the average contemporary white American youth?

The answer is *no*. As against the panty-raiding, goldfish-swallowing college kids of past generations, today's crop looks good. Looks good to the casual eye, that is. One cannot deny that the emergence of even a small number of militant and articulate white youngsters is encouraging. It's better than none, to be sure, but I'm afraid that the truly committed and involved are very few in number.

The rest of them, the overwhelming majority, are just along for the ride, and only part of the ride at that. Most of them are swept along on demonstrations and picket lines without really digging what it's all about, or they go through the motions with the gang but don't really mean it, or they have a ball with the language and costumes of the times and gain a feeling of "belonging" to the "New Thing" by being part of the "New Bag" without any understanding or commitment to it. And now, under the influence of the hippie movement, most of those who were involved in some sort of social action have retreated to a drop-out position of noninvolvement. Barricaded behind a wall of drugs, flowers, Eastern pseudo-mysticisms, and bizarre costumes, the hippies proclaim love for all mankind but are not interested in lifting a finger to straighten out a society they recognize as all wrong. It is estimated that Negro participation in the hippie movement amounts to about one per cent. The paradox here is that white youth seems to want to drop out and black youngsters are striving to get in.

Young singers and songwriters of the present era come complete with costume and hair style. Record stars Bob Dylan, Barry McGuire, and Sonny & Cher come equipped with a whole new "inside look." Their records become popular, they are seen and heard on television today, as against yesterday's stars who were heard on radio only. Their hairdos and costumes are as much a part of their performance image as the songs they sing or their musical accompaniment. Fans begin to gather. Soon an army forms, and the army is strictly in uniform. The only trouble is, most of the troops know only the melodies to the marching songs, not their meanings.

From Joan Baez, whose delicate beauty is reflected in her wistful performance, to Sonny Bono, image impressions are created. Thousands of young girls, whether it fits their facial contours or not, wear their hair pressed long and stringy. Boys sport beards or Beatle mops or boots or Liverpool caps or whatever. But the "whatever," you can bet, must be part of the "New Bag." So, it is not at all unlikely today to see a line of demonstrators protesting against conformity, and all the pickets are wearing beards, boots, stringy long hair, and bell-bottomed trousers.

I'm not so sure most of them are protesting at all. Granted, there is a nucleus of sociopolitically motivated students, who, by their zeal and dedication have attracted the attention and captured the fancy of large followings. But, again, I suspect that the followers are simply enjoying the costumes and the togetherness, not to mention the kicks involved in shaking up the adults.

It will be interesting (and probably painful) to watch what

will happen to this mass of "progressive-minded social-reform-ers" when the Establishment closes in on them as they reach adulthood. I wonder how recognizable many of today's idealistic young civil rights champions will be a few years from now when the combined forces of big business, organized religion, and their neighbors and relatives have had a chance to flog them back into line.

TWENTY-ONE

Your Mama!

"People couldn't even walk up and down the street, not unless the police stop 'em and ask 'em where they going, or take 'em to jail because they thought they did something. Not that they could prove it, but they just take 'em in to be taking 'em in." — *Young boy, interviewed during the Watts riots.*

A FEW YEARS BACK some members of a college rooting section built a giant papier-mâché finger. They smuggled it into the football stadium piece by piece the day of the game, reassembled it in the stands, and at the opportune psychological moment, held it high in the air facing the enemy across the field. Americans in general, when rubbed the wrong way, and at times even playfully, tend to give each other the finger. The average Negro is more apt to talk about your mama. This mother-insult pattern, in addition to being a severe affront, can, under certain circumstances, take on the characteristics of a frivolously rude poetry game. It is called "paying the dozens." Back in the thirties there was even a recorded song entitled "The Dirty Dozens," in which talking about somebody's mama was refined into a rhythmic blues melody:

> ". . . *You're a liar and a cheater, and a dirty
> mistreater . . .*
> *And your mama don't wear no drawers!"*

If this is the first you've heard of "the dozens," chances are that whether you are black or white, you have been "slipped in 'em" at one time or another. And it is also possible that you earned the whispered "MF" or the subtle reference to your sister, even though you don't feel that you deserved it. I should point out that your mama is not the only one who can be verbally compromised if you are "slipped in the dozens." In addition to the classic Motherfucker, which is a by-word both in and out of the ghetto and has the most opprobrious implications, there are other lesser-known and less shopworn phrases which, when employed by a skillful dozens player, can involve any member of your family. They include, Granny Dodger, Uncle Jumper, Sister Snatcher, Father Tricker, and a milder version of the granddaddy of them all, Mother Grabber.

An average person in the mainstream of white society will use the words "goddammit" or "son-of-a-bitch" in a burst of profanity, while Negroes tend to use "motherfucker." It is just as improper and vulger to use MF in Negro circles as it is to use SOB in white, but more and more, particularly in sports, show business, and other "hip" environments, whites are beginning to make use of MF. Maybe it's because, as the late John Mason once pointed out, "It has more rhythm to it."

Sports Illustrated magazine commented on this social phenomenon in a lengthy article which examined the effects Negro and white athletes have upon one another. Whites have always copied Negro music, dancing, and humor, and now it seems there is even something highly contagious and captivating about the profanity. *Sports Illustrated* explained that certain white ball players, in emulating their brownskinned teammates, had picked up a unique insult that had "maternal incestuous" meaning. The phrase had become so much a part of one white ball player's vocabulary that he got carried away and applied it to an umpire. He was tossed out of the game.

If it were legal to copyright a colloquial phrase (even a vulgar one), and if it were possible to log and collect payment for its use, then MF would surely be one of the top money-makers of all time. I would like to have the royalties accrued on the number of times the phrase was used in Watts alone to describe the white police, landlords, bill collectors, summons-servers, merchants, and politicians.

But the *biggest* "motherfucker" anyone has ever been called in history was the one the Negro rioters called "Whitey" in mid-August, 1965, in Watts. And the final tally reflects it. There were more than 30 dead, 700 injured, thousands arrested and jailed, $624,511 in city payroll overtime, approximately 1,000 fires, and $200 million in property damage.

Anyone who doesn't see the deep racial overtones in the Watts uprising is kidding himself or trying to kid others.

More than 1,000 Negroes migrate to Los Angeles each month. Most of them, because of racial discrimination in jobs, apprenticeship programs, labor unions, or housing, wind up unemployed in the Watts area. Watts has the highest population density in the nation.

There's something deadly about being ignored. It's more devastating than overt rejection. The Negro has long been the "invisible man" in America, as Ralph Ellison so aptly described the situation in his book. The disadvantaged Negro of Watts had become less than an invisible man; he had become less than part of an amorphous mass. He was ignored, unnoticed; he had ceased to exist. The *San Francisco Chronicle* observed that all this had led to Watts being "a little like a pressure cooker." Unfortunately, however, the local Los Angeles press failed to view Watts as even a tiny, lukewarm saucepan.

Anyone who lives in the Los Angeles "ghetto" area knows that police brutality in its various forms does exist. We also know that it was not the main cause of the holocaust. It was an ever-present ingredient that helped trigger the disorders. We are also aware that when the temperature hits ninety plus, people are likely to be more irritable than usual. The excessive heat during the week of rioting has been advanced as the cause. This is nonsense, too. The heat contributed to the explosion but it didn't cause it. It was the same 92 degrees in Bel Aire and Beverly Hills. It is simply that one segment of our population was so utterly oppressed, forgotten, and ignored that it spontaneously blew up.

The civil rights movement in Los Angeles, with its well-intentioned (and well-fed) Westside leadership, has never been able to involve the real victims of American racism in its programs. You can't spend nonviolent protests, and many of the people of Watts were, and are, broke. You can't eat orderly picketing demonstrations, and many of the residents' children go to bed hungry at night.

The elected representatives, black and white, had failed to provide meaningful legislative and community programs that would offer some hope of relief. Feeling was running so high against politicians during the disorders that a couple of the elected officials had to hole up behind police protection.

A man who has been completely oppressed in the past, is being economically strangled in the present, and who has no hope for the future, has nothing to lose by going berserk. The riots started as a small chain of accidental incidents, but they were related in the sense that the people of the area were primed for the explosion. They were primed not by any pre-planned, organized, sinister, and subversive foreign force, as was suggested by certain officials, but by degrading and cruel conditions imposed by a callous white supremacist's Establishments.

The people who participated in the rioting and looting did not necessarily have age, sex, IQ level, or education in common, but they did have *something* in common: they were all victims, in one way or another, of the white man's inhumanity to the black man. They all felt abandoned, isolated, abused, insulted, hurt, outraged. Though pent-up, these emotions were felt daily and deeply. Here was a chance to get in a lick of protest, to draw attention to their dilemma, to act out their rage and outrage, to dramatically call the uncaring and cruel white man a big MF publicly. Some people set fires but did not loot; some looted but did not throw rocks. Some shot, some shouted encouragement, some just watched; some were in Watts, some in the Central Avenue area, a few on the Westside. But no matter where and under what circumstances, *all* were related to one another by a common history of oppression and a united feeling of rage.

Occasionally, a member of the Negro community will testify publicly that he or she has never personally experienced racial discrimination. I've tried to imagine a Negro living in America and never having had a brush with the color line. It seems to me that you would almost have to have lived in a vacuum, or not have lived at all, to honestly make this claim. I find it impossible to believe that a Negro can live in America and claim he has never been discriminated against.

If discrimination exists, it applies to all of the members of the group at which it is aimed. Therefore, if you are black and discrimination is practiced against black people, you have been victimized, whether you recall a specific personal incident or not.

It need not be a case of denial of job opportunity or segregated schooling. It might be an experience with finding a place to stay, like the time at the motel at Lake Isabella.

IT WAS MY second trip to Lake Isabella. Sonny Love and I had caught some nice catfish here just two weeks earlier. This time I had the camper plus the whole family with me. Jackie Gober was along. So were our close friends Bardu and Tila, who had rented a house trailer for the three days at the lake. The family and I (Janice, Laura, Shuggie, Phyllis, and four-month-old Nickey) were all going to stay in the same little motel where

Sonny and I had stayed recently. It was right on the lake. Jackie was going to sleep in the camper. We were all set, and it promised to be a groovy three days.

"Hold it there, Jackie, while I go in and rent the rooms. Then after we unload you can take the camper and follow Bardu to the camping ground."

As I walked around the corner of the building to the motel office, I could see the same little woman who had rented Sonny and me a room two weeks ago. She remembered, and after a few pleasantries I paid her for three days, and she gave me a receipt.

While we were unloading, I noticed that she had been joined by her twin sister, and they were watching us from the office doorway. I didn't pay any mind because I was used to whites staring. They don't always mean anything by it. Sometimes they are just curious, particularly in out-of-the-way places where they see few dark skins.

I got Phyllis and the kids into the rooms and then climbed back into the camper cab to have a last word with Jackie before he left. Up came the woman with a look in her eye and a tightness around her mouth that always rings a little bell in my mind. But *no*, not here. After all, I thought, this is California.

"I'm sorry, I'll have to ask you to vacate the rooms. You lied to me in the office," she said.

"What do you mean, lady, I lied to you?" I asked.

"You said it was for six. Now you're bringing in seven, and I'm giving you your money back, and I want the rooms vacant at once!"

Was it possible, I asked myself, that this was all there was to it? That she thought I had tried to ring a seventh person into the deal? If so, I could take care of it by explaining that I wasn't welshing on her.

"No, I didn't lie to you. There are only six people in my family. Five and a half really, counting the baby. This man is not staying. In fact, he was about to drive over to the camping grounds. He is staying in the camper."

"Well, I'm sorry, but you'll have to vacate the rooms. That way there's no misunderstanding, no trouble."

Oh, oh! What had I done to deserve this mess? And if fate owed me a kick, Phyllis and the kids didn't deserve it. The first vacation in years! They had *waited* for this weekend, *counted* on it. The twin sister had walked up behind the first lady now. Her mouth was even tighter, and that peckerwood look was blazing away in her eyes. My impulse was to call them both a sack of honky bitches and check out and leave, but I thought to myself, hell, I'm not going to let them spoil our long-awaited vacation. I'm gonna be cool . . . cool.

"Listen, lady, I know exactly what this is all about. You feel frustrated because you didn't know you were renting to Negroes. Well, better luck next time, but I'll tell you something. I'm NOT going to move out. So forget it."

She finally got off my back, but it threw a sour note into the vacation.

An old man, a local trout "expert," around Reno, Nevada, once told me in all seriousness that you had to be "at peace" to catch fish successfully. "If you're upset they feel it in the water. It goes down the line and they won't bite." Maybe he was right. I didn't catch one fish during the whole three days.

TWENTY-TWO

Poverty and Politics

"I haven't been working since March fifteenth, 'cause all the places I went to they tell me, you know, you see the ads in the paper and they say they train. . . . I go down there and they say they don't have enough men to start training and they have to have experienced men and stuff like that. Well, there's a guy that I went to school with, he didn't have as much experience as I did, and he got the job. So, I didn't say anything about that, I just go on to other places and the same thing happens. And from March to now, it's a pretty long time to go without working."
—*Young man, interviewed during the Watts riots.*

IN 1964, THE YEAR BEFORE the Watts blow-up, the President's Council of Economic Advisors wrote:

"Poor parents cannot give their children the opportunities for better health and education needed to improve their lot. Lack of motivation, hope and incentive is a more subtle but no less powerful barrier than the lack of financial means."

Thus, long before the riots occurred there was evidence that the powers that be, at least those in Washington, were aware of the harsh consequences of economic oppression. "Poverty breeds poverty" the report advised. What they didn't know or failed to mention, however, was that poverty could also breed revolt, bloodshed, and destruction.

"A poor individual or family has a high probability of staying poor," the President's advisors went on. "Low incomes carry with them the high risks of illness, limitations on mobility and limited access to education, information and training."

If they were to write this type of report today, they would, in all likelihood, be obliged to include the high risk of human explosion. At any rate, like many other reports, both before and after the riots, it may have lacked in definitive fulfillment, but it served as an instrument of persuasion, and it helped convince Congress to appropriate $800 million to launch a new form of attack on poverty.

On November 23, 1964, not quite two months after the appropriation, the Los Angeles Youth Opportunities Board was granted $2,729,683 in Federal funds to implement a series of community action programs. The Youth Opportunities Board, a joint governmental agency of city, county, and state governments and city and county schools, had been formed in 1962 to coordinate youth programs on Federal funds. It received an additional $1.9 million on December 16, 1964 to finance a Neighborhood Youth Corps for six months.

The highly touted and anxiously awaited War on Poverty had begun in Los Angeles, and the area waited to see and feel the beneficial results. It wasn't long, though, before the local politicians bogged the program down with their bickering. Rumblings were heard and accusations of patronage, boondoggling, misappropriations of funds, exorbitant salaries, and exclusion of minority-area representatives in the administration of the programs began to fly through the already smog-thickened air. Harlem's Adam Clayton Powell, then Chairman of the House Labor and Education Committee, holding hearings into the national poverty program charged the program was ". . . marked by wildly unrealistic salaries for those directing it, by excessive planning and little action and by giant fiestas of political patronage."

Matters were further complicated when the proposal to merge the Youth Opportunities Board with the Economic Opportunities Federation was opposed by City Hall. This prolonged the struggle for control of the local antipoverty funds and programs.

New projects and proposals were screened and approved but money was held up in Washington, pending the outcome of the political hassle.

Finally, after listening to arguments and wrangling from both sides, Sargent Shriver's national poverty office in Washington issued an edict to the opposing agencies to merge or neither would be recognized as the screening agency for handling the community action programs.

In January, 1965, both boards voted to merge, and in February they agreed to accept a draft of a document that would bind them together as the Economic and Youth Opportunities Agency. All that remained now was the ratification by the five parent government bodies. But a verbal blast from the Mayor's office set off the haggling all over again, and so it went while activists in the Negro and Mexican-American communities became more bitterly vocal, and disenchantment with the poverty program began to filter down to the waiting, proposed beneficiaries.

To suggest that the political squabbling that bogged down the LA poverty program was the one cause of the Watts riots would be a mistake, but to say that it had no contributory impact would be even further off the beam.

In talking to people involved in the administration of the various poverty programs, one gets the impression that even without the big Los Angeles political hang-up, there were already seeds of bitter discontent. These flowed from the actual limitations of the poverty program itself against the all-encompassing panacea that so many of the poor believed it to be.

To the average citizen, and certainly to the very poor, the OEO, YOB, CAP, EOF, NAPP, NYC, EYOF, etc., are confusing and meaningless garble. What *had* made a strong impression, however, was the publicity surrounding the Great Society's plans for the poor—plans that evoked bright visions for the future among some of the utterly deprived. Among those, that is, who had not lost all confidence in the future in a white man's land.

The fact that the actual amount of money available to conduct the war against poverty was just a drop in the bucket, considering what it would take to make a meaningful dent, was understandably lost upon the multitudes who took literally the lofty political pronouncements and promises.

An old man, calling out from the audience of a recent meeting, startled the speaker who had come to Watts to explain the workings of the various agencies of the poverty program.

"We don't know nothin' about YOB, RON, DON, and nap and cap and crap. Where's the money? And where's the good of it? I don't see nothin' at all bein' done for the poor people!"

Los Angeles County Economic and Youth Opportunities Agency Director Joe P. Maldanado considers the goals of the poverty program to be: "To provide local communities and neighborhoods with resources so that they can implement programs that will provide poor people with the opportunities to improve economically and educationally."

But he is quick to add, "We must dispel the impression that there are unlimited dollars available, and that all one has to do to receive funds is to ask for them."

But dispelling such an impression is easier said than done. All the people know is that the Great White Father in Washington has promised that a great new day is coming, and they want to know what's holding it up.

"For one reason or another," the McCone Commission Report says, "the records of the ethnic mix of the membership of many unions have not been furnished despite our repeated requests."

If this development is a mystery to the McCone Commission, it is part of a very old and well-known story to Negroes in the Los Angeles labor movement. To supply ethnic breakdown lists would be to reveal their dirty linen publicly, and this the lily-white and near lily-white unions will not do if they can possibly help it.

While there is general agreement that joblessness was the major cause of the riots, and that jobs must be made available to the people of the depressed areas of the city, too little attention has been focused on the unfair practices of many racially-segregated unions.

The prolonged struggle waged by local Negro labor leaders to fully integrate Los Angeles unions has brought some gains, but there remain vast, murky areas of fraudulent and tricky racial preemption.

Among some of the worst offenders are the building-trades unions. Conspiratory hiring-hall procedures, loaded aptitude tests, and labor-management "sweetheart" agreements are some of the methods used to keep the black man out of competition for thousands of well-paying jobs. In many cases it is just plain refusal to admit Negroes to union membership.

Attempts to break down discrimination in lily-white locals often get bogged down in the sly, bouncing-ball game, a game that has been sharpened to a fine art through years of chicanery. Management blames labor, and labor blames management, and in the back-and-forth sham, frustration and white supremacy triumph. In this game, management and labor publicly and piously display fair-employment-practices policy statements, but behind the scenes they practice collusion and blame the situation (when they are forced to admit that a situation exists at all) upon one another. The lily-white workers, once again protected from fair and open competition with black men and women, maintain their traditional posture of cupidity. Meanwhile, the Negro labor leaders are once again worn out by battle fatigue or are mired down in litigations that slowly go nowhere.

Seven years ago, a fully qualified sheet-metal worker with years of experience and letters of recommendation from another state, began a long, painful, and, to date, unsuccessful campaign to join the union of his trade.

"With my background," he stated, "I would have had no great difficulty becoming a union member and eventually finding gainful employment in my field—if I were a white man."

He came to Los Angeles, like so many others, hoping to find a better life, and ran into the dead-end of a racially-segregated local.

"They're not going to discriminate against you openly," he explained, "but you'll just die waiting to get in."

Those who manage to get in sometimes "just die" waiting to get out of the hiring hall and into a job.

It is not only the individuals and organizations on the liberal side of the ledger who take note of the discrimination in certain labor unions. The late conservative Senator Robert Taft once observed that putting an end to discrimination against the Negro in the nation's labor unions would be one of the most important answers to racial imbalance.

The foes of organized labor often pounce upon this sordid state of affairs to embarrass and discredit the labor movement.

Barry Goldwater, in a syndicated column, observed: "This double standard (discrimination in labor unions) is still in operation. It was fully evident at the recent AFL-CIO convention in San Francisco, despite the pious-sounding resolutions and speeches on equal opportunity for Negroes. One newsman counted the Negro convention delegates and found only twenty out of a total union representation of 922, and most of the twenty were from New York City."

This is a strange statement to come from the man who inspired the most segregated Republican Convention of modern times, which also took place in San Francisco. But it only serves to point up the mileage that can be gained by the enemies of labor while labor continues to operate with dirty hands.

TWENTY-THREE

Go North, Young Man

"There go my people . . . I must catch them, for I am their leader."
                                                    —*Mahatma Gandhi.*

TEEN-AGERS throughout America view California as the glamour spot for youth. It's not all myth, either. It is the land of surfing, skiing, hot-rodding, motorcycling, rocking and rolling, and Hollywood. Certain industries favor California because the climate gives them increased production. Farmers and ranchers enjoy a year-round crop advantage. Religious cults find fertile fields here, so do way-out political kooks.

Southern California is the unchallenged center of extremist organizations. John Bircher and neo-Fascist raw material (human) flows into the area in a steady stream, and Bircher and neo-Fascist material (printed) flows out by the ton. Individuals with way-out, right-wing ideas are everywhere in America, but in Southern California they find each other, form into groups, organize chapters, and swing. Any nut who hates Negroes or Jews or the Supreme Court can pick up followers if certain ground rules are observed. Everything must be done in the name of anti-Communism, the order of the day is hocus-pocus rationale coupled with ultra-emotional, pseudo-scientific, "inside information," and the whole package is wrapped up in the American flag. Some of these professional bigots are making millions.

For Negroes wishing to escape the indignities of the South, Los Angeles has had great allure. The promise of "sunny," "free," "cosmopolitan" Los Angeles has brought thousands of southern immigrants into the LA ghetto in the span of a few short years. In our travels throughout the South I can't remember a city where people didn't ask us wistful questions about Los Angeles.

For most Negroes, however, the bubble bursts once they arrive. The "promised land" becomes a bitter trap. Los Angeles can be far more disillusioning than Chicago or New York. Much has been written and reported on the roaches, rats, and cops that plague the black population in Harlem and the South Side of Chicago, but the misery of Watts was relatively unknown. Until the lid blew off, many thought of Los Angeles as a "nice" place for Colored to live.

Some of the prime offenders in building the myth of "democratic Los Angeles" have been certain Negroes themselves—middle-class Westsiders and hilltop members of the local "Black Bourgeoisie." Far removed both geographically and emotionally from the heartache of Watts and the southeastern end of the ghetto, the Negro "haves" generally thought of the "have nots" as indolent and unwilling to hustle in order to make it—that is, if they thought of them at all. Big spreads in the Negro magazines and newspapers showing the LA silk-stocking set living it up with champagne sips and swimming pool dips and Beverly Hilton extravaganzas painted a picture of paradise in Los Angeles for Negroes.

But while the privileged few party, a vast legion of black souls in the city wonder where they can find a decent house to live in, or when they will find a job, or what, if anything, the kids are going to eat tonight. Another great mass of residents within the heart of the ghetto are beyond even this. They have lost all hope. The long trek from Alabama, Mississippi, Arkansas, and other southern states has ended in shattered dreams. The past has been a desperate struggle. They have now lost confidence in the present, and there is no faith in the future.

On Friday morning during the riots I was in a store on the Westside. I overheard a young Negro society matron complain to a friend, "Isn't this a pain, girl? We had to cancel our affair because of those niggers in Watts!"

"They oughta send them all back to Mississippi where they came from!" her lady friend answered.

"I'm glad they live way out there in Watts!" the first one concluded.

What the outraged young socialites couldn't know at the time was that the store would be reduced to ashes during that very night.

The feeling was not all directed against "Whitey." At the height of the frenzy, Negro State Senator Mervyn Dymally (then an Assemblyman) urged a young rock-thrower to "cool it."

"Whose side you on, man?" the youth asked.

"I'm with you . . . the people," Dymally answered.

The kid handed Merv a rock. "Then throw!"

DURING World War II and the early postwar years, there seemed to be great hope in America for all who yearned for equality and democracy. In Los Angeles we saw a massive influx of Negro people. Thousands upon thousands of hopeful individuals came to California to reap the harvest of opportunities the war had created. Here was the glittering promise of jobs and the chance to live in those lovely Southern California neighborhoods, to bask in the sunshine of the legendary, cosmopolitan "land of freedom," freed from the oppressive way of life which had been their bitter lot back home. And perhaps most compelling of all, a chance to give their children a full and integrated education, and to give their kids that which they had never enjoyed in the South: an equal shot toward fulfilling their potential and a brimming measure of human dignity.

Hopes and aspirations ran high in those days. Truman had integrated the armed forces. Many Negro men had learned valuable skills while in service. Many others were learning trades and professions and going to college under the G.I. Bill. The defense plants had trained many Negro men and women for jobs that previously had been denied them. Many times I heard the observation that the Germans and Japanese had freed the American Negro.

It looked good for a while, but gradually the shiny illusion faded. It became increasingly apparent, as we moved into the fifties, that the people of the exodus had traded the degrading paternalism and tyranny of the South for the icy heartlessness of the Los Angeles urban metropolis.

The Negro population of the Los Angeles area rose from 75,000 in 1940 to nearly 600,000 in 1967. Today there are many Negro neighborhoods with lovely homes and impressive surroundings. There is one particular Los Angeles hillside area that rivals the finest neighborhoods in Beverly Hills. While it is true that many Negroes live in style in Los Angeles, the overwhelming majority do *not*. In fact, most live in sub-standard circumstances and an appalling number live in abject poverty. But in spite of the bitter disillusionments and the deplorable conditions in the ghetto, people still pour into Los Angeles, seeking the promised land that exists only for a privileged few.

Integrated housing has never actually existed in recent times in Los Angeles. A neighborhood may become integrated briefly, but it stays that way only as long as it takes the white residents to get out; then it becomes a part of the main body of the ghetto. The periphery inches out at a snail's pace and the ghetto gradually expands, but integrated housing remains an idealistic theory.

To the casual observer, Negroes in Los Angeles appear to have attained a relatively comfortable middle-class position. In reality, though, there are two separate and distinct groups living within the Los Angeles Negro ghetto. In recent years they have been distinguished from one another in various ways: the black bourgeoisie and the black masses, the middle class and the working class. In the latter classification, it is interesting to note that the strongest identifying feature of the middle class is the fact that it is working, and a distinguishing mark of the so-called working class is the massive unemployment that plagues it.

Above the middle class and appearing to form yet a third distinct group is the self-appointed aristocracy of the Negro community, sometimes referred to as the "silk-stocking set." These people, the "cream" of the black bourgeoisie, exert every effort to create an illusion of majestic preeminence. They are aided in this attempt by the local and national Negro press with its concentrated campaigns of glorification: photographs, features, and social columns. This perpetual preoccupation with the upper crust's conspicuous consumption, grossly exaggerated reports of affluence and influence, titles and degrees, lofty civic and social achievements, and extravagant cotillion balls and functions, fails to raise them more than a cut above the middle class because of the dogged persistence of the color-based American caste system and the virtual absence of an authentic and powerful Negro capitalist class.

It is not at all uncommon for the silk-stocking set to find that their neighbors are doctors, pool-hall owners, preachers, pimps, school teachers, bookies, lawyers, or ex-numbers racketeers.

This peculiar ghetto housing democracy doesn't make matters any easier for those who are trying almost hysterically to prove to the white world that they are exceptionally excellent culturally and high on the hog financially.

The Negro middle class in the Los Angeles area, while it is quite large, creates the impression of being a much greater part of the overall black population than it actually is. The disadvantaged folk who make up the black masses of the working class far outnumber them.

Beyond the economic factors that qualify members of the ghetto for middle-class status are the social attitudes that tend to bind them together as a class. The dominant characteristic is their common rejection of the social heritage of the Negro people and their straining to find status symbols to compensate for their deep inferiority complex and to gain acceptance in the white world, a world that compounds their neurosis by keeping the door slammed shut.

The social strainers of the Negro middle class would feel it beneath their station and dignity to hire a Negro "folk" orchestra, secure a hall in the ghetto, and have an ethnic good time. They think nothing of renting the grand ballrooms in the biggest white hotels, where they are viewed with amusement and contempt and soaked thousands of dollars for extravagant facilities, so that they may put on their glitteringly ostentatious, and often ludicrous, displays of social "arrival."

A Negro waiter overheard the manager of a plush Los Angeles hotel say that he felt he could sell tickets to the white spectators who line the lobbies to view the procession of society Negroes arriving at their functions in full-dress, mink-and-jewel finery. He referred to this new pastime, in which the whites delighted so, as "nigger watching."

The polarization of the two groups within the Negro community is almost as severe as that which exists between the overall white and black communities. The isolation of the Negro "haves" and "have nots" from one another is established and perpetuated as much by the upper class's rejection of the "folk" and its striving to "live white" and be accepted by the majority, as it is by the economic conditions that preempt the black masses.

The contempt that upper-class Negroes feel for their disadvantaged cousins is more than matched by the black masses' heartfelt disdain for the "phonies" on the hill. The distance be-

tween the "haves" and "have nots" can be measured by the rioters' reaction to the middle-class "leaders" who tried to cool them
down during the Watts uprising. There were no leaders who
wielded influence over the people in the streets. Local figure-
heads were ignored and even threatened. Martin Luther King
met with stony silence and a few catcalls and jeers, and Dick
Gregory came away with a bullet wound in his leg in answer to
his plea for peace.

The middle-class-oriented leadership, which has been guid-
ing the civil rights movement for the past ten years, got a rude
awakening from the people they thought they were leading, the
people in whose behalf they were supposed to have been marching, picketing, and demonstrating.

Since the riots, a myriad middle-class-led groups have
emerged and struck off in many directions. A number of these
are tied to the revival of interest in "Negro business." Once
again, as has happened periodically since the formation of
Booker T. Washington's National Negro Business League in
1900, great emphasis is being placed upon the theory of Negro
business as the salvation of the race. And again, as in the past,
the promulgators of this alleged cure-all are usually members of
the upper echelon of the black bourgeoisie. That Negro business
supplies jobs to some Negroes is a foregone conclusion. But to
project and promote the idea that Negro business is the basic
answer to the black man's problem in America is as colossal a
fallacy (if not a bare-faced lie), as the Booker T. Washington
nonsense notion that a "separate-as-fingers-in-a-glove-and-menial-
labor-way-of-life" for Negroes would make everything all right.

It is sheer nonsense to suggest to a people who are short-
changed in education, job opportunities, health care, housing,
and who are devoid of a true capitalist class, that Negro-owned
business is the key to equality and justice.

Most of the titled and privileged individuals who are using
the emotion of the day to promote their Negro-business panacea

schemes are not concerned with the appalling plight of the trapped black masses. They are interested (whether they admit it even to themselves or not) in the perpetuation of the Jim Crow institution, which gives them a monopoly on a ghettoized, captive audience and enables them to profit from these thousands as patients, clients, and customers. In the meantime, most of these middle-class professionals take their profits, just as surely as the white opportunists do, out of the poor community, usually to the Westside hills where they live in relative splendor with their wives and families who wouldn't be caught dead among the black masses who make it possible for them.

The members of the black bourgeoisie who maintain offices or businesses in the poor black belt and live in the privileged hills, generally hold "key" memberships in the larger Baptist churches in the heart of the impoverished ghetto. This gives them a favorable image among the people that is good for business. It has nothing to do with their spiritual persuasion, however, because when public relations does not dictate periodic visits to and technical membership in the churches of the folk, they are to be found in the more staid and conservative Methodist, Presbyterian, and Catholic environments. Many maintain a standing in the ghetto Baptist churches for business expediency, while their wives and children attend Methodist services across town for purposes of social status.

A local, white-owned Negro-audience-oriented radio station regularly programs a "Negro progress" feature which exalts the achievements of Negroes who have made "outstanding contributions to this country's greatness" in the fields of politics, medicine, music, and sports. Market survey experts tell us that most upper-class Negroes who listen to the radio tend to favor general-market radio or jazz-format FM station programming. We can assume, therefore, that the "inspiring" Negro progress messages fall, for the most part, upon the ears of members of the Negro working class, who are tuned in because the station plays the rhythm and blues and gospel music of the folk. The Negro progress reports are fraught with the kind of symbolic compensation that soothes the inferiority complexes of the bourgeoisie class; but since we are informed that they are not listening, one cannot help but wonder what kind of reaction this all-American, Horatio Alger propaganda elicits in the minds of the listening members of the black masses, so many of whom are living in hopeless and abject misery.

TWENTY-FOUR

The Great White Father

"Nowadays, everybody knows that if a cop catch you on the street, you don't have to be doing nothing to get knocked up-side the head; and down in Watts, they beat you up for nothing." — *Man, interviewed during the Watts riots.*

As I WRITE at this point in time, August 20, 1966, I can't help noticing the distinguishing character that separates white street mobs from black. By the time this book is published, I realize that the distinctions I shall attempt to describe may have undergone kaleidoscopic transformations, but this is how it seems to shape up now.

The sharp difference is that Negro mobs seem to possess a group will which, though directed generally against "Whitey," is acted out specifically against inanimate *things*: cars, stores, windows. The white mob, on the other hand, is possessed of a murderous character bent on personal attack.

There is no doubt that there have been individual members of Negro mobs whose goal was to kill whites, just as there have been individuals in the white mobs who were not out for blood. But, basically, the black mob has been expressing its rage by attacking the symbols of ghetto misery and oppression, while the white mobs, their hatred fanned to white heat at the sight of civil rights marchers invading their pure white citadels, and urged on by their Nazi and Ku Klux Klan comrades-in-arms, have spat out verbal poison and erupted into murderous violence against people.

The civil rights marchers, including the sprinkling of whites who usually participate, are not, as many of them think, hastening the day of integration. What they do—and it is a valuable contribution to the overall struggle—is dramatize the black man's plight in America and, perhaps even more significantly, cause the white man to reveal his basic gut attitude as far as integration is concerned.

The Negro middle-class leaders have succeeded in mounting a passive-resistance movement which has served to focus attention upon the cancer of American racism and has tended to get the ball rolling, but in the process, they have been guilty of perpetuating the false dream of American integration and brotherhood. This cruel hoax sets back the black man's struggle for human rights because it causes so many Negroes (and the handful of sincerely dedicated whites) to attempt to operate under the delusions and unrealities of a colossal myth. When I say "sincerely dedicated whites," I mean the few white people, here and there in America, who feel strong human compassion for their enslaved black brother and are prepared to do what they can to help free him. I don't mean the "Great White Fathers" and the "African Queen" types who feel paternalistically compelled to "lead" or "advise" black folk.

I decided to run for the Assembly from the Los Angeles 55th Assembly District, in the June, 1966, primary. I had half convinced myself that if elected I could work for meaningful legislative programs that would relieve the misery of the ghetto: bills to relieve unemployment, to build low-cost housing, etc. That was all right as far as it went, but what I wasn't keeping in mind was that *working for* and *accomplishing* are two different things. The fact still remained that the white men who controlled the Democratic and Republican parties shared the same attitudes toward black Americans. So, you either programmed abjectly with the party leadership and were rewarded with authorship of watered-down civil rights bills, or you tried for the real McCoy and were slapped down. But in spite of all the hard evidence to the contrary, I thought that maybe now, after the riots, an elected official from the ghetto could get something done.

I had run for office previously in 1960, and although I lost I remained politically active. In time I was elected to the County Central Committee and was eventually appointed Chairman of the Speaker's Bureau for the Los Angeles County Democratic Party.

The campaign started just after I had begun writing this book. I would campaign in the evening and return around midnight to work on the book. I would ask myself: What am I doing asking people to vote for me and promising them things I am going to do when I'm elected, and then going home and disputing the whole myth in my book? I was living a contradiction. I began having severe headaches. They would usually start at about seven in the evening, just before I would leave for a coffee klatch or meeting, and would last until one or two in the morning, making it impossible for me to work on the book. I would try not to tell the damn lies that politicians often tell in their zeal to gain votes. But the whole thing was a lie and I knew it.

One night, during the question-and-answer period following my pitch, a young black man asked me, "Do you really believe that the Negro community can ever make meaningful progress under the white man's Democratic or Republican parties as they function today?"

I thought about it for a moment. *As they function today,* the young guy had said. I hemmed and hawed for a moment. My head began to throb painfully. Finally I answered, "No."

"Then what are you doing?" he asked.

"That's a good question," I said.

It was a good question because as long as the vast majority of the members of the State Legislature viewed the black man's problems with indifference or hostility, there was really nothing that one or two ghetto representatives could actually accomplish. A shocking example of this same kind of indifference was the almost frivolous fashion in which some members of Congress helped defeat the rat-control bill during the 1967 session. Things *can* be done to ease and ultimately cure America's racial troubles, but the American white people and their elected representatives must first *want* to do these things. It would mean, for one thing, uncorking the lid on the treasury, and I'm just not convinced that at present the average American realizes how much the country's domestic tranquility and stability depend on the need to relieve the black man of his miseries, or how much hard cash it would take to do the job.

The big urban cities in America will continue to become more and more populated by black people. The problems of the ghettos, because they have been unattended for so long and have reached such massive proportions, will become more and more severe. The situation will become messier and messier. Barring a miracle—and that's what it will have to be, when one takes into account white society's refusal to do the very costly and, to them, painful things that must be done—*violence will become* even more the order of the day.

Sooner or later, as these seemingly inevitable things come to pass, the white man will be forced into a definite course of action. When the racial picture has become messy and violent enough, he will probably be willing to consider even the extreme and now totally unacceptable idea of a separate territory for black Americans; or he will embark upon a campaign of genocide to get the black man out of his hair once and for all.

Not many people will admit the possibility of either of these extreme alternatives. That is because Americans have lulled themselves into thinking that as late as it is and as bad as things are, the good white people will triumph over the bad and the miracle of full equality and integration will occur before the situation becomes irreconcilable. Or they imagine that a few more civil rights acts and war-on-poverty programs will bring about a tolerable compromise wherein the black masses will settle down and accept, as they have in the past, a less than equal status in American society.

As inconceivable as these things appear, I, for one, am quite convinced that they could happen. The more inconceivable of the two drastic alternatives is, I believe, the idea that the white man would ever, no matter how rough it became, give up any American territory to the black man. And even if he did, I'm sure that many Negroes would prefer to stay with the Great White Father, no matter how he degraded them. But he wouldn't give up an inch, let alone a state. He might think about it and even debate the idea, but in the final analysis, I'm sure he would choose to attempt to exterminate the black man. After all, it hasn't been *that* long ago since he did the same thing to the American Indian.

An interesting thing happens when this idea is expressed among people who have not, for one reason or another, given it any previous thought. I find that most black people think for a moment and agree that it is possible. Most white people immediately reject it as unthinkable. The reasons advanced against the possibility of genocide are, "The rest of the world wouldn't allow it," or "The American leaders would prohibit it."

TWENTY-FIVE

The Big Black Crack
in the American Dream

"Well, they know that they couldn't get even with the police. They know they couldn't do that regardless of how dirty the police do them; they always and they always take the police's word before they would our word." — *Woman, interviewed during the Watts riots.*

ON SUNDAY EVENING, February 13, 1966, I watched a Los Angeles TV panel discussion show. The participants were the Chief of Police, the head of the County Human Relations Commission, a representative from the Mayor's office, and a representative from the Governor's staff.

It was announced that the panel would discuss the implementation of the McCone Commission Report.

The discussion actually amounted to a meeting of minds on the subject of Southern Negro migrants bringing with them to Los Angeles a deep-rooted antipathy toward police. This is an interesting observation and doubtless it has some basis in fact, but what was *not* examined was the antipathy that so many racist-minded Los Angeles police officers project against Negro residents, whether they be of Southern, Northern, Eastern, or local origin.

The sweeping assumption that the problems between the Los Angeles Police Department and the Negro community begin and end with the imported attitudes of Southern Negroes is a convenient way to avoid facing the full facts of the matter. It is also a lie.

So many Negro people come into the Los Angeles community from other parts of the country, hoping that they are moving to a better way of life. They soon learn that unemployment, ghettoized housing conditions, and sub-standard educational opportunities are the bitter facts of life. They also learn that "Mister Charlie" with the badge and the gun in Los Angeles is very much like "Mister Charlie" with the badge and the gun in Mississippi. When confronted by the police in Watts, our Southern arrival learns what we native sons and daughters already know: that while some of their methods vary, the local police often display the same attitudes and hostilities as the Southern cop.

The TV show also seemed to agree that somebody should inform the newly-arrived Southern Negro that LA police are okay and are only trying to do their job.

A new arrival might believe this propaganda for a while—until some local cop, seething with anti-Negro venom, calls him a nigger and goes up-side his head with a billy club. But it would be awfully difficult to convince those of us who have been here any length of time and know better.

It is not the newly-arrived Southern Negro who influences the local scene as much as it is the way of life that molds the immigrant.

It's not a matter of who's mad at whom; it's a matter of history taking a new turn. For hundreds of years white society has been on the offensive against the black man. This historical attitude has not changed. What *has* changed suddenly and quite drastically is the reaction, the attitude of the Negro community. What sociologists and historians have held out as a sooner-or-later eventuality has begun to manifest itself in a mass manner.

The moderate voices of the Negro optimists calling for patience and foretelling justice and equality in the not-too-distant future have finally lost what impact they may have had. As these voices fade into the background, new, strident, angry voices rising from the masses are shaping the emotional and intellectual tone of the community.

This is social revolution. The old ground rules no longer apply. Black people have developed a common will of purpose. It is a singularly uncompromising posture, in spite of the impression of disunity created by the varied programs and approaches of the many groups involved in the struggle. In short, the common will of the people says that the time has come for an end to the American color-caste system and the hell with the consequences.

The white majority will be forced to decide upon a clear-cut approach . . . and soon. It is either *really* the beginning of the end of the color line and all its ramifications, or race war. Anything short of full freedom is unacceptable. Timely, contrived civil rights "crumbs," political manipulation, glowing promises for "tomorrow," economic intimidation, or physical terror are doomed to failure. These devices have worked in the past, but they will buy less and less time as the days go by. They were an efficient formula for placating and disciplining yesterday's black Americans. They are difficult to implement today, and they will be impossible to foist upon the coming generation.

The American dream has a big black crack in it. The moment of truth is at hand. The white majority can believe that white supremacy will prevail, or that *all* Negroes are not angry, or take comfort in their superiority of numbers, or whatever. The age-old American "race problem" is coming to a head, and no amount of false-promising, sabre-rattling, crumb-throwing, or head-in-sand-hiding will make it go away.

The American white man has had at least three historical

opportunities to remedy the situation. The first occurred during the Reconstruction Era after the Civil War. The second was after World War II when Negroes were inspired and receptive to a meaningful accommodation. The third chance . . . if it is not already too late . . . is now. Three strikes and you're out.

The Black Muslim movement grew out of the American color-caste way of life. If the white man dislikes it he has no one to blame but himself. He made it possible. If American Negro masses veer toward Communism at some future date, either on a "my enemy is your enemy" basis or through political motivation, the white man can likewise take full responsibility. After all, he has branded the Negro leaders Communists and Communist-inspired from the beginnings of the struggle.

Summary

WHITE America stands at a critical crossroad. She can meet ghetto disorders with increased police power in the belief that oppressive punitive actions will make the problem go away, or she can start getting at the economic and social causes of the riots. Unfortunately, but typically, the trend is toward punitive police power. But even if the nation decided to spend the billions necessary to remove the causes, black people would be a long time believing it because whites have conned, lied, and swindled for so long.

But if the problem is to be effectively dealt with, billions of dollars and long years of straightaway work must be spent to raise the living conditions and economic opportunity in the ghetto until they are on a par with other American communities.

There is a growing number of people in the black community who feel logic dictates and history confirms that violence is the only avenue of escape from ghetto sub-life and its inherent discriminations. Surely the Negro leaders who work for integration have less impact on the black community today than they had a few years ago. Dr. Martin Luther King was one of the organizers of SNCC, but he has long since been replaced as its idol by Malcolm X. The court actions, freedom rides and marches, sit-ins, and nonviolent demonstrations of recent years did not change the economic or social status of black Americans and certainly did not hasten integration. Black people increasingly distrust whites and have hundreds of years of empty and broken promises upon which to base this growing lack of faith. The Martin Luther Kings, Whitney Youngs, and Roy Wilkinses were unable to deliver any meaningful victories, and more and more Negro eyes and ears are turning toward younger, more militant and radical leaders.

Because a group like SNCC has a relatively small membership, it is a mistake to dismiss it as uninfluential in the Negro community. Whites would do well to understand that the SNCC's increasingly truculent mood accurately reflects a swelling Negro frustration over failure to gain equality in jobs, education, and housing.

Even if billions of dollars were suddenly available to make the ghettos livable and to create jobs and to do all the things that would be necessary to close the opportunity gap between white and black Americans, I'm sure that riots and violence would not stop overnight. But eventually, as conditions visibly improved and the people of the ghetto began to see a future for their children and black economic and political power became a reality, things would begin to settle down.

Whites on the liberal side should ask themselves what they are basically concerned with: the idea of integration or the welfare of millions of oppressed black people? In working to get the nation moving on a multi-billion-dollar program to bring justice to black people, they should forget about integration and get at first things first. Once the black community is economically equal to other segments—and it is inclined to do so—the theory of racial integration in America might be reexamined.

If the country continues to drift toward increased police power as an answer to riots, I am convinced that more and more black people will be drawn into what UCLA Professor Dr.

Nathan E. Cohen calls "pride in aggression." And one need not be a professor to realize to what bloodshed and eventual race war this road can lead.

America should move at once and with all the vast resources at the nation's disposal to the task of raising the black community to an equal position. First, because it is the right thing to do and is long, long overdue. And, equally as important, because violence and tragedy are the grim alternatives.

Perhaps the basic lesson to be gleaned from the Watts rebellion is the knowledge that the *whole* community was involved and angry.

During the riot, Watts NAACP President Ed Warren said:

"There's nobody in this city who has taken a stand. They always condemn. Mayor Yorty, when he spoke: 'It's the hoodlums.' Chief Parker: 'The hoodlums.' I say both of them are lying. It's the people in general who are dissatisfied, and the hoodlums are only the overt. But the people in the houses are just as mad as those kids are in the street, and if you learn this, you'll understand Watts."

The young Muslim said, "We'll all see each other face to face in the street."

But it is not *only* the Muslim youth who are prepared to meet the "man" face to face in the street. And when you learn this you'll better understand the situation throughout the land today.

Johnny Otis, an American blues and R & B drummer, pianist, vibraphonist, singer, and bandleader, was elected to the Rock and Roll Hall of Fame in 1994. He is a painter, a sculptor, the author of several books, and until recently the host of "The Johnny Otis Show" on Pacifica Radio (KPFA Berkeley).

George Lipsitz is professor of black studies and sociology at the University of California, Santa Barbara. He is author of, among other books, *Footsteps in the Dark: The Hidden Histories of Popular Music, Time Passages: Collective Memory and American Popular Culture,* and *American Studies in a Moment of Danger,* all published by the University of Minnesota Press.

Preston Love (1921–2004) was a renowned alto saxophonist, bandleader, and songwriter from Omaha, Nebraska.